PRINCE OF THE CITY

STARRING
TREAT WILLIAMS

EXECUTIVE PRODUCER
JAY PRESSON ALLEN

PRODUCED BY
BURTT HARRIS

SCREENPLAY BY
JAY PRESSON ALLEN AND SIDNEY LUMET

BASED ON THE BOOK BY
ROBERT DALEY

DIRECTED BY
SIDNEY LUMET

AN ORION PICTURES/WARNER BROS. RELEASE
Thru WARNER BROS. A Warner Communications Company

PRINCE OF THE CITY

THE TRUE STORY OF A COP WHO KNEW TOO MUCH

ROBERT DALEY

BERKLEY BOOKS, NEW YORK

PRINCE OF THE CITY

A Berkley Book / published by arrangement with
Houghton Mifflin Company

PRINTING HISTORY
Houghton Mifflin edition published 1978
Berkley edition / October 1981

ISBN: 0-425-09789-7

A BERKLEY BOOK ® TM 757,375
Berkley Books are published by The Berkley Publishing Group,
200 Madison Avenue, New York, NY 10016.
The name "Berkley" and the "B" logo
are trademarks belonging to Berkley Publishing Corporation.

PRINTED IN THE UNITED STATES OF AMERICA

10   9   8

But if thou wilt offer a holocaust, offer it to the Lord.

JUDGES 13:16

And Samson said to the lad who guided his steps: Suffer me to touch the pillars which support the whole house, and let me lean upon them and rest a little.

JUDGES 16:26

About the Author: Robert Daley was born in New York City in 1930. His work as Publicity Director of the New York Giants resulted in his first novel ONLY A GAME. He served as foreign correspondent of the New York Times in Paris and other locales in Europe and North Africa. During this time Daley wrote his second novel, THE WHOLE TRUTH. In 1971-72 Daley served as a New York City Deputy Police Commissioner. His bestselling novels TARGET BLUE and TO KILL A COP followed. Subsequently, he wrote PRINCE OF THE CITY: The True Story of a Cop Who Knew Too Much. Several of Daley's other books were inspired by his unusually adventurous personal experiences. THE CRUEL SPORT and CARS AT SPEED are about auto racing; STRONG WINE RED AS BLOOD, winetasting; THE SWORDS OF SPAIN is a photo essay on bullfighting; and TREASURE deals with diving for treasure in the Gulf of Mexico.

As well as being a successful novelist and journalist, Daley is an avid photographer whose works have been exhibited in The Baltimore Museum, The Art Institute of Chicago and other galleries. His photos, in addition to numerous articles and short stories, have appeared worldwide in such publications as *Esquire, Vogue, Life* and *Paris Match.* He lives in Connecticut with his wife and three daughters.

Author's Note: All of the events depicted in this book are a matter of factual record, and the people are real. No names have been changed. The dialogue has either been taken from concealed tape recordings made at the time the events took place or been carefully reconstructed through interviews with the participants.

Book One

1

THEY WERE NOT ordinary detectives, nor even ordinary narcotics detectives. They were SIU detectives— Special Investigating Unit, New York Police Department—and during the long wait in crowded arraignment courts they stood out, and this was by choice. Their appearance was special, their prisoners were special, and their evidence was special.

Other cops, waiting, were in uniform, or else, if detectives, they wore street clothes: usually lumber jackets, sweaters, corduroy pants, or jeans—the rough clothing of rough men. SIU detectives had adopted a kind of uniform of their own. In winter they affected full-length suede or leather coats, and a number of them, underneath, wore business suits and vests. In summer, SIU detectives tended to sport Italian knit shirts and forty-dollar tailored slacks and loafers. They were forever observing and approving of each other's attire. Also, their fingernails were usually manicured, and in some cases lacquered. They tended to smell of strong scents, and they gave the appearance most times of having just stepped up from a barber's chair—an expensive barber's chair—and in fact, this was often the case. It had become ritual for SIU detectives to spend an hour or two under hot towels, pampering themselves, immediately after breaking a case.

Their prisoners, caged in nearby holding pens, were as extraordinary as themselves. Other cops arrested common thugs, or in narcotics cases, street junkies. The thugs, caged, looked as feral as beasts. The junkies huddled in corners, snot and tears caked to their faces, sitting sometimes beside pools of vomit.

SIU detectives did not bother with junkies, and they came in contact with thugs only by accident—if they happened, for instance, to witness a crime on the way home. Their prisoners usually were expensively dressed and often somewhat glamorous, being Frenchmen or Turks or South Americans, or high-ranking New York Mafiosi. These were the wholesalers, importers, and executives of the narcotics trade, and most of them, waiting caged with common criminals, were trying to puzzle out how the SIU detectives had ever got on to them.

As for evidence, other cops, as they waited, clutched a single gun or knife or crowbar—the weapon with which one or another caged defendant had stuck up an old lady or a store, or burglarized a house. Or, in narcotics cases, transparent evidence envelopes lay on the cops' laps. The envelopes could be seen to contain one or two, or four or five five-dollar bags of heavily cut heroin. Whereas SIU detectives held or sat beside brown paper bundles—or suitcases, or occasionally a steamer trunk—containing pure junk, uncut junk. Whatever the receptacle, it was filled to the brim with narcotics worth maybe a million dollars or more on the street.

Ordinary cops, waiting in court, were sometimes bloody and torn after violent arrests. SIU men always cleaned themselves up first. Court was, in a sense, their stage, and on it they were impeccable. Besides, they were so slick in the taking of prisoners that violence seldom was necessary.

Of course they were too close to the street to avoid it entirely, and certain of their exploits approached the status of legend among ordinary cops. Detective George Bermudez, driving along, one day witnessed the stabbing and robbing of one man by another. Leaping out of his car, he grappled with the assailant, who stabbed him in the heart. Bermudez not only did not die, he hung on to the assailant until help came.

Detective Eddie Codelia, having made an undercover buy in a Harlem tenement, was assaulted in the hallway by four men, who menaced him with guns and a hunting knife pressed to his face. Codelia fell to his knees weeping. He groveled. He begged for his life. He spilled money to the floor. The last thing to spill from his pockets was his gun, with which he shot all four men, killing two instantly.

SIU detectives disdained medals, and rarely put in for them. They were too good for medals; they didn't need them. But sometimes official recognition came anyway, and Codelia was awarded the Medal of Honor, the Police Department's highest decoration.

SIU detectives carried themselves with a kind of presence. They seldom mixed with other cops. In the police world they were as celebrated as film stars, and they were aware of this. In court, when the judge at last mounted the bench, whichever of them was senior would step forward and identify himself by full title: "Detective So-and-so, Special Investigating Unit, Narcotics Division."

He would then cut into the head of the line. Invariably, other cops and detectives would let him do it.

When major crimes, particularly homicides, occurred in the city, commanders often borrowed SIU detectives in hope of breaking the case quickly. Detective Robert Leuci, for instance, once brought in a wanted murderer named Johnny Loco singlehandedly at the end of only two days. But it was against the strange code of the SIU detectives to take credit for such arrests. Invariably the murderer was turned over to some squad detective, while the SIU detective went home, or back to the narcotics case from which he had been taken.

To other cops SIU detectives reeked of success. They had style; also, obviously, they had money, more money than cops were supposed to have. But for a long time no one in authority noticed this, or wondered where the money might be coming from.

Of course they were the object of envy.

Not because they had rank. They did not. Like all detectives, they were patrolmen who had been designated to serve as detective-investigators. They held authority over no one. The newest sergeant outranked the most senior first-grade detective, and the newest patrolman was, technically, his equal.

The envy existed because the SIU detective, though

perhaps still in his mid or late twenties, had reached the top of his profession; there was no other assignment as good as the one he had. The rules and procedures of the department, which weighted down every other cop, he ignored.

He was virtually unsupervised. SIU headquarters was on the third floor of the First Precinct station house, but some SIU detectives did not go near this office for months at a time, not even on pay day—they would send someone in to pick up their checks. Some of them, in effect, worked out of their houses or their cars.

They were rated on results only. All they had to do was keep making big cases, big seizures of heroin. That they worked hard was never questioned. They were men who would sit on wiretaps or surveillances for days, even weeks at a time, virtually without relief, and never put in for overtime. They were hunters. Theirs was the most elusive game of all, and the kill was always close—maybe tomorrow, maybe even today. They disdained overtime as much as medals or credit for arresting murderers.

But once a narcotics case was made, the major violators arrested, the heroin seized, once the ritual barbering had taken place, many would award themselves, unbeknownst to the Police Department, two weeks' vacation. Then, looking tanned, fit, and as expensively dressed as always, they would come back to work, begin a new case, a new hunt.

They had citywide jurisdiction. They chose their own targets and roamed New York at will. Someone once called them the Princes of the City, for they operated with the impunity, and sometimes with the arrogance, of Renaissance princes. They could enforce any law or not enforce it, arrest anyone or accord freedom. They were immune to arrest themselves. The Princes of the City—they liked this, and adopted it.

The Narcotics Division of the New York Police Department numbered, at the start of the sixties, less than two hundred detectives, all focused on street corner junkies and pushers. In October 1961 two such detectives, Sonny Grosso and Eddie Egan, stumbled upon a Mafia supply ring that imported heroin direct from France. A small squad of the best narcotics detectives then available was thrown together—never more than twenty men in all —and that was the start of the Special Investigating Unit.

Working in conjunction with federal narcotics agents, SIU detectives over the next several months put together their case, effected their arrests, and seized ninety-seven pounds of heroin—the largest street seizure ever up to that time—and in so doing they destroyed the Tuminaros as a major Mafia family. This famous case became a best-selling book in 1968 and an Academy Award-winning movie in 1971. Although the world knew it as *The French Connection,* inside SIU it was always spoken of as the Tuminaro case. Conceptually it became the case every detective sought to match. And on the operational level it made possible the extraordinary freedom of movement SIU detectives came to enjoy; it dominated SIU for the twelve years the unit lasted.

During the sixties, as public outcry swelled and as the Narcotics Division expanded, SIU expanded too, though it never exceeded ten percent of the division's comple-ment. From 1967 to 1972, the period of this story, it stood at about sixty detectives.

One captain, one lieutenant, and five sergeants comprised its command structure—not nearly enough to exert supervisory pressure over so many detectives working alone or in small groups in obscure corners of the city. Several commanders over the years attempted to put in controls, all of which were bitterly resisted by the star detectives, and all of which failed.

The sixty detectives operated normally in four-man teams. One member of each team usually was ac-knowledged by the others as team leader. It was the team leader's job to pick the target of each investigation and to give out assignments each day.

The team leaders were the elite of the elite. Most were in some way unique. Detective Carl Aguiluz, born in Honduras in 1935, and a naturalized American citizen only from the age of twenty-two, was an exceptional wire man and bugger, the best in SIU. An electronic technician before he became a cop, he knew telephones.

He had never been a patrolman in uniform, for immediately after graduation from the Police Academy he had gone to work undercover for BOSSI, a super-secret police intelligence squad, and he had infiltrated a communist cell in the East Village. When that assignment ended, he went immediately into the Narcotics Division as an arresting officer, and in time was promoted into SIU.

Most SIU detectives could tap a phone at the box in an apartment house basement. But Aguiluz could find the pair of wires that he needed four or five blocks away from the suspect's house. He could read where telephone lines went, and find the binding post. He could bridge his tap onto a dead line so that even experts—the FBI or telephone security—couldn't find it. Planting bugs inside suspects' houses was another of his specialties. He was a good burglar, and he understood the principles of directional transmitters. He left no clues, and no bug he planted was ever discovered.

Also, he spoke Spanish. He was among the first SIU detectives to concentrate on major Hispanic importers, and he quickly developed the technique which, in a later case, led him to the most monumental seizure of all, an entire closet load of heroin and cocaine straight from France. One of his partners was Joe Novoa, who was of Spanish extraction and spoke Spanish with a Castilian accent. Novoa, however, was fair skinned—he looked Irish or even Scandinavian.

In the presence of prisoners, Aguiluz would address Novoa only in English. He would then curse the prisoners roundly in Spanish, and angrily leave the room.

Invariably, the prisoners, as soon as the door slammed, would turn toward each other and begin to discuss their predicament in Spanish, never suspecting that the fair-skinned Novoa, staring stupidly off in some other direction, was at the same time drinking in every word.

Thus it was Novoa who learned of the existence and location of the secret closet, and its secret contents. But it was Aguiluz's ploy, Aguiluz's case.

The next day a newspaper photo went up on the SIU office bulletin board: eight or ten grinning detectives, arms around each other, standing behind a table on which reposed a hundred kilos of narcotics. Over this photo was pasted a hand-lettered headline: CAN YOU TOP THIS?

Detective Joe Nunziata, born in 1932 and raised in Brooklyn, had scarcely ever seen a horse before entering the Police Department. Nonetheless, he became a mounted patrolman in midtown, and it was on horseback that he made his earliest reputation. He seemed to understand everything about horses just as, when he came into Narcotics, he immediately seemed to understand everything about the drug scene, too.

As a team leader, Nunziata was a detective of extraordinary vision. He had instincts, and he obeyed them. He knew how to pick targets, and as soon as he had fastened onto one, he immediately saw the entire case as it would eventually take shape. Most times he was able to puzzle out, once arrests had been made, where the narcotics must be concealed. He once tracked down eighty-eight pounds of heroin hidden in the bottom of wine bottles in the McAlpin Hotel.

Nunziata had an exceptionally open and engaging personality. Everyone liked him at once. Without trying, he tended to dominate every gathering he attended. At a party, before long, everyone in the room would crowd around Nunziata, for he exuded magnetism and charm. This same charm he used as needed when breaking cases. He could talk his way inside private places, and when he went looking for information, whether to the state parole board, or to one or another agency, the men he addressed were always anxious to give him whatever he wanted. Of all of the detectives in SIU, he was the one most admired by the others.

Detective Robert Leuci, as team leader, had more and better informants than anyone, for he was willing to spend as much time as was necessary to win a potential informant over. Once, when he learned that a certain dealer was about to enter his territory, he mobilized sixteen or seventeen junkies, furnished them with a description of the dealer, and stationed them at strategic places. Then he simply waited in the station house for the phone call that would tell him where his quarry had holed up.

Born in 1940, he was much younger than Aguiluz and Nunziata—also much younger than the other three members of the team that he led.

Though not as good a wireman as Aguiluz, he was adequate. Though not as magnetic as Nunziata, he was charming and perceptive, and when he went to people for information or help, they were anxious to accord it. He worked always against the biggest names in the narcotics trade, and he produced a great number of arrests, a great many seizures of substantial—as opposed to spectacular—bundles of narcotics. He had the best organized crime connections of any SIU detective, because his first cousin, John Lusterino, was a captain in the Colombo Mafia family.

In the street Leuci was known as a compassionate cop. He was the type of cop to whom vicious fugitives, fearing a savage beating from other cops, sometimes chose to surrender. They knew he would not hurt them.

All of the detectives mentioned so far are part of the fabric of this story, but its principal actor is Leuci—with Aguiluz and Nunziata as chief supporting players, and various prosecutors in the role of Greek chorus.

Leuci prided himself on being a tough cop—they all did—but in the end he proved far less tough than any of the others. Perhaps he had more conscience than they did, or perhaps he merely was more troubled by what all of them were doing. In any case, he was the one who stepped forward, and, in so doing, brought on the ruin of everyone else. It was almost biblical. Like Samson, he first did penance, and then he pulled the temple down.

2

IN MID-FEBRUARY of 1971 Detective Leuci was called before the Commission to Investigate Alleged Police Corruption—the so-called Knapp Commission.

He was a few days short of his thirty-first birthday. He had a wife of seven years, Gina; a son, Anthony, who was five; and a newborn daughter named Santina. He lived fifty miles east of the city in a Long Island town named Kings Park, in a tract house in a development of tract houses, and six of the nine houses on his street were owned by New York cops. Thousands more cops lived in that town, and in surrounding towns just like it, and their cars, like an invading army, advanced on the city every day.

Leuci, both on and off duty, was a cop among cops.

A few months earlier he had been routinely transferred out of SIU, and his team routinely dispersed. He was now a precinct detective investigating common crimes, and his past, he had resolved, was behind him.

But he had been summoned to the Knapp Commission offices, where he was made to wait for an hour in a starkly furnished waiting room. He could see into certain offices. People came and went carrying dossiers. The purpose of the Knapp Commission, of those people, of those dossiers, was to send cops to jail.

The Knapp Commission had nothing on Leuci, but he didn't know this. He was waiting to be interviewed by a man named Nicholas Scoppetta, whom he had never met. As he waited, he had become increasingly tense.

Scoppetta, a former assistant district attorney under Frank Hogan, appeared at last in the waiting room.

"Bob Leuci?"

"Yes."

Scoppetta, thirty-eight, had a flat nose and looked like a light heavyweight prizefighter.

"Come into my office."

Leuci, though afraid, flashed a boyish kind of smile.

Scoppetta had expected to meet a case-hardened detective. Instead he was surprised at how young Leuci looked, and by the disarming smile. Leuci's countenance, Scoppetta thought, was almost cherubic. Though thirty-one, he looked as innocent as a choir boy.

Scoppetta's office was as stark and temporary as the waiting room.

"Why don't we talk for a bit? Let's talk about what we, the Knapp Commission, are doing here."

Leuci's fear had gone over into a kind of ingratiating anxiety. "I'd like to get out of here, personally," he said lightly.

Scoppetta at the filing cabinet was replacing folders. "Don't I know you?" he asked over his shoulder. "Didn't we put some cases together in Manhattan?"

He was trying to put Leuci at ease, but failed.

"No," said Leuci.

Scoppetta had studied Leuci's personnel folder, but it told little. He decided to switch away from Leuci to other cops.

"Let me ask you some particular questions. What about Carl Aguiluz? What about Joe Nunziata?"

"Outstanding detectives."

Scoppetta glanced at him sharply. "There have been a lot of allegations of misconduct against them."

Leuci said, "There are allegations against federal narcotics agents too."

"That's true. We can talk about that later. But for now we ought to talk about cops."

"Obviously. We are easy, aren't we? Cops are easy."

This interview, Scoppetta saw, was going nowhere. But the intensity of Leuci's anxiety was interesting. What, the prosecutor wondered, was behind it?

Scoppetta was, at this time, an unknown but ambitious lawyer. He had grown up in an orphanage. Later he worked his way through college, and through law school, working during the last three years for the Society for Prevention of Cruelty to Children. When he went to work as an assistant D.A., he showed himself to be a dogged but successful prosecutor.

Twice he had left public service to join law firms at big salaries; each time he had returned to low-paying jobs like this one with the Knapp Commission. The career he sought—the prestige, the relatively good money—he was determined to find while also contributing to the public good. The Knapp Commission was, to Scoppetta, either a six-month interlude before returning to private practice, or his best chance yet at a successful public career.

He decided to invite Leuci home to dinner.

"How about coming over to my place," he said. "My family is away. We'll have dinner. Maybe you can give me some tips on how I ought to approach my investigation."

Their eyes met across the desk.

Scoppetta began to refill his briefcase. "We'll ride up there now," he said decisively.

In Scoppetta's West Side apartment, Leuci walked around studying the pictures on the walls. Most were blowups of Scoppetta's wife and children. They were of exceptional quality, and they had been taken by the prosecutor himself.

"Tell me," called Leuci to Scoppetta, who was in the kitchen, "what do I call you?"

Scoppetta's head appeared in the doorway. "Call me Nick."

"Nick, what is it? What is it you want to ask me? I didn't do it, whatever it is."

"You're not under investigation. What are you thinking about?" Leuci had been identified to him as a totally honest detective who might be able to cast some light on corruption in Narcotics.

"Apparently you got something on your mind," said Leuci. "I wish you would tell me about it, and let me deny it and leave."

Scoppetta's head again appeared in the kitchen doorway. He smiled. "No, it's nothing like that. How do you like your steak?"

"Why don't you spend some time doing something important?" asked Leuci, feeling somewhat reassured. "Like investigating lawyers. You were in the Manhattan D.A.'s office, right? I'm sure there is all sorts of corruption in that office."

"There is no corruption in that office. I never heard even a hint of it. But maybe you know something I don't."

Leuci snorted derisively. "You're kidding."

"This conversation is starting to bore me," said Scoppetta, and he strode back into the kitchen.

But Leuci followed him. "The conversation immediately becomes boring when we talk about corrupt lawyers and district attorneys. You want to talk about cops."

Scoppetta put steaks and salad onto the plates and carried them to the table. As soon as the two men sat down to eat, Scoppetta resumed talking about corruption in the Narcotics Division.

But Leuci interrupted.

"Why don't we talk about lawyers I know to be corrupt," he said. "Why don't we talk about district attorneys that are corrupt?"

"Well, if you know anything about lawyers and D.A.'s I'd love to hear it. We'll work on that. But you know the Knapp Commission is here to investigate cops."

Neither was eating.

"Is it common practice to sell narcotics in the Narcotics Division?"

The detective's anger appeared genuine, though how could the prosecutor be sure?

"Those are the kinds of asinine stupid things that people write in the *Village Voice* or the *New York Times*. We don't sell narcotics. Dope dealers sell narcotics. We're not dope dealers, we're policemen."

"It's hard to distinguish between the dope dealers and the policemen sometimes," retorted Scoppetta.

Leuci said, "Why don't we talk about corrupt lawyers? Why don't we talk about how we can approach that?"

Scoppetta began to cut through the steak on his plate. "Why don't we eat;" he said, "and forget all the bullshit?"

During dinner Scoppetta's questions became personal,

and there was no talk of corruption. The experienced prosecutor, probing for a weakness, asked about Leuci's schooling, about his wife and kids, about his feelings for life, love, and the police department. About the Italian heritage both men shared.

From the age of sixteen, Leuci had had no other ambition than to become a cop, he said. He had passed the Civil Service test at nineteen, and had gone into the Police Academy at twenty-one in the first class for which he was eligible. Five months later there he was, a cop in uniform patrolling the streets of the city, and even the borough—Queens—in which he had been born.

There was no wife or kids or tract house yet. He lived with his parents and with his younger brother and sister in a quiet house on a quiet residential street. His father, formerly a semi-pro pitcher known as Hooks Leuci, was foreman in a pipe factory. His mother worked in a sewing-maching plant. They were honest, hard-working people who had come up out of an Italian ghetto in Brooklyn, and the day their son graduated from the Police Academy was possibly the proudest of their lives. They saw him as a police captain one day.

There were Mafia elements all around them, even within their own family, but they avoided these people, and they tried to instill their contempt for them in their son. Hooks Leuci, whenever he was in the presence of his sister Rosa Lusterino, realized that his son was a policeman, whereas Rosa's son Johnny was usually in jail.

Detective Leuci was the first member of his family ever to finish high school, and it was a big family—there were nine aunts. By police standards he was highly educated, for at eighteen he had gone to Baker University in Kansas to play football. He was a chunky, five-foot-nine-inch fullback. In Kansas, surrounded by prairies and by middle-class Wasps, he was miserably homesick. He yearned for the streets of New York, and when freshman year ended he hurried home to wait to be old enough to become a New York cop.

\ Every squad to which he was assigned he had led in arrests, and so his rise was quick. In February 1966, after less than four years in uniform, he was promoted to detective third-grade, and he got second grade in August 1969. These were pay grades only; as a second-grade detective he was earning sergeant's wages.

By then he had moved up into SIU, and was one of the elite. His street nickname had been Babyface, and now Scoppetta asked him about it.

Part of his success as a cop had been due to his exceptionally innocent appearance, Leuci replied. He always looked far younger than his years. As a rookie patrolman he could pass as a teenager, and even as he neared thirty he still looked very young. Hoodlums and dope pushers often failed to take him seriously until it was too late.

After dinner Scoppetta and his guest moved to the living room, and the interview continued. Scoppetta was searching for tidbits of information. But Leuci continued to refuse to talk about corruption, or about SIU.

"You're a very disarming guy," Scoppetta said. "I heard a lot about Bob Leuci before I met him today. The tough detective I heard about was nothing like the one I met and that I'm talking to now. The Bob Leuci I heard about I never would have invited to my home."

Scoppetta was still probing, still choosing each word carefully, still watching closely for each reaction by Leuci.

"All cops are like me," responded Leuci. "I'm no different. I represent what we all are."

"There are cops that are criminals," Scoppetta said. "There are cops that are real criminals. They have destroyed you. They have destroyed this Police Department."

Scoppetta probed more deeply still. "I know there is more to you than people think. First of all, some people think that you are a totally honest guy. I don't think that's true."

Leuci stared him in the eye. "I go out there and do what I have to do. I do my job."

Earlier, Scoppetta had extinguished all illumination within the apartment except for one lamp burning on the end table beside Leuci. Its circle of light enclosed both men. They were as isolated as characters on a stage. Beyond was outer darkness—the dark apartment, the darker city. Scoppetta had not contrived the lamp, he merely noticed it, recognizing its importance to Leuci's mood. It shut out the world. It established the intimacy of a confessional. Leuci was about to confess something, Scoppetta was sure of it. Whatever Leuci might confess only his confessor, Scoppetta, would hear.

Scoppetta said, "There's a lot going on inside you. I don't know what it is exactly, but certainly you feel guilty about something. Do you want to talk about it?"

"If I did talk about it, I would destroy myself."

"Not necessarily. You ought to think about telling me what's bothering you. You ought to think about a new beginning. A new life."

Leuci grasped at this notion. "You mean there's a potential that I could start over again?"

"You could cooperate with us, wipe the slate clean. Will you think about it?"

After a moment, Leuci said, "I'll think about it."

It was nearly dawn when they walked to the door. "I want you to go home now," Scoppetta said, "and I want you to ask yourself some questions. How do you visualize yourself? What do you see reflected in the mirror in the morning? What does your wife think of you? What are your children going to think of you three or four years from now when they're old enough to decide for themselves what you are? That's what we'll talk about tomorrow."

The two men watched the dawn come, Scoppetta from his window overlooking Central Park, Leuci as he made the fifty-mile drive out onto Long Island. Leuci, driving, wondered what he had started to tell Scoppetta, and why. His own willingness to talk, which he did not understand, was frightening, because he did not know where it would take him.

Scoppetta, on the other hand, was elated, and planning tomorrow's day. Leuci perhaps represented a breakthrough, the Knapp Commission's first. After six months no significant corruption had yet been proven by the commission. Where other commission lawyers had failed, he perhaps would succeed. He sensed an enormous potential in Leuci. The Police Department files were full of allegations about serious corruption in the Narcotics Division, and Leuci seemed on the verge of talking about it.

3

THEY TALKED the next night away, and also the next.

Yes, Leuci admitted, there was massive corruption in the Detective Division. There was massive corruption in the Narcotics Bureau. He was nodding vigorously. There was also massive corruption at every stage of the criminal justice system, starting with assistant district attorneys who helped detectives prepare wiretap orders, and routinely told them to perjure themselves, to lawyers who met them in hallways wearing three- and four-hundred-dollar suits, and came over and whispered that this case didn't mean anything, here's $50, $100, $500, $15,000, let's forget it.

The two men stared at each other.

Scoppetta said softly, "What are you going to do about it?"

"I can't do anything about it," Leuci cried. "What are *you* going to do about it? You are the guy who has the power to do something about it."

Scoppetta was an extremely skillful interrogator.

"Let's talk about my family, and your family, and the comparison," he said. "We are the same blood." It was an abrupt switch in mood, and it worked.

"Yeah, we are the same blood," agreed Leuci after a pause.

What about Leuci's brother, his sister, Scoppetta asked.

It was as if there was a switch concealed somewhere inside Leuci that Scoppetta, without knowing it was there, had somehow tripped. The detective began to talk about his brother Richie, who was five years younger, and who almost from infancy had had to wear thick glasses. The boy's parents had regarded this as a deformity—no

19

one in the family had ever had to wear glasses before—and Hooks Leuci and his wife had been consumed by shame. They went to doctors to be assured that Richie's deformity was not hereditary, not their fault, and because of their shame, they shamelessly coddled the child, seeming to prefer him to Bobby, who was strong and would grow up to become a policeman.

But their shame over Richie's eyesight was as nothing compared to their shame when they discovered only a few months ago that he was also a heroin addict. Leuci's voice became husky as he described his brother's suffering, and his parents'. Richie had lost all manhood. He wept, he groveled, he would not work or even keep himself clean. He lived from fix to fix, and constantly begged his brother, the narcotics detective, for heroin with which to feed his habit.

Worst of all, said Leuci, and tears started to his eyes, he himself was being blamed by his parents for Richie's habit, for the disgrace and misery that had come to the whole family. According to Hooks Leuci, it was cops like his son who had allowed it to happen, cops like his son who allowed dope pushers to do their business, to hang around and infect innocent children.

Now Leuci began to describe a backyard barbecue. He had invited a number of narcotics detectives and their wives to his house, and suddenly, unexpectedly, his father had appeared in the garden. He had been out for a ride, and decided to stop by and see his son. Accepting a drink, he began to speak to the detectives. At first he seemed pleased with them, commenting, "These are nice Italian boys." Then he began to notice how well-dressed they were, and how their pinky rings flashed in the sun; he listened to them talk about their trips to Miami and Las Vegas. His smile faded, he put his drink down, and he sought out his son, saying, "These guys are corrupt cops, and you're a corrupt cop."

Hooks Leuci had been a neighborhood hero, and of course a hero to his son. It had been Hooks Leuci's respect that Robert Leuci had always coveted most. Now Hooks strode to the door with Leuci calling after him, "Dad, you'll never understand. I couldn't begin to tell you what it's like, and what I have to do."

But his father went out, slamming the door behind him.

Scoppetta, listening, had been moved, partly by the story itself, and partly by Leuci's suffering as he told it. Tears had overflowed Leuci's eyes, and he had begun to weep. What did his parents expect of him? It wasn't his responsibility to watch Richie. They should have watched him themselves.

After a time, his tears dried, and he began to get angry. His parents understood nothing about the pressures on cops, and neither did Scoppetta, he said. What gushed forth next was, mostly, Leuci's shame. It was impossible to tell what exactly he was confessing to, or if in fact he was confessing to anything at all.

You people on the Knapp Commission, he said, are focusing on the Police Department. You tell cops that you are out to catch them taking meals, taking Christmas presents, giving drugs to junkies. It's absolutely incredible. Cops are looking at you and saying: You bastards. It's you guys, the assistant district attorneys, lawyers, judges who run the system, and the whole fucking thing from top to bottom is corrupt. We know how you become a judge. You pay $50,000 and you become a judge. We see stores open on Sunday on Fifth Avenue, but they can't be open in Little Italy. And then you wonder why cops stick together. The only people that know us, care for us, love us, are other cops. You people are just looking to hurt us. You want to lay on us the responsibility of fucking up the system.

Do you know what it's like to be a narcotics detective, Leuci continued. Do you have any conception? Do you know what it's like on a February night in South Brooklyn a block from the piers with two addict informants in the back of the car, both of them crying, begging you for a bag of heroin? Do you know what it's like going home fifty miles away, and getting a phone call five minutes after you're home saying, I blew the shot, please come back and give me another bag. And driving fifty miles back in, and watching him tie up, and walking out of the room. Then working with him the next morning and locking up some dope pusher that's just as sick as he is. It's an insanity. And going into the office and the lieutenant says you have to make five arrests this month. Do you know what it's like working six, seven days a week? You have to be one of the best, otherwise you go back to swinging a stick.

Scoppetta's every nerve was attuned to Leuci's mood. But his mind was racing, looking for the key word, each time Leuci paused, to keep him talking.

You're in Westbury, or West End Avenue, Leuci ranted on. We're in El Barrio, we're on 125th Street. You want us to keep everybody inside the barricades so you can stay outside. I'm on Pleasant Avenue and 116th Street at three o'clock in the morning, just me and my partner and Tony somebody that we have been following for three weeks, and he's going to offer me money, and me and my partner are going to decide whether we'll take it or not. You don't care about me. Some black revolutionary is going to whack me out if he gets a chance. Some newspaper is going to call me a thief whether I do it or don't do it. The only one who cares about me is my partner. It's me and him and this guy we caught. We're going to take him to jail and lock him up. We're going to take his money. Fuck him, fuck you, fuck them.

Scoppetta listened, waiting.

I see what kind of man you are, and I see what kind of man my partner is, and there's just no comparison, see? I'm going to side with him. He tells me it's okay Bobby, hey Bobby, it's you and me against the rest of the world. You guys are eating in the Copa six nights a week. We try to get forty dollars expense money, and the department won't even give us that.

Leuci swallowed painfully.

You're winning in the end any way. We're selling ourselves, our families. These people we take money from own us. Our family's future rests on the fact that some dope pusher is not going to give us up, or some killer, some total piece of shit, is not going to give us up.

To you, cops are detestable kinds of people. But the vast majority of cops are good, honest, law-abiding, family-loving, decent men. Some of them do criminal things once in a while, but they are the only people between you and the jungle.

The long monologue ended. It had been dramatic but unspecific. The only thing clear was that the young detective was in the grip of extremely powerful emotions which Scoppetta might somehow be able to harness.

He said calmly, "Why don't you do something about it? You have knowledge. You can provide evidence. You can make cases."

"I can make all kinds of cases. I can make cases against lawyers, too. I can make cases against district attorneys, I can make cases against people who pay cops. Why don't we do that?"

The Knapp Commission, Scoppetta said firmly, was obliged to concentrate on cops.

"Then fuck the Knapp Commission."

The following night Leuci was calmer, and the two men discussed in detail the type of investigation Leuci might be willing to undertake. First, said Leuci, Scoppetta should leave the Knapp Commission and set up a separate office.

Scoppetta nodded. It could perhaps be done. He saw himself accorded funding by the Justice Department and setting up a separate office, perhaps under the U.S. Attorney for the Southern District of New York State.

Leuci meant to work primarily against corrupt lawyers, he declared. He wanted to put in jail district attorneys and judges who regularly solicited bribes, and defense lawyers who regularly seduced cops. If the focus was to be strictly on the cops themselves, then he would not take part. Any corrupt cops whom he might, so to speak, stumble over would go to jail too. But they would be incidental to his investigation. And he would not work against cops who had been his friends and partners in SIU. He was willing to wear a recording device. He was willing to handle marked money. He was willing to play a role, to risk his life for however many months or years the investigation could be kept secret.

Scoppetta was jubilant. "Do you realize how important this investigation can be? We'll do it together. I'll be with you every step of the way. What kind of cases can we make?"

As Leuci began to outline possibilities, it became clear to Scoppetta that what he was sketching were real cases, cases involving police misconduct. Leuci then selected one specific case, and painted in most of the details.

An SIU team, he said, had conducted a long investigation into a Mafia drug ring, but had failed to come up with enough solid evidence to obtain an indictment. The team then decided to contact the subject of the investigation, and offer to drop the case—which would have been dropped anyway—in exchange for money. Legally this was certainly bribe soliciting, and probably it was extortion—the line between the two crimes is somewhat blurred.

Leuci, because of his superb Mafia contacts, was enlisted by the team to make contact with the subject. He did this, and when the drug dealer agreed to pay $10,000, the case was dropped and Leuci collected a commission, though he did not tell Scoppetta how much.

Scoppetta had listened grim-faced to his tale. "What else?" he demanded, when Leuci had finished.

He had been involved in two other similar situations, Leuci said. He did not elaborate. He was watching Scoppetta carefully. He was not worried about being prosecuted. If Scoppetta tried it, which was inconceivable in light of the investigation offered, Leuci could always recant in court.

Nonetheless, he had just admitted to crimes, an admission he did not have to make, and there were some later who found this amazing. His motive, it seems clear, was twofold. First, he was sorely troubled by his past. Guilt and shame afflicted him like a disease. He wore remorse like a heavy overcoat everywhere he went. In making confession, he had hoped to assuage this crushing burden. And indeed, he did feel lighter after speaking out. Second, he was attempting to establish his credentials with Scoppetta; he was saying that, because his own past was dark, the investigation would work—he would be able to get close to some very bad men.

"Three things," said Scoppetta grimly. "Is that all you've done all these years?"

"Nick, that's it," said Leuci.

Scoppetta studied him carefully, then pounded his fist into his hand. "We're going to do something important," he said enthusiastically. "What this investigation has going for it is a real detective."

4

THERE IS ample evidence that Leuci himself was deeply troubled by what he had decided to do. After talking each night away with Scoppetta, he floundered by day through the city, seeking advice from other cops incompetent to give it, one of them a sergeant noted for his incorruptibility, another a former partner who was quite the opposite, and in both cases he risked blowing his cover before it was ever assumed.

There were long, tormented conversations with his wife, most conducted by dawn light as the infant Santina, on Gina's lap, alternately gurgled and sucked at a bottle. The words spilled out of him—words that, to Gina, sounded dangerous.

She had come from Europe at twenty to visit a cousin, and had met Patrolman Leuci. "Talk to her, Dad," Leuci had said proudly the first time he brought her home. "She speaks beautiful Italian."

She still had her Italian passport.

"Gina," she heard her husband say now, "I think I may have found an important friend. Tonight I wanted to tell him everything. I wanted to get it all out. All the things I've been uptight about, sick about over the last several years."

"Who are you going to hurt?" she said. She began to mention detectives Leuci had worked with: what about his three former partners? What about Joe Nunziata, Carl Aguiluz? "Are you going to implicate them? Are you going to ruin their lives?"

"I'm not going to implicate any one close to us."

"Do you think they will allow you to do whatever you choose to do? Do you think they will say: Okay, Bob, whoever you want to tell us about. You decide. I don't think they will allow you to do that."

After a moment she added, "I know you feel guilty. Stop feeling guilty. Other people are responsible, not you. They are guiltier than you are."

In a low voice he replied, "I want to end this life I have been living."

"Then quit the Police Department."

But he loved the Police Department. "And do what? Sell insurance? Work in a bank?"

Gina said, "I know you. It's going to kill you. They will force you to hurt friends, people who have done no harm to you, only good. When you were sick, they all came. They called me every day. I know what kind of man you are. I know what you can live with and what you can't live with. This will kill you. You tell me the feelings you have for informants, and now you are going to be an informant. How are you going to live with that? How am I going to live with you, as you live with that?"

Leuci said, "I am going to make the decision. You are going to decide to stay with me, or not to stay with me. But I am going to make the decision."

This conversation sent him rushing to Brooklyn to see Detective Frank Mandato, one of his ex-partners from SIU. Mandato lived in a new highrise building on Ocean Parkway. He lived on a detective's salary, but there was a doorman downstairs and from his balcony one looked out over New York harbor. Mandato let him in, and they stood in the kitchen while Mandato cooked up a pot of espresso coffee.

Mandato, then thirty-five, had black curly hair, black eyes, and a sculptured black beard. Behind his back, he was sometimes referred to by other detectives as Jesus Christ, or else as The Devil.

Leuci's other two partners had been Les Wolff and Dave Cody, but he felt closest to Mandato, and so it was to Mandato that he had come. He and Mandato had been partners for five years, and they were both Italians.

"I walk into a courtroom," Leuci told Mandato. He was pacing Mandato's living room, tiny cup in hand. He was obviously agitated. "I walk into a D.A.'s office. Guys don't call me Leuci. They smile and say, how's Babyface? It's not funny any more. Because to me Babyface represents the most vile kind of guy."

"What do they know?" Mandato asked soothingly. "Do they know anything about you?" He put his cup down on the coffee table.

Leuci went out through the French doors onto Mandato's balcony. The other detective followed. They stared out over the harbor.

"Remember, Frank," Leuci said, "how we would get together in a restaurant the night before we planned to hit some place? You and me and Les Wolff and Dave Cody. We would have these great spaghetti dinners, and I think we were all afraid. Because the next morning we were going to be kicking doors down. We needed each other. We would talk about the guy we were going to take, and someone would always say: Tony, or Marco, or whatever the guy's name was, I hope you're getting laid tonight, because it's going to be the last time for a long time."

Mandato was watching him carefully.

"Do you understand, Frank? Maybe there are guys doing that right now with you or me, or Wolff or Cody. And I don't want to live that fucking life now. I don't want you to be nobody's fucking target."

This was only part of what Leuci felt: the fear. His remorse was much harder to explain.

Mandato said, "Are you afraid that one of us will turn on you? Is that what it is? Les? Or me? Or Dave?"

"I'm not afraid of you guys turning on me. I'm afraid of me turning on me. I just can't take it any more."

Leuci's voice began to rise until he was yelling. "I don't want to be anybody's target. I don't want to be anybody's target."

Mandato said, "Come on inside. It's cold out here."

It was cold outside the old partnership, outside SIU.

Back in the living room, Mandato said quietly, "What are you going to do, Bob? Should I go perch myself on a ledge right now? Are you going to let me know before they come and drop the safe on me?"

Leuci gazed at his friend. In the last five years he had

spent more time with Mandato than with Gina, had shared more emotions with Mandato than with Gina, and it was possible even that he loved Mandato more than Gina.

"Frank, I'm not going to do anything. What the fuck can I do?"

These scenes show something of Leuci's suffering, something of his indecision, though they fall short of explaining his motivation satisfactorily.

In the end he went back to Scoppetta. It was Scoppetta who projected the strength he was looking for. It was Scoppetta who had sworn to uphold the same laws as himself—and who was doing it. It was Scoppetta who seemed to him to understand all that could not be spoken.

Leuci certainly did not think it out in any reasoned way. He went into the investigation with his eyes firmly closed. He was arrogant enough to believe he could control Scoppetta, could control any prosecutor, could protect himself, could protect his former partners, could protect all of SIU.

He seems to have imagined he could create a new Robert Leuci. "And then I met Scoppetta," he was to say later, "and we changed what I was."

Scoppetta, about to fly to Washington to request funds for the new office, needed some sort of dramatic evidence to bring with him.

By then Leuci had made up his mind. "What would you say," he asked, "if I told you that with a single phone call I can buy the location of every wiretap in the city?"

Scoppetta refused to believe him.

Leuci made the call—to Detective Bernie Geik in the Criminal Investigation Bureau—and later Leuci met with Geik on a midtown sidewalk while wearing a recording device. Scoppetta himself taped the conversation on a machine lying on his lap in a car parked half a block away.

Both horrified and elated by this awful tape, the prosecutor hurried to Washington for meetings at the assistant attorney general level. The funding he needed was accorded, backup agents were assigned him, and arrangements were made to swear him in as a special assistant U.S. attorney in charge of the Leuci investigation. There were later meetings in New York with Justice Department officials, and with Whitney North Seymour, U.S. attorney for the Southern District, and there was a long and rather poignant meeting at Whitman Knapp's club at which the Knapp Commission formally gave Leuci, its prize catch so far, over to federal authorities, and to Scoppetta.

And so the Leuci investigation was begun.

5

SCOPPETTA SET UP his office in the same building as the Knapp Commission, and he began to coordinate his plans with E.M. Shaw, aged thirty-four, seven years a prosecutor, head of the Anti-Corruption Unit in the office of U.S. Attorney Seymour.

Since Leuci could not afford to be spotted in or near any building housing the Knapp Commission or prosecutors, nor in the company of Scoppetta either, strategy meetings began to be held at night in Shaw's apartment in Brooklyn Heights. Shaw's wife Margaret would serve dinner. Afterward the two prosecutors and Leuci would sit around the living room, plotting. Usually Margaret sat cross-legged on the rug, listening with fascination.

Boston-reared and Harvard-educated, Shaw stood six feet five inches tall, and he had the absolute assurance that family lineage and family money sometimes confer. Shaw was a man who could look wealthy even when wearing paint-spattered blue jeans and a T-shirt.

Leuci, though basking in so much attention, was now having second thoughts about his ability to control the directions the investigation might take. He was worried. He wanted to climb up into the criminal justice system as high as district attorneys and judges, but without banging into someone lower down that he cared about. He was trying to figure out how this could be done. He knew he would have to use cops to work his way up higher. He knew he was going to have to implicate cops. But he wanted to be selective. He wanted to pick his targets himself.

Shaw was in a hurry. "Where do we start, and how?" he kept saying, and he kept proposing ideas. But many of these were unacceptable to Leuci.

One of his first plans was to call in the leaders of each of the city's five Mafia families. We tell them, Shaw said, that they may be prosecuted for tax evasion. Then Bob, here, reaches out to them through his organized crime connections. He lets it be known that he has access to the IRS files. Then he meets with them, and they bribe him to get these files. Then we arrest them for bribery of a police officer.

"I can't do that," Leuci protested. "That's a total frame."

Mafia guys were no different from accountants living in Scarsdale, he explained. Tell a man he's being audited by the IRS, and he panics. Sure a Mafia guy would pay Leuci money. So would the accountant in Scarsdale. So would Leuci's next door neighbor, or Shaw's.

And how would Leuci reach these organized crime people? he asked rhetorically. Through his cousin John Lusterino, right? And what would happen to Lusterino afterward? The whole story would be a fabrication, and when the fabrication came to light, Lusterino would be killed.

"What you can't do to organized crime guys," Leuci told Shaw earnestly, for he knew these people, and Shaw did not, "is embarrass them in a make-believe situation, fool them, emasculate them. If there is a real situation, and they come to me, that's another story. My cousin would be clear, even though he recommended me originally. Whenever he introduces me to somebody, he always says, 'Remember, this guy is a cop.' Being a cop is a sickness to Johnny. Anyone who wants to put people in jail, anyone who wants to take someone else's liberty away—there is something wrong there. My cousin always made that clear. All cops are rats. That's the bottom line."

Leuci continued: "But this income tax fabrication you're talking of—that's a total frame, and he would definitely be killed."

Shaw nodded, and the tax idea was dropped.

Leuci's car, a new 1971 Pontiac, was driven up to Boston to Bell and Howell. A false wall was built into the trunk with a tape recorder behind it. A telescopic microphone was planted in the ceiling of the car, one so sensitive it could pick up even whispers. The on-off switch was built into the buckle of the safety belt.

Leuci began to insist that he be transferred back into SIU, so that he could move freely about the city, so that he would stand constantly with lawyers, judges, D.A.'s in situations where big money existed and payoffs tended to occur.

But no one had ever been transferred back into SIU. Scoppetta would have to go directly to Police Commissioner Patrick Murphy, and this seemed a dangerous step.

In his public statements the new commissioner had proclaimed himself a foe of corruption. But Murphy, underneath it all, was still a cop. A single second-grade detective now threatened possibly to tear Murphy's department apart, and Murphy could not be expected to be handed this knowledge and then do nothing. He would have to tell someone, at least his first deputy, and total security would be over. It was too risky. If Leuci's cover was blown, the investigation was blown—all that time, work, money wasted. Furthermore, if Leuci got caught wearing a recording device while gathering evidence against corrupt people, he could get killed.

So Shaw returned to the idea of Lusterino. Lusterino was a captain in the Colombo family, Shaw noted. As such he represented a rich source of potential intelligence. Shaw asked if Leuci would be willing to make secret tape recordings with his cousin, provided certain conditions were met.

The recordings would be used for intelligence purposes only—for whatever insights they might provide into the Mafia. Shaw would personally listen to them himself. The tapes would be kept in his personal safe. Under no circumstances would they be made public, or used as the basis of a prosecution. There was no way that the tape or tapes could hurt Lusterino, who would never know they had been made.

"You want me to secretly tape my cousin," cried Leuci angrily. "I won't do it."

Scoppetta at such times had a way of putting his head

in his hands. Or else he would look down and rub his eyes. He was afraid Shaw would scare Leuci away. In private conversations Shaw and Scoppetta would agree to be patient with Leuci. Still, they had to get this investigation moving.

Shaw was interested only in the Mafia itself, he told Leuci. Not Lusterino at all: Lusterino was safe with him. But how did the Mafia work? How were new soldiers inducted? How was money moved from one place to another? How did the different families get in touch with one another?

When Scoppetta and Leuci had left Shaw's apartment, Scoppetta said, "He knows better than to push you on that. We'll talk to him some more about it."

Shaw kept pleading. The Lusterino tapes would provide law enforcement with invaluable knowledge.

Again Leuci refused. "My father would despise me. He has no great love for Johnny, but it's his nephew. It's his sister's son. Johnny's my cousin. Do you follow me?"

To Shaw, Lusterino was a forty-two-year-old mobster who had already served more than fifteen years in prison. But all he said was, "Of course I do. Please believe that we will never force you to do something that you can't live with."

6

IN MARCH 1971, with the Leuci investigation barely two weeks old, two FBI agents presented themselves at the Bureau of Criminal Investigation, where they were received by Detective Bernie Geik. They asked to research the files on Mikey Coco.

Mikey Coco had been, in his youth, a Mafia street enforcer. Now forty-eight, he moved in the hierarchy of organized crime. He operated a luncheonette at 100th Street and Central Park West, and was believed to own part of a Bronx travel agency. He was allegedly part of a group of organized crime figures who, using strong-arm methods, were taking over legitimate businesses on Long Island, including bars, restaurants, used car lots, and garbage companies. He was seen frequently at the Blue Lounge, Chez Joey, and Sleepy's Lagoon Clam House, all in the Bronx, all known mob hangouts, and all kept under almost permanent surveillance by law ·enforcement agencies. He was reputed to be attempting, through a front, to gain control of the Clam House.

His associates were almost exclusively Mafia figures believed to be involved in drugs: Joe Indelicata, Dom Trinchera, David Petillo, Anthony Novello, Sal Panico. Previously Coco had been closely involved with Frank Mari, a Mafia underboss and drug dealer now missing.

Coco himself was a major narcotics importer. He lived in the suburb of Dobbs Ferry with his common-law wife Phyllis, who had once been wanted for questioning in the shooting of Detective Vince Albano outside Chez Joey.

Coco's cousin, Oscar Ansourian, was believed to have shot Emmanuel Morris, and to have dumped the body on the lawn of Joseph "Bug" Bugliarelli in Dobbs Ferry three years before. Coco was believed to have been involved in this murder and in numerous others, including that of Frank Salzberg, who died of multiple stab wounds in the back in 1968. More recently a gang of young hoodlums had kidnapped Mafia figures and held them for ransom. Certain law enforcement figures believed Coco and several others had trailed this gang to Louisiana and killed four of them. Altogether, police intelligence files connected him with up to seven murders.

Coco was unusual among high-ranking Mafiosi in that he was not Italian. He was the son of Armenian immigrants, and his legal name was Murad Nersesian. He had been a teenage paratrooper during World War II and had seen bloody fighting in North Africa. He had won medals for killing Germans. When he came back from that war, never having learned a trade, knowing nothing, he went into the streets. He went back to the one trade he knew: he went back to war.

The war he came home to was not much different from the one he had left. The late forties were tumultuous for the New York underworld. Mafia families reached for power, and the streets were full of corpses with Italian names. Young thugs who had seen heavy fighting in Europe were lining up on the different sides, not only for or against the five major families, but also for or against various family segments. Mikey Coco had sided with Joey Gambino's people in the Bronx.

There was a group of these freelance shooters and they were called the paratroopers. Carmine Persico, Mikey Coco, Alphonse Indelicata, Sonny Pinto, Joey Accafelli. These were all ruthless young men, some of whom developed into cold-blooded killers, but they were also more intelligent than most street hoodlums. Their allegiance was to Joseph Gambino, and through him to Carlo Gambino. When Carlo Gambino came out on top as *capo di tutti capi,* the paratroopers became, as Mafia jargon had it, "made" men, and after that they had few worries. Money began to come to them from loan-sharking and gambling. Coco during the fifties was earning up to $1000 a week.

Being an Armenian, he always sensed that he was not

totally accepted. "I'm more of an Italian than all of the Italians," he would say. "I have more heart than all of them."

He had enjoyed a big reputation. He was brave and he was vicious.

"A tough guy is not someone who can pull the trigger," he said once. "A child can pull the trigger. A tough guy is someone who can go out and eat a good dinner afterwards." He pointed to Carmine Persico, who was almost a cripple, as a tough guy.

He himself was a tough guy also.

Before long Frank Mari, a major narcotics dealer who was having trouble collecting, took Coco in as partner. Once customers knew they were dealing with Mikey Coco, there was no longer any problem collecting.

Overnight, narcotics made him a wealthy man. Within two months he was earning $5000 a week—some weeks $10,000 or even $15,000—without doing much for it. He made certain arrangements. He went to Florida a lot to close deals. He never went near a package himself.

He had no great understanding of narcotics personally, no idea how drugs were processed, or even how they were used.

"Marijuana makes you stupid," he said once. "Why would I use marijuana? I'm stupid enough already. I should take marijuana to make me more stupid? What do these addicts do with it, anyway? I know they smoke it. But they also shoot it up, don't they?"

He was a big spender. At one time he drove a Rolls-Royce. He was capable of leaving a waitress a fifty-dollar tip. Since he was frequently under surveillance, friends called such behavior outrageous and remonstrated with him for bringing attention onto himself.

But attention was what he wanted. "What else am I living this kind of life for?" he asked. "I walk in here next week and she'll remember me. They will all remember me. I'll do my time in jail when they catch me. Meanwhile, I'm out here. I'm an important guy. If I can have one year on the street, I'll do five years in jail any time."

He had been sentenced at age sixteen to three years for

armed robbery, and in later cases he drew a three-year term for possession and sale of counterfeit money, and an eight-to-ten-year term for sale of heroin. Other arrests were for disorderly conduct, for possession of an illegal gun, for violation of the gambling laws, and for contempt of court. When subpoenaed to testify anywhere, he regularly refused to answer questions; at least once he was jailed a month for civil contempt.

Most of the foregoing information the two FBI agents found in Coco's file, while Detective Geik hovered nearby, paying close attention to their conversation. As soon as they were gone, Geik phoned his friend Leuci.

"They were trying to associate Coco with someone else," Geik reported, "someone who is also an organized crime guy, only they don't know his name. They were trying to identify this other guy. He is supposed to be short and stocky, in his early forties, with mixed gray hair." There was a pause. Then Geik said, "You know Coco. I'd like to sell this information to him. I'd like you to reach out for him for me. See if he is interested in it."

Leuci did know Coco, and after hanging up, he thought about Geik's proposal—and about Coco—for a long time.

To reach Coco, one dialed the number of Sleepy's Lagoon Clam House and left a message. Leuci did this, and in due time his own phone rang. He picked it up. Coco had numerous aliases, but on the phone, for unknown reasons, he always identified himself as Sidney.

"Bobby," he rasped, "this is Sidney." It was a voice like broken plates grating together in a sack.

They agreed to meet at night in the parking lot of the Baychester Diner in the Bronx. Leuci, as he drove his altered Pontiac toward this meeting, was as troubled as if he were on his way to entrap a fellow cop. He had known Coco so long that the man was almost a close friend. Leuci in no way romanticized Coco, yet he had from the beginning been fascinated both by the man himself, and by the glimpses he permitted into the Mafia world. In addition, Coco had always been nice to him, and concerned about him. Most of Leuci's other Mafia contacts were crude, vicious men, and some were psychopaths.

His earliest meeting with Coco had been set up by Lusterino, who had told him, "Mikey Coco wants to meet you. I don't know what about."

So he and Coco had sat together in a booth in a diner in Queens. Coco, Leuci noted, not only had the voice of a Mafia enforcer, he also looked like one. He was five feet ten, weighed 210 pounds, and was built square. His hair was black, his eyes were deep-set and black, and his flat nose had been broken many times. He had a dark pockmarked face. Both his arms were tattooed: two eagles, a tiger, a dagger, and the words "U.S. Army."

Of course Leuci knew of the tattoos, and of Coco's reputation as an enforcer, only from the files.

The drug dealer had been wearing a leather zipper jacket, but it was an expensive one. His shoes and trousers were expensive too. Leuci judged that Coco's outfit had cost about $500. Despite his burly build and pockmarked face, the mobster looked, to Leuci, very nice, and he had asked, "What did you want to see me about, Mike?"

It seemed that Coco and his partners had just been shaken down by two SIU detectives: pay or get arrested. They had paid. Now a third detective was demanding money too. "I'd tell him to fuck off," Coco said, "but I'll meet him if I can trust him. Everybody's got to earn. I like to see people earn, but I'm not going to meet some cop that turns out to be a rat, too. You come on a very high recommendation from your cousin. I want you to tell me if I can trust him. His name is Detective Bell."

Leuci had said carefully, "If you'd like, I'll meet him for you."

"No, I want him to look in my face one time. I want him to see my eyes once."

Leuci said, "Are you as bad as everyone says you are?"

Coco said, "A lot worse."

Reaching into his pocket, Coco had withdrawn a wad of bills, which he handed to Leuci.

But Leuci said, "Mike I don't want money from you. You're asking me if you can trust Dick Bell? You can trust him. Is that such a big deal? You don't feel good unless you give me money. Feel good. I like you. We'll be in touch with each other."

Coco laughed. "You're pretty good," he said.

After that first meeting, Leuci had begun to meet Coco from time to time. The mobster wanted to know what life was like in the police world, and in exchange he talked often about his own life and code.

Now, four years later, as Leuci in his car in the parking lot waited for Coco to appear, these memories and others crowded his head, and he attempted to give himself a pep talk. He was not betraying anybody here tonight. He was doing his job. Mikey Coco was a major Mafia drug dealer. Geik was a corrupt cop. Leuci was about to put together a case involving the sale of confidential police information by the corrupt cop Geik to the Mafia drug dealer Coco. It was the perfect kind of case, the kind he really wanted to make.

After tonight, Coco would go to jail. It would be an easy case. The reason it would be easy was because Coco trusted him.

As Leuci's fingers toyed indecisively with the switch built into his seat belt, a new Mercedes pulled into the parking lot. He watched Mikey Coco jump out, cross the lot, and slip into the seat beside him.

The drug dealer was glad to see him, and greeted him warmly. Freeing his hand from Coco's grip, Leuci reached down to the seat belt, and threw the switch. He then began to explain about Detective Bernie Geik, about the FBI investigation, about the man with the mixed gray hair whom they were trying to link to Coco but who was otherwise unidentified.

Coco said, "Forty years old with mixed gray hair. It could be anybody. This is a fucking puzzle. You brought me a fucking puzzle. Is this guy I'm supposed to have met in junk?"

"No, gambling."

Above their heads the concealed microphone plucked their words out of the air, and behind the dummy panel in the trunk the tape recorder preserved each one.

"Gambling is worse than junk. You have more people watching you for gambling than anything else." Coco took a roll of bills from his pocket. "Here's a thousand dollars. Give it to this Detective Geik. Tell him I'd like to get together with him. You take whatever you want from there."

Leuci nodded politely. He thought of the tape turning, and of the money in his fingers. Two solid pieces of evidence. The case was solid. Coco, already in prison for half his life, faced more of the same.

Business concluded, Coco began to talk about other subjects. Black revolutionaries, he had read in the paper, had begun shooting at cops from ambush. A gruff affection came into his voice. The article had made him worry about the safety of his friend Bobby.

"You cops spend all your time chasing guys like me around, looking to give us aggravation," Coco continued, "while some black son of a bitch is looking to come up and blow your brains out. Those are the guys you should be worried about. We'll never kill you." Suddenly he grinned, having found a solution to the problem. "Give me a year or two, and one day I'll poison the packages and kill a million of the bastards."

Very funny. Leuci was laughing. But a jury, he realized, probably a jury with one or more black jurors on it, would soon listen to this tape, and they were not going to laugh. Secret tapes, Leuci reflects, represented insights into a defendant to which juries normally were not entitled. He was guilty of betraying Coco more deeply even than he had imagined, of exposing to jurors even the man's casual prejudices.

"You know why I don't carry no gun?" said Coco amiably. "Because every nigger I know has got a gun. You got a gun, you get in trouble. I don't need no gun. I got a little hatchet that I keep under the seat of my car. Some son of a bitch bangs into my car, I jump out and beat him with the hatchet."

This time Leuci only smiled.

Coco, lounging against the car door, began to talk about stool pigeons, how much he loathed them. The drug business was plagued by them, he said. A stool pigeon was a rat, a cancer. The only solution was to eradicate every one you found, for there was no lower form of life.

It made Leuci squirm in his seat. He has learned to like me, Leuci thought, and to trust me, but tonight, as far as he is concerned, I have become a stool pigeon, indistinguishable from any other.

Leuci had fallen silent. The drug dealer, noting this, was immediately concerned. "You're not yourself tonight, Bobby. What's the matter? Don't you feel well? Is it your job? Would you rather be a steelworker? I can get you into the steelworkers' union. But you've got to be nuts to want to be a steelworker, and go up there and break your back."

When Leuci remained despondent, Coco said soothingly, "We need you where you are, Bobby. You know we need you. We trust you. These other cops are out to suck our blood. Not you. You got to stick around because you're the only one we can trust."

An hour later in Scoppetta's living room, Leuci threaded the tape onto the machine, and they sat listening to the gruff-voiced mobster.

"Here's a thousand dollars. Give it to this Detective Geik..."

That one line was enough, Leuci realized. Coco would go to prison because of a forty-year-old guy with mixed gray hair whom he couldn't even remember. He'd go to jail because of a thousand dollars, and by his own lights he wasn't trying to bribe anyone, he was just buying goodwill.

Scoppetta had stayed up late, reading a book of short stories, waiting for Leuci. Now, listening with considerable excitement, he kept saying, "This is a great case."

But Leuci said, "Tonight I felt like a snake that had crawled into this guy's bed, and I struck out at him. I have difficulty handling this thing."

Scoppetta turned off the machine. Watching Leuci closely, he said, "That's why you are so important, Bob. That's why you are about to make such a meaningful contribution to society. No ordinary undercover cop could get involved in this at the level you can. Do you realize what you have done here today? You have a cop in an extremely sensitive position selling confidential information to an organized crime guy. A guy who has killed a number of people."

But Leuci shook his head. "Going out and making cases against people I don't know," he said, "developing new situations—I have no trouble with that. But I don't know if I can handle much more like tonight. The conversation on that tape"—he gestured toward the machine—"was not between a cop and an organized crime guy. It was between two people who knew each other. Maybe I don't belong inside his world, but I was there with him tonight, and he was totally disarmed. He wasn't guarded in his conversation. He trusted me totally. He's going to pay for that."

Scoppetta said, "Coco's a killer. Think about the times he sat in the back seat of a car, and some unsuspecting guy was sitting in front of him, and they drove the guy some place. He did that to a number of guys. You know he did. He lives in a world that we've got to get rid of."

Later, as he slid into bed beside his sleeping wife, Scoppetta felt pleased with himself. He thought he had handled Leuci's misgivings carefully and well.

Leuci thought this also. When he got home he said to Gina, "Nick was very good tonight."

Nonetheless Leuci lay awake for a long time. To reinforce the case he would have to meet Geik and hand over the bribe. After that he would have to set up a meeting between Geik and Coco, putting them together on the same tape. Two bad characters would be put out of circulation, justice would be served. He foresaw no risk, because Geik and Coco both trusted him. In the interest of a higher good he would betray two men who trusted him. He lay in the dark feeling depressed.

7

AS ALWAYS, Scoppetta sat with a legal pad on his knee, alternately reading from and jotting down notes. Across the room, the tall, skinny Shaw lay on the sofa with his shoes off, his long legs hanging over the end, and he watched Leuci over steepled fingers.

"What about Captain Tange?" inquired Scoppetta.

Daniel Tange had commanded SIU during Leuci's years there; in fact it was he who had promoted Leuci into the elite unit in 1967. Then only thirty-six, Tange was one of the youngest captains in Police Department history, and one of the most brilliant as well. It was predicted that he would one day rise to chief of detectives at least, if not police commissioner.

Tange had been sent into Narcotics on temporary assignment at first. His job was to investigate allegations of misconduct against detectives. He took over office space and began summoning detectives. Word spread quickly through the division: this guy Tange is bad news.

Leuci's turn had come. Captain Tange was not smiling, and he did not invite the detective to take the empty chair beside his desk. He showed a letter that had come in signed by a man named Carti. According to Carti, Leuci had planted narcotics on Carti's cousin, arrested him, and taken money from him.

"It's all bullshit, captain," said Leuci. But he was scared. All detectives, guilty or innocent, were scared of investigations like this.

There were a number of similar allegations against Leuci, Tange said, and he had been studying them for several days. "They can't all be bullshit," he declared.

He was dressed in sports coat and slacks, with a buttondown collar and rep tie. He was college-educated, articulate, handsome. Being of Irish Catholic extraction, he fitted easily into the Police Department power structure, but he seemed to represent—as opposed to the boorish, cigar-smoking officers of the past—the best of the new young officers now rising to the top.

Allegations against active detectives were not unusual. Friends and relatives of men they had arrested often wrote scurrilous letters to the police commissioner or a district attorney. The defendants were fighting to stay out of jail after all. The vast majority of allegations were false, and, in the past, no detective had had much to worry about. The allegation would be bucked down to his own lieutenant, who would interview the complainant and usually try to arrest him. The street people knew this, and were loath to make allegations at all. Even if, after investigating an allegation, the lieutenant believed it to be true, still he would probably bury it, for the alternative was to arrest one of his own detectives, and this, in 1967, just was not done.

Captain Tange began mentioning to Leuci names of other allegations against him. Had he ever given narcotics to these people? But Leuci had denied every charge.

Beginning the next day Tange went out and himself interrogated certain of the complainants, after which he informed Leuci that every allegation lacked corroboration. Therefore he was closing them all out.

"But the next time," he threatened, "I'll have your head. You can tell every detective out there that if I catch anyone one inch off base, they are going to jail. I don't care how things were done before I came here, but they will be done differently from now on." Then he added, "I'm recommending that you be moved up into SIU."

Midway through 1967, Tange himself was appointed commander of SIU. For several days he walked in each morning wearing his freshly shaven face and his nice collegiate clothes, walked past all the detectives without so much as a nod, entered his office, and closed the door. Everyone was concerned. What would he do?

A message went up on the bulletin board: Office meeting for tomorrow morning at ten o'clock.

The detectives were waiting nervously when Tange strode to the front of the room and demanded order.

"Apparently this office is made up entirely of superstars," he began, once they were silent.

For the last several days he had been studying their case folders, he told them. Though they might be superstars, their case folders proved some of them incompetent and inefficient, and suggested that others were corrupt. Well, the incompetents were about to get bounced out of SIU; those who stayed had best understand his feelings about corruption. He hated it. He would arrest without a qualm any cop he caught.

The assembled detectives began sliding down in their seats, and when Tange had left the room they gathered, shaken, in small groups. Mostly these groups broke down along ethnic lines, for that was the way close friendships tended to form in SIU. Leuci talked it over with Nunziata and Mandato while Aguiluz, Codelia, and the other Hispanic detectives conversed volubly nearby in Spanish. Nunziata at this time was already the most magnetic and respected cop in SIU, but Aguiluz, his monumental seizure still two years in the future, was not yet even a team leader. Instead he worked on the fringe of Nunziata's team whenever a wireman or translator was needed.

Nunziata was extremely worried by Tange's tough speech, he told Leuci. He was convinced that Tange was straight—straight enough even to lock up another cop. Leuci was worried too, but he was also in some strange way elated. A man like Tange could change SIU into the efficient, incorruptible, elite unit it was supposed to be. He could turn them all back into knights on white chargers again.

Tange's first order was to clean the office up. He wanted the floors swept, the files organized. No longer aloof, he moved through the corridors with his sleeves rolled up and his tie down, giving orders. He talked to his detectives in small groups, giving them direction, promising money to make buys, money to pay informants. He promised new equipment too, especially radio equipment. He made them rewrite their wiretap and search warrant applications, and more of these began to be accorded than ever before.

A number of detectives were afraid of Tange. A number watched him shrewdly, waiting with a certain cynicism to see him show his true colors. And a number, Leuci for one, were delighted with the young captain, and with the sense of mission he had brought to their lives.

Next Tange tried to put in controls. He wanted at least one member of every team in the office every day, and he gave orders to this effect. But the detectives screamed loudly that the dope dealers were out there, not in here. They protested so much and resisted so hard that Tange rescinded his order after about two weeks.

One night, about two months after Tange had taken command, Sergeant Jack Hourigan passed the word to several detectives: Tange wanted to meet them, separately, in Jimmy's bar across the street. "The worm has turned in the apple," said Hourigan cryptically. "You have a new partner."

Leuci went to confer with Nunziata. "What's going on, Joe?"

Detective Nunziata, grinning broadly, was shaking his head back and forth. He had to meet Tange at 6:30, he said, thirty minutes before Leuci. "I think the guy is Italian, and he changed his name," Nunziata joked.

At seven o'clock Leuci sat opposite Captain Tange in a booth in Jimmy's bar.

"Would you like a drink?" inquired Captain Tange.

Tange, in civilian clothes, began by praising Leuci's work. There were only a few SIU teams who knew their jobs, he said. One of the best was Leuci's team. Leuci was an outstanding detective.

Leuci's drink was set down before him.

As for himself, Tange said, he would not remain a captain long. He was the youngest captain in the job. His future was unlimited. To Leuci the inference was clear. Every detective needed a rabbi to help his career along and Tange figured to be as good a rabbi as Leuci could hope for.

"But I've got a long way to go," Tange said. His hand toyed with his glass on the table. "And I just bought a house out in Northport. I went way over my head."

For Leuci a light dawned, and he understood at last what was coming. He had heard enough other cops, who had never taken money before, try to rationalize doing it. Tange described his house: it was on four acres overlooking Long Island Sound, he said, and had to be seen to be believed. "I thought I could afford it. But I can't."

"What are you trying to say, captain?" asked Leuci bluntly.

"You have a new partner, and it's me," said Tange. He was studying his glass. "I get an equal share of anything you do."

Now it was Leuci's turn to stare at the table top. He had never committed a dishonest act in his life, he said, and he didn't know what Tange might be referring to.

Tange only nodded. His voice grew hard and he sounded like a commander again. "If I find out that you have done anything and haven't paid me my share," he said, "I'll not only have your job, I'll have your head." The money was to go through Sergeant Hourigan, who would serve as bagman.

Tange served three years as SIU commander, and during that time had no difficulty meeting payments on his house in Northport. Meantime, with each major heroin seizure by SIU detectives his reputation soared within the department, and shortly before the Leuci investigation began he had been handed a new and choice assignment—command of the Twenty-eighth Precinct in Harlem, one of the most sensitive jobs in the department and one calling for deputy inspector rank. He was still only thirty-nine. His rise to the top had begun.

But now Scoppetta, studying old SIU rosters, had chanced to notice his name and, with Leuci sitting across the room, had asked, "What about Captain Tange?"

At first Leuci defended Tange as a fine and honest man, adding, "He'll be chief of detectives some day."

But Scoppetta rejected this remark. "If there was corruption in the unit," he said doggedly, "and if Tange was so bright, then he should have known about it."

Scoppetta studied Leuci. The detective was a good actor—the tapes with Geik and Coco proved it—but a bad liar, for his emotions were close to the surface, as now. In his shifting eyes, in the pinch of his mouth, Leuci's inner conflict showed.

It was a question of loyalty, Scoppetta judged. Loyalty to Tange and SIU versus loyalty to Scoppetta. Scoppetta had never yet betrayed Leuci. Had Tange?

After a moment, having made his decision, Leuci muttered, "He'll take money."

Though Scoppetta and Shaw immediately tried to interrogate Leuci, he refused to say how he knew this about Tange, or what his experiences with Tange had been. Instead, he demanded $500. He would hand $500 to Tange and would make a recording, he said. If Tange took the money, this would prove him a crook. There was no need to go back into the past.

But money to Scoppetta was money. He was afraid someone would judge his investigation too expensive and shut it off. Certainly he now wanted to nail Tange if possible—who else had nailed a police captain?—but he wanted to do it cheaply.

Also he wanted more information from Leuci, and he went on questioning him. What possible grounds did Leuci have for handing Tange money, he demanded? And when Leuci declined to reply, he added, "I mean, you can't just hand him five hundred dollars for no reason."

"Don't tell me what I can do and what I can't do," Leuci retorted. "I don't need a reason to give him money."

Scoppetta sighed, and the next day signed out the money and, in a disgruntled mood, handed it over to his undercover detective. This was no way to conduct an intelligent long-term investigation, he told himself. It would never work. But for the moment he had no choice. Leuci, he realized, had begun to try to take control of the investigation into his own hands—a drift that would have to be stopped at once.

*　*　*

That night Leuci drove up into Harlem. He had $500 in his pocket and an appointment with Captain Tange. It was raining. The streets were wet and glistening.

You could have led us, captain, Leuci brooded as he drove along, windshield wipers swishing. We were the best detectives in the city. You could have given us purpose, you could have won us the kind of honor and respect we had never had before. Instead of that, you set yourself up as a partner. You appointed Sergeant Hourigan as bagman. Hourigan was a lovely guy, but he was weak, and he was a drunk. He was a bad drinker, a dangerous drinker. Dealing with Hourigan was like dealing with dynamite.

A leader must be able to pick his subordinates, captain. And who did you pick? You picked Hourigan, a crony from your days as a motorcycle cop. What kind of a captain is that? Did you ever hear Hourigan's great line, captain? "The worm has turned in the apple." He not only told me, he told the clerical man, and the switchboard man. Once he walked into an office containing nine SIU detectives. Nine men stood up in unison and chanted, "The worm has turned in the apple." This was Hourigan's big secret—and yours—that he was telling to everybody.

Leuci parked outside the station house, and felt himself briefly. The money made a bulge in one pocket, and the transmitter made a bulge at his belt. He ducked through the rain into the station house, and went into Tange's office. Tange seemed glad to see him, for his handshake was firm, his greeting effusive.

The two old friends chatted about recent transfers and other department gossip. Leuci remarked that he hoped to get back into SIU soon. Then, claiming that he had something personal to discuss, he invited Tange for a ride in his car. One can't hand over money inside a station house.

The two men drove along in the rain. A captain in the Police Department is like a Mafia don, Leuci thought, as he tried to explain to himself what was about to happen. I will give him money on general principles, and he'll take it. I will give him money because he's the reason I'm in this mess. He's the reason I'm betraying cops. He could have saved all of us.

Not that he was trying to punish Tange for the past, Leuci assured himself. All Tange had to do was refuse the money. If he did, then Leuci would never tell anyone about Tange's past, about going into partnership with his men. If Tange refused the money tonight, then he was in the clear.

It was Leuci's game, and he had begun changing the rules because these new ones were the only ones he could live by. Because Scoppetta's were too strict. It was complicated, and, to anyone else, incomprehensible.

And if Tange took the money? If he took it, then his career was over at thirty-nine, and to some extent his life. But if he takes it, Leuci told himself, it will not be me ruining Tange's life, it will be Tange ruining his own life.

And so, taking one hand off the wheel, Leuci put it into his pocket and found the wad of money there. He brought it out.

"Listen, captain, I did something last week," he said. "I want to give you something," and he handed across the $500.

Tange took it. "I appreciate that," he said. "Do you want to play golf next week?"

In Shaw's apartment later that same evening, Leuci played the recording for the two prosecutors. "I don't hear the money being passed," Scoppetta said, listening hard. "I don't hear him receiving the money."

Leuci pushed the reverse button on the machine, stopped the tape, then started it forward again. "I tell him, 'I want to give you something,' and he answers, 'I appreciate that.' There, hear it?"

Scoppetta heard it, and it made him angry. "That's no good in court, and you know it," he snapped. "You never even mentioned money. When you hand somebody money, tell him, 'Here, here's the money'. Count it, dammit, say something to show you're giving over money."

"I'm the cop," asserted Leuci. "I'm the undercover

agent. If I say to him, here's the money, Tange will either go into shock, or he'll jump out of the car and call Internal Affairs. He'll do something crazy, because I've never spoken to him like that before. No one speaks to someone like that when giving money." Leuci snorted derisively. "Here's the money. Don't tell me how to pass money to someone."

Both had lost sight—Shaw too—of the essential fact revealed: how did Leuci know all this?

Scoppetta stomped angrily about the room.

Leuci had been searched by his backup agents before leaving to meet Tange, and then had been handed the $500. The two agents had never lost sight of him, except while he was inside the station house. After he had left Tange they had searched him again, and the $500 was gone. This was good evidential procedure. Still, if Tange ever came to trial, his defense lawyer could always suggest that Leuci had secreted the money inside the station house, or even thrown it away.

Scoppetta said, "That's $500 wasted. Maybe you don't want to make a case against Tange. Is that it? You'll have to meet him again. There's not enough here."

Leuci, furious, stared at the back of Scoppetta's head.

"We want him solid," said Scoppetta, turning to face the detective. "And from now on I want to hear money exchanged. If you're going to exchange money I want to hear it."

The two men glared at each other.

Shaw, reclining on the room sofa with his shoes off, said, "Calm down, Nick."

Scoppetta was very upset.

"He's a police captain, Bob," said Shaw. "In a one-on-one situation the jury would believe him, not you. You'll have to get a better recording."

8

IT WAS Leuci's job to set up another meeting with Coco, this time putting him together with Detective Bernie Geik.

To this meeting Leuci wore a one-watt Kel transmitter that was about the size of a Zippo lighter. Together with its small but powerful batteries, it was taped flat to his waist. The bands of tape had been wound as tightly as he could stand them around his middle, so that transmitter and batteries were pressed into his body. Afterwards the tape had been patted as smooth as careful fingers could make it. There were no rough edges. Anyone giving Leuci a casual search would feel what appeared to be just another roll of flesh.

The tiny microphone was taped to the middle of his chest; it could be mistaken for a button, or for medals or jewelry hanging from his neck by a chain. The microphone wire running up his belly and sternum was under tape, and two antenna wires, which ran up over his shoulders, were taped in place also. Leuci believed himself safe from discovery unless someone ordered him stripped, or unless he was carefully patted down by someone who knew what he was looking for.

His backup agents were two IRS men lent to Scoppetta for this purpose. Their job was to stay close enough to Leuci to record his transmissions, which carried only a block or two, and also to rush forward as bodyguards if needed. But they were men used to catching crooked accountants and tax cheats. They were not street people and they were incapable—as was about to be proven—of maintaining a difficult tail.

Tonight's meeting place was again the parking lot of the Baychester Diner. The difference was that this time, instead of climbing into Leuci's car, Coco invited Leuci and Geik, who had arrived together, into his Mercedes. He then accelerated in a squeal of rubber, made a violent U-turn, jumped the divider, and sped north out of the city—maneuvers the IRS backup team failed to follow.

Leuci, wearing his incriminating gear, was now alone in the night in a car with a corrupt cop and a Mafia enforcer. There was nothing he could do about it. He settled back in his seat and tried to calculate his options. Both these men faced jail terms because of him. If they were suspicious of him, what would they do about it? His biggest risk was that they would demand to search him, and he tried to figure where and how this would be done, and what his reactions should be.

Geik was armed. Coco was possibly armed.

Geik, chatting amiably in the back seat, did not seem suspicious. Coco was silent. He drove normally now, and as he gazed out over the wheel his pockmarked face revealed nothing.

Had he spotted the backup car back at the parking lot? If not, why all those violent turns? Did he associate the backup car with Leuci?

Geik was a detective, Leuci reflected. Geik knew about wires. If Geik patted him down, he would find it.

As he considered all this, Leuci became increasingly nervous, with the result that he began to sweat, and almost immediately he became conscious of a sharp burning pain near his navel, where his batteries and transmitter were taped. The excessive sweat pouring off him seemed to have set off a short circuit. The batteries and transmitter were burning him, but there was nothing he could do about this either, unless he wished to rip open his shirt and yank off that tape.

Coco drove steadily north. Leuci beside him sat perfectly still, his mind focused now on the pain at his waist.

In Yonkers, thirty minutes later, Coco pulled into the parking lot beside an Italian restaurant. The three men walked inside, took a table, and ordered dinner.

Excusing himself then, Leuci carefully stood up, and went carefully out through the tables and into the men's room. Once inside, he looked for a way to bolt the door, for he wanted to get his fingers under the tape, to get that transmitter away from his flesh.

Unfortunately there was no bolt, no way to lock the outer door at all. There was no door on the one toilet stall either. To get at the tape around his middle he would have to open his clothes, but Geik or Coco at any moment might walk in on him. He couldn't risk it. Standing at the urinal with his fly open, he reached upward and tried to dig his fingers under the tape. But the gum had melted. He tried to pluck the transmitter, which felt now red hot, away from his belly, but he failed. The tape would not come free. He could not get his fingers under it.

So he went back to the table. He had been gone a long time, and Coco, watching him approach, looked worried. "You don't look too good," said the mobster solicitously. A candle burned on their table. The flame sent strange shadows flickering across the flat nosed, pockmarked face, imparting to it the look of a friendly satyr. "Are you sure you're okay, Bobby?"

Leuci managed a smile. "Sure, Mike."

Reassured, the mobster began to eat. Leuci watched him devour a huge mound of fettucine swimming in clam sauce, followed by a plate of dripping cannelloni stuffed with veal and sausage. Salad was served. Then dessert.

At last the bill was paid, and they were crossing the parking lot toward Coco's Mercedes. Coco started the car and steered back toward the city. Leuci's pain seemed to have doubled in intensity. He was trying to hold himself very still, thinking that if he once began to squirm, he wouldn't be able to stop. Coco and Geik were talking about electronic surveillance. Geik was revealing all the department's secrets. Coco, driving slowly, was listening with fascination.

Leuci's pain had become terrific, and he was trying, as inconspicuously as possible, to slip his fingers through his shirt and under the tape. But the transmitter remained inviolable. Afraid Coco might notice, Leuci brought his fingers out of his shirt. But they soon went back in again, trying and failing to dig under the tape. Also he had began—only slightly for the moment—to squirm.

Presently Coco began to sniff the air. "There's a terrible stink in this car," he said. "Did someone step in some dog shit or something? Hey, this is an expensive car. Check your feet." He pulled over to the curb, and the overhead light came on. Three grown men examined the soles of three pairs of shoes.

"I don't know what it could be," Coco said, driving on, "but there's still a terrible stink in here."

Leuci, focused in on his pain, had at first smelled nothing. But the odor got through to him now and he recognized it. It was burning flesh, his own, and this realization made him squirm worse than before.

Half an hour later the neon sign of the Baychester Diner at last came into view. Coco drove into the lot and parked beside Leuci's car. By then sweat was pouring down Leuci's face, and the mobster, after turning off the ignition, noticed it. Reaching over, he felt Leuci's forehead. "I think you got a fever," Coco told him. "You're coming down with something."

"My God, your whole back is soaking wet," said Geik. He was leaning over the seat, his hand on Leuci's back.

"You better get home and get to bed," Coco said, his face showing great concern. Leuci didn't want advice; he wanted Coco to leave, and Geik to leave.

Coco at last drove off, but Geik still waited beside Leuci's car. He was waiting to be driven home. Leuci was scarcely aware of this.

"I have to go to the bathroom," he mumbled, and ran. He ran into the diner and through into the men's room, where he closed the door of the toilet stall, tore open his clothes and, with his trousers half way down his legs, tried to rip the tape from his body. But it was still stuck to him, and the pain had made his fingers blunt and inaccurate. At last it began to come free. He kept pulling at it, ripping it off his skin, until at last the Kel set and the batteries were revealed. The transmitter, he saw, had slipped out of its pouch and was stuck to his flesh. When he had peeled it carefully off himself, he saw it had burned away a patch of skin the size of a half dollar.

Now that he had the belt off, he didn't know what to do with it. He couldn't just leave it in the toilet stall—it would cause talk and this was a place Coco frequented. So he put it back on—gingerly. He patted the tape back down, tucked his shirt back into his trousers, and went outside to Geik.

In the parking lot he told Geik he was sick, and to grab a cab home. But Geik protested that he didn't really know where he was, didn't know how to get to his apartment from here. Punishing himself, Leuci drove the corrupt detective all the way home.

The night was not over. He still had to report to Scoppetta, who had been waiting up. "How did it go tonight?" he asked when Leuci walked into his apartment.

"Terrific," Leuci said, "There's no recording. Those IRS guys lost me."

Scoppetta became angry.

But Leuci was in such pain he barely noticed. Undoing his clothes, he once again removed the belt of tape, the transmitter, the batteries. He peered down at the circle of raw flesh where the skin had been burned away.

"We've got to find something else, some better gear. I just can't wear this belt," he said.

Scoppetta stared with sympathy and horror at the terrible burn.

Once the pain had abated somewhat, Leuci began begging for New York City cops as backup men. "If you don't get cops who know the street, this is going to happen all the time. We're going to lose many valuable recordings. We've got to get cops."

Leuci had brought this up before. But Scoppetta couldn't arrange backup cops without going to Police Commissioner Murphy.

Then go to him, Leuci insisted. Besides, only Murphy could transfer him back into SIU—where he would have the jurisdiction and freedom he needed to make big cases.

Big new cases, Scoppetta silently amended. Cases against people he didn't know, rather than against these ghosts who haunted his past.

"All right," Scoppetta said, "I'll talk to Murphy."

An hour later and fifty miles east, Leuci lay on his bed on clean cool sheets while Gina smoothed salve onto his wound. She was gentle and concerned, and spent a lot of time on it. Leuci told her how the transmitter had begun to burn him, how much he wanted to work with fellow cops, not IRS agents. He wanted this to be a police investigation, not an IRS investigation. He wanted other cops in it with him.

He wanted not to feel so guilty.

In the middle of the night he awoke and remembered tonight's terrible pain, and he wondered how much of it might have been self-induced. What he was doing, though good, nonetheless felt evil. Perhaps subconsciously he believed that he deserved such pain. And he began to fear that every time he put that belt on it would burn him again, because that's what he deserved and perhaps even desired.

9

A NUMBER of new detectives had been assigned to SIU in Leuci's absence, but many he had known were still there, some of whom regarded him with suspicion from the moment he sat down behind his new desk. For he had accomplished what no detective had ever accomplished. He had come back to SIU.

But other old-timers were friendly to him, and one even greeted him with a bear hug. He looked around him. His own former partners had been rotated out of course. Nunziata was gone too. But Aguiluz was still there, his team intact, and so were Eddie Codelia, Jack McClean, and other old friends.

All of these Leuci intended at all costs to avoid. Leuci knew he would be assigned partners. He was determined that they should be men he had never met before.

The next day these partners were introduced to him: Detectives Jim Sheridan and Bill Hubert. Both had been working in Narcotics in Harlem, had compiled good records there, and had just been promoted into SIU.

He met Sheridan first, a tall blond Irishman from Belfast, who spoke with the heaviest brogue he had ever heard. Leuci was determined to keep this relationship strictly professional. He didn't want to know about Sheridan's family. He didn't want to know about his problems. Because if he turned out to be a corrupt cop, he was going to jail.

But the Irishman greeted him with such an open, bubbling kind of personality that Leuci thought at once: I'm going to be in trouble with this guy. It's going to be impossible to keep him at arm's length.

Later he met Hubert, who seemed, in contrast to Sheridan, a blunt, tough cop. It was Hubert who suggested the Leuci join him and Sheridan for dinner that night. The three of them should get acquainted, and drink to the future successes of their new team.

But Leuci walked away, saying, "I have other things to do."

The first job for any detective beginning a new assignment was to contact the junkies, ex-convicts, and other street people he had known in the past. And to probe for information.

Leuci did this, and before long he learned of a man in the Bronx named Joseph Andretta who was supposed to be selling drugs. Andretta, though only a mid-rank dealer himself, was supposed to be buying from a man with access to vast quantities of heroin.

Hoping to be led to this connection, Leuci, Hubert, and Sheridan set up surveillance outside Andretta's house. Working in relays, they sat for hours in parked cars waiting for him to come out, and when he did they trailed him wherever he went. But days passed, and Andretta led them nowhere.

Sheridan and Hubert were stumped; they did not know what to do next. But to Leuci, this was a typical SIU case; it was just beginning to get interesting. The only way they were going to find Andretta's connection, Leuci told them, was to wiretap his phone. And they certainly didn't have enough evidence to get a legal wiretap order.

Sheridan agreed. "Let's get on his phone. Let's find out who he's calling, who he's doing business with."

But an illegal wiretap was a federal offense, and Hubert was reluctant. "Do we have to do that? If we get caught we'll get locked up."

Back in the station house they conferred with their supervisor, Sergeant Norman Cohen. It was decided they should check out Andretta's basement. They would find and look over his phone box, and would make their final decision then.

Driving up to the Bronx to Andretta's address, they picked the entrance door lock, then descended to the basement, where they pushed through dim corridors looking for the phone box. An easy phone to tap, Leuci told the others when they had found it. They would come back tonight and do it. Leuci also checked out the nearby storeroom, which was clogged with bicycles, baby carriages, and unused appliances, and when the others asked what he was looking for, he told them they would soon find out.

·That night the three detectives crept down into Andretta's basement. A quick jerk on the telephone box cover revealed the wires inside. The pairs stood in rows. In some buildings the pairs were marked by the apartment they serviced. These weren't. Leuci would have to find Andretta's pair. Removing a hand set from his bag, he attached its two alligator clips to a random pair of terminals. He could now make an outgoing call, and he did so, dialing Andretta's number. As the dial spun back from the last digit, Andretta's phone began to ring upstairs.

In the cellar Leuci licked the tips of his fore and index fingers, and ran them up and down the pairs of terminals, waiting for the mild shock. His hand jumped back as he touched the pair on the bottom right side. "That's it," he told Sheridan and Hubert, and he yanked his hand set loose. Andretta, if he had picked up his phone at all, had just been disconnected.

With needle point pliers from his bag, Leuci loosened the two terminal bolts. Selecting a coil of telephone wire from his bag, he stripped one end and attached the terminals to the two screws. This wire he ran up through the hole in the top of the box, entwined it with the telephone company's wires, and shoved it through one telephone company leader after another until he had reached a point opposite the basement storeroom. Branching off here, he led his own wire into this dark, junk-cluttered place. Running his wire as far as a derelict stove, he attached it to the jacks on his Craig tape recorder, then slid the tape recorder into the oven, and closed the door on it. Walking back to the telephone box, he dialed Andretta's number again. But as soon as the phone began to ring, he pulled his hand set free.

Returning to the storeroom, he opened the oven door

and studied his self-starting tape recorder. The reel had turned one full time. The phone tap was made, the tape recorder was working perfectly. Leuci closed the oven door and pushed a refrigerator up in front of it.

As the three detectives left the building, Hubert said anxiously, "This is all very exciting, very new to me. It's terrific that we are going to be able to get this kind of inside information. But if we get caught, we're going to get locked up."

There was no way they could get caught, Leuci assured him. Hubert was now an SIU detective, was he not, and this was the way SIU detectives worked. He then explained the rest of his plan. His informant would order heroin from Andretta. Andretta would telephone his connection for the merchandise. Since they would be listening in on the conversation, they would know where and when Andretta would take delivery. They would tail him to this meeting and arrest both him and his connection. It would be easy.

The two less experienced detectives were awed by this plan, but Scoppetta, the night Leuci revealed it to him at his apartment, was furious. The prosecutor paced the rug. "That's an illegal wiretap," he fumed. "You're breaking the law. You can't do that."

"Nick," Leuci fired back. "I didn't do it. They did it and I went along. If I am going to be believable as an SIU detective, then I have to be allowed to go along with them. And in a case like this, every SIU detective I know would tap Andretta's phone. They wouldn't think twice about it. How do you think they made all those big cases? If you want to burn me, then just tell me I should blow the whistle on this illegal tap."

Scoppetta, shocked, stared at Leuci. After a moment he admitted the validity of Leuci's logic, but the law was the law. He did not have the power to give Leuci permission to break the law. He would talk to Shaw; he would talk to U.S. Attorney Seymour.

Scoppetta was greatly troubled by what he was learning about SIU. There were serious questions that Leuci must be asked, and Scoppetta would soon have to ask them.

A number of conferences took place the next day involving Scoppetta, Shaw, U.S. Attorney Seymour, and other prosecutors as well. A consensus was reached. To preserve Leuci's cover, and to gather evidence of illegal wiretapping, his team would be permitted to continue the tap on Andretta's phone.

The Andretta case went forward. The informant duly met with Andretta and ordered the heroin. The detectives, sitting in surveillance in a parked car, watched this meeting, then tailed Andretta back to his house. As Andretta entered his apartment upstairs, they were already in the basement pushing the refrigerator away from the stove to get at their tape recorder in the oven. Even as the oven door flopped open, the spools began to turn.

Andretta had telephoned someone named Joe at a poolroom. He and Joe had agreed to meet the following night on Boston Road in the Bronx. Joe would have with him an eighth of a tire.

Leuci snorted derisively as he heard this. "Tough code to break," he muttered.

As the three detectives walked out through the lobby of Andretta's building, Hubert said, "Is it going to be that easy? Are we going to go up to Boston Road, and wait for this guy to show up with an eighth of a kilo of heroin?"

"It's going to be that easy," Leuci said.

And it was. The following night the three detectives and their supervisor, Sergeant Norman Cohen, arrested three men: Andretta, Andretta's shotgun rider, and Joe, whose name was Joseph Marchese; and they seized an eighth of a kilo of heroin.

It was still a typical SIU case: imaginative, efficient, illegal. And it remained one to the end. Once in the station house, Marchese offered Sergeant Cohen "a couple of thousand" to secure his release.

Cohen, drawing Leuci aside, reported the bribe offer. Immediately the room went electric with tension. Everyone was whispering. Everyone was staring at everyone else. Sheridan and Hubert had overheard a word or two, and had guessed the rest.

Cohen, still whispering to Leuci, said, "I don't trust

Hubert. As a matter of fact, Leuci, I don't trust you. There are a lot of rumors about you."

"If you don't trust me," Leuci said, "forget about it. We'll lock the guy up. I don't give a shit."

Sheridan now drew Leuci aside. Leuci was team leader, he said. He and Hubert would agree to whatever he decided. "This Marchese has a lot of money," Sheridan added. "Did you notice his fucking shirt? That shirt cost more than my whole wardrobe."

Marchese came over to them. He owed money in this precinct, he said, and wanted badly to leave at once. It was worth $4000 to him.

"Sold," said Cohen.

There remained the problem of Hubert. "I don't want to do it," he said. "What are we going to do, arrest the two shit heads? And let the connection go?" He glanced from Cohen to Leuci to Sheridan, seeking support.

Stepping across to Hubert, Cohen snarled, "This guy is a businessman. He owns a taxicab company in Yonkers. We're letting the guy go. He owes people money and wants to get out of here before they come looking for him. That's the reason we're getting the four thousand, not because he's the connection."

Hubert stared at the floor.

"You don't belong in SIU," Cohen told him. "You belong back in the fucking field group, chasing niggers up in Harlem, that's where you belong." And he strode angrily away, leaving Hubert still staring at the floor.

I've got a good case here, Leuci thought, as he watched the disconsolate Hubert. I got Marchese. I got Cohen. I got Sheridan. And I'm going to have Hubert. "Bill, listen," Leuci said, "do you want to take the money or not? You tell me what you want to do. I'm not your father. Don't expect me to make decisions for you. You make your own decisions. Whatever you want, I'll do. If you want to lock the guy up, then we'll lock him up."

"I hate this fucking thing," Hubert said. "This is the nicest collar I ever fucking made. And so quick. I've kicked in a thousand doors. I never saw that much junk before. All I ever got before was little bags, four or five little bags at a time maximum. I work with you two days, and in twenty minutes I got a fucking Mafia guy. I got an eighth of a kilo of heroin."

Leuci watched him.

"I'll do whatever you do," mumbled Hubert miserably. "But I don't want to talk to that little fuck of a sergeant again, because I might punch him out. This prick will put me back in the fucking field group tomorrow unless I take the money. And after that back to uniform."

Thirty minutes later Marchese was on the street, and Leuci drove him to a bar and grill. Double-parking outside, Leuci waited with the motor running until Marchese came out carrying a paper bag. The drug dealer handed the bag in through the car window. Leuci felt that it was full of money.

"Will you drive me home?" Marchese asked pleasantly.

"Fuck you," said Leuci, and drove back to the station house.

Hubert was waiting for him on the sidewalk. Sheridan and Cohen had gone ahead to the restaurant where the money would be split up. Hubert got into the car beside Leuci.

Leuci, as he accelerated down the street, pushed the paper bag across the seat. "There should be four thousand dollars in there. Count it."

Hubert, counting, said, "This makes me sick, Bob."

Leuci did not look at him. "You mean to tell me you've never done this before?"

"Nothing like this. Never."

"How much money is in there?"

The answer was $3600. Marchese had beaten them out of $400.

"Take nine hundred for yourself," Leuci said. "And take a share for Sheridan. I'll give Cohen his."

The two detectives went into the restaurant, where they slid into the booth opposite Cohen and Sheridan. Reaching under the table, Leuci passed Cohen $900. Cohen, as he gripped the money, began chuckling happily. Hubert passed over Sheridan's share, but as he did so, he was trembling.

The next day, meeting with Scoppetta, Leuci handed over his $900 to be vouchered.

"That's a solid case," said Scoppetta, very pleased. "You've got the Mafia guy and the sergeant solid. You got the two detectives solid. All you need to do is get corroboration."

The prosecutor decided that Leuci should go back to all four men wired, and talk over the case. This would be all the corroboration needed. But when Scoppetta looked up he saw that Leuci's face was grim.

"I want to tell you right now," Leuci said, "that if you try to prosecute Hubert, I'm finished. Let's find out right now what kind of guys you are. I will not allow Hubert to be prosecuted."

Scoppetta studied him. Each of these crises of conscience, these pangs of guilt or remorse, called for a separate judgment by Scoppetta. Would he overrule the detective, or humor him, or what? "Did it happen the way you're telling me?" Scoppetta asked.

"Exactly that way."

"I don't believe you. If Hubert was totally honest, he wouldn't have taken the money."

This produced another emotional monologue by Leuci. "You don't have the faintest idea what it's like to be a cop, do you?" he cried. "After working years in a precinct, you finally get a chance to come into the Detective Bureau. You finally get a chance to work in Narcotics. You finally get into SIU. And then your whole career goes out the window because you run into some thieving little sergeant who is ready to bust you back to uniform. Do you understand the pressure that Bill Hubert was under? And then he looked to me for direction, and the direction I gave him was: Take the money. Now you want to prosecute this kid. If that's what you're going to do, I quit."

After a moment Scoppetta said, "Prove to me this kid is honest, and we won't prosecute him."

Leuci said, "I'll prove it to you, and after that you're going to get him transferred out of Narcotics. You're going to send him some place where he can do his fucking job."

Scoppetta shrugged. "Let's see what happens."

Corroborating tapes. Leuci wanted three that proved criminal guilt, and one that would be exculpatory.

So he met again with Marchese, who talked about handing over the bribe. Leuci's battery transmitter picked this up and it was recorded in the car of his backup team.

Again wearing a wire, he spoke with Cohen. Cohen was cagey, but enough went down on tape to corroborate the case.

Leuci's third meeting was with Sheridan. Sheridan was no problem. Sheridan was entirely open, trusting, ebullient, friendly. But Leuci didn't want to be friends with Sheridan. It was easy not to be friends with Cohen, but with Sheridan and Hubert it was another story.

Leuci phoned Hubert, and they met in Leuci's car. Leuci pushed down on the seat belt, activating the secret tape recorder. They began to talk about the money from Marchese. The unsuspecting Hubert said into the tape recorder that he hadn't been able to spend the $900. He wanted to give it back. It made him sick when he looked at it. He couldn't face his wife, his kids. He wanted no part of this shit. He just wanted to be a cop and do his job.

Leuci rushed back to Scoppetta with this tape, threaded it onto the machine, and started it forward. Scoppetta listened carefully until the tape ended, then said, "You led that whole conversation. The case against Hubert is a prosecutable case."

"I don't care if it's a prosecutable case," Leuci cried.

Recognizing the state Leuci was in, Scoppetta agreed to talk it over with Shaw.

By this time, Leuci in his undercover role was conducting several cases simultaneously. He was meeting with and making secret recordings with two other Mafia drug dealers, and with two suspect lawyers. He played golf with Captain Tange while his backup team trailed in a golf cart recording their conversation. In addition there were constant strategy meetings with Shaw and Scoppetta.

As a result Leuci often missed meetings with Sheridan and Hubert, who were not experienced enough to operate without him. They began to complain. They were cops, they wanted to make cases. Leuci gave them excuses. He had to meet a confidential informant. He had to go to the dentist. He had to meet a girl.

Eventually they ceased to believe him. They got angry. They gave him an ultimatum. Either he would show up for work tomorrow morning or they would report him.

But the next morning Scoppetta summoned Leuci to an urgent strategy conference.

Knowing Sheridan and Hubert would be furious, Leuci phoned SIU and left a message for them. His son had been hit by a car. He couldn't meet them.

When he reached home that night, Gina was in tears. "What are you doing?" she wept. "You're driving me crazy. I can't stand this any more. All day long I've been getting phone calls from this lovely Irish lady, and this lovely Irish man with a beautiful accent. They want to come out to the house. They want to know how badly hurt is my child."

Leuci was appalled.

"The phone has not stopped ringing," Gina sobbed. "They call me every hour. I sound nervous to them. They will drive out from the city. Sheridan said to tell you not to worry. You should take the week off. He'll cover for you. I talked to this Bill Hubert. He said he's your partner. You shouldn't worry. He'll cover for you."

Leuci was unable to speak.

"Horrible. Horrible," she said. "You're going to hurt these people."

When Leuci reported this to him, Scoppetta attempted to soothe the anguished detective. He had talked to Mike Shaw, he said. "Shaw thinks you are absolutely right. We decided that there may not be a prosecutable case against Hubert if he agrees to cooperate against the others."

A little later Leuci learned that Hubert was being transferred to Intelligence. Scoppetta and Shaw told him they had not instigated this. Leuci thanked them anyway, and rushed to tell Hubert.

"You ought to go to Intelligence," Leuci told him. "Work on big-time cases."

"I'd love to go to Intelligence." But Hubert's voice fell. "I'll never get there."

"Don't worry about it, Bill. You're going to get there."

When the transfer came through, Hubert phoned Leuci. "I don't know how the fuck you did it," he cried exultantly, "but I've just been transferred to Intelligence."

Some months later an enormous Mafia roundup was made by Hubert and several other Intelligence detectives. Attempting to buy his release, one of the Mafia figures handed over to Hubert and his partner $120,000 in cash. Hubert and his partner rearrested the subject on a bribery charge, and turned in and vouchered the $120,000.

Meanwhile, Leuci continued to suffer with Jim Sheridan, who stood constantly beside him, wanting to be friends. Leuci asked for a new partner, saying he wanted no part of Sheridan, a clod. But Sheridan was not a clod, Leuci well knew. He was a brave, tough guy. He invited Leuci to his home many times. Always Leuci refused. He showed Leuci pictures of his daughter, pictures of his wife. He talked about his years in the IRA. He had been in jail in Ireland as a revolutionary. He said that his ambition was to make enough money to get out of New York, "to leave this fucking miserable city and go back to Ireland."

Leuci kept trying to hold him off: He could not afford to become friendly with Jim Sheridan.

10

HIS THREE FORMER PARTNERS—Frank Mandato, Les Wolff, and Dave Cody—Leuci had scrupulously avoided for months, fearing to ensnarl them.

Once, early on, it almost happened. He had an appointment to meet Mikey Coco and was wired. He had just got into his car when the other door opened and Mandato jumped in beside him. All Mandato wanted was to ask Leuci to use his apparent influence to get Mandato back into SIU too.

"I can't talk to you, Frank," Leuci had protested, immediately turning the radio up loud. "I got to go up to the Bronx."

"I'll ride up with you," said Mandato, turning the volume down.

Behind them trailed the backup car, one IRS agent driving, the other adjusting the dials of the tape recorder that lay open on his lap, spools turning.

Leuci kept turning the radio up, Mandato kept turning it down. Leuci was trying to talk his ex-partner out of the car. Mandato would not go. He didn't mind riding up to the Bronx, and he wanted Leuci to get him back into SIU.

In the Bronx Mandato moved to the back seat, and Mikey Coco slipped in beside Leuci. By then Leuci was in a panic, worried not only about what Mandato might say, but also about what Coco might say that Mandato might hear and not take action on. Dereliction of duty. A felony.

Leaning across Coco, Leuci turned the volume up as high as it would go.

In the back seat, as he grasped what must be happening, Mandato stiffened. Leuci saw this in the mirror. Beside him the gravel-voiced mobster merely spoke louder, his conversation overriding the music. But

Mandato in the back seat remained rigid, and spoke not one further word.

Leuci had stayed away from his former partners ever since.

But now a case they had made two years earlier brought them suddenly together again. The trial would begin the next day, and they were led into a small room in the Bronx County Courthouse by the assistant district attorney who would prosecute the case.

The D.A.'s name was Carl Bornstein. He ordered them to study their memo books, and to get their stories straight. This was an extremely important case, Bornstein told them, but there was a problem with it, a very serious problem about which he would interview them shortly. Bornstein was a young man with the smooth untroubled face they saw often on lawyers, and his attitude toward cops was familiar too, a combination of arrogance and contempt. Their case had become his case. He was the star now. He wished he didn't need them at all, but unfortunately he did need them. He needed their testimony. And he needed an explanation from them about this "problem."

Bornstein went out. The door slammed.

The four former partners looked at each other, and for a moment no one spoke.

Leuci had been hoping to be greeted with the warmth and intimacy of the past. From Cody, who was an older man and different from the other three partners, this was exactly the greeting he had got. But from Mandato and Wolff came a certain coldness, a certain reserve, and he looked into their faces and saw that they did not trust him. They seemed to be waiting for an explanation of some kind.

The tension became so pronounced that even Cody noticed it, and he began to glance from face to face trying to puzzle out what it was he sensed.

Mandato and Wolff were both thirty-six years old, five years older than Leuci, but Cody was forty-five. He was, in the police world, of a different generation. He had been in the navy in World War II, and often talked about "the war"—each time making the other three glance up sharply, wondering which war he was talking about. To them, Cody's war was ancient history.

Cody was a thin, almost emaciated man, and in contrast to most SIU detectives he wore out-of-date, baggy clothes. He slouched. He looked sickly, even undernourished, which perhaps he was. He had never married, didn't eat properly, and took many of his meals in bars. Since he had no wife or kids to go home to, he was the one whom the others often left behind to sit on surveillances half the night. They would leave him, saying, "Don't get hurt, Dave." They were always concerned about him, for he looked so frail. But in the macho police world, any expression of affection had to be tempered at once, and one of the other partners would always add quickly, "Because if you do get hurt, we'll be filling out forms for the next three days."

Mandato, with his sculptured black beard and expensive clothes, seemed more Jewish than Italian. He much resembled a young Jewish businessman. The son of a court stenographer, he had been among cops most of his life, and it was his father who had urged him toward the Police Department. Paper work bored him. So did early stages of any investigation, when he sometimes did not come to work for days at a time. But there was a certain brilliance about him. He was rich in ideas. Once Mandato borrowed a black detective as chauffeur, and hid himself in the trunk of a rented limousine in order to get inside a Harlem garage where narcotics were believed to be hidden in derelict cars.

The black detective parked inside the garage and went away. Mandato let himself out of the trunk and waited alone in the dark until the dealer, who was heavily armed, entered the garage and approached his stash. Mandato took him alone. No violence. No problem of any kind.

The stolid, hard-working member of Leuci's team had been Wolff, who often disapproved of Mandato and Mandato's ways, and said so. Both were muscular six-footers. Mandato was often taken for a Jew, and Wolff was in fact a Jew, but in dress and personality they were very different. Mandato dressed with considerable elegance. Wolff, though born and bred on the streets of New York, favored clothes with a western flair, much of it leather. He often wore boots, and sometimes looked like a cowboy.

For all of their differences, these four men had been, emotionally, extremely close. In police terms, they had been tremendously effective too—they put a great number of major narcotics dealers in jail. When, almost a year ago, their partnership had been dissolved for no very good reason by order of higher authority, all four had been filled with regret.

But now they were together again in a small room preparing to testify in an old case, and if there was suspicion of Leuci on the part of Wolff and Mandato, this was Leuci's own fault, and he knew it.

However, these tense opening moments passed. No one articulated them. Instead the four men began to discuss the old case that was about to come to trial; it was one of the best they had ever put together. It was an important case, but it was rich in laughs too, and as they discussed it their faces brightened, they began to chuckle, and the old warmth and intimacy began to reassert itself. They also knew what Bornstein's "problem" was, but they were not worried about this themselves.

The case was this. A man named Raymond Acervedo had owned a drugstore at 116th Street and Madison Avenue, out of which he sold principally quinine, the basic ingredient in narcotics mixing. He would sell quinine in thirty- or forty-pound sacks. Mandato, Wolff, Leuci, and Cody had begun an investigation of Acervedo, who, they learned, also owned a large drug discount store in the Bronx.

Presently the four detectives requested a legal wiretap on this discount store. When the wiretap was accorded, they set up their gear in a basement around the corner and, working in relays, they began monitoring Acervedo's calls. It was a good narcotics case. They felt professional. They were enjoying it.

But a call came in unrelated to narcotics. A rough,

Italian-sounding voice said, "Raymond, I'm going to come to your store tomorrow. I need your store only for a couple of days."

Acervedo had a quiet, almost faint voice, and he spoke in Hispanic cadences. He said he wasn't sure he understood.

"We need a place to unload a truckload of television sets."

The four detectives, eavesdropping in their basement plant, looked at each other in shock. The man was talking about hijacked TV sets, and they couldn't believe he would say such a thing right over the phone.

The Italian voice continued, "I don't know how many sets. Maybe three hundred television sets."

Acervedo's voice, showing panic, said, "I just opened this store. It's a drugstore. It's only open a couple of days."

The Italian voice said, "We'll be there tomorrow."

The four detectives stared at each other. A truckload of hijacked television sets was about to be unloaded into the middle of their investigation.

But they had no time to discuss this, for the tape spool began turning again, and they listened to Acervedo's plaintive telephone calls to friends. The Hispanic was nearly in tears. "These Mafia guys are going to come in and lay these television sets on me," they heard him say. "I don't know what to do with them. I got no room in the store. They are going to fill up all my aisles with television sets."

Silence. In the basement room the spool stopped turning. For a moment the four detectives were silent. Then the discussion began. Their narcotics case had just become a hijacking case. What should they do?

After checking out cameras with telescopic lenses, they talked their way into an apartment directly across the street from the drugstore.

The apartment was upstairs above a tailor shop, and it belonged to the tailor, an aged Jew whose language was Yiddish, not English. It was Leuci who convinced the tailor to hand over the keys to his house. Leuci never mentioned narcotics, nor Mafia, nor hijacked TV sets, for these subjects might have terrified the tailor. Throwing in Yiddish phrases, claiming to be a Jew himself, Leuci invented a story about black revolutionaries who planned a weapons drop here in this white neighborhood. The tailor looked into the open, engaging countenance of Babyface, and did his civic duty. He handed Leuci the keys.

Once installed upstairs, the detectives began photographing everyone who entered or left the drugstore. They planned, when the truckload of television sets arrived, to film the entire scene. Simultaneously, one or another of them would continue to monitor the tapped telephone in the basement around the corner.

At four o'clock in the afternoon the truckload of television sets arrived. What happened next was, to the watching detectives, almost unbelievable.

The truck pulled up. Wolff and Mandato began taking pictures. Three men got off the truck. Three others got out of a car. Not one of them, the detectives judged, was wearing less than a five-hundred-dollar suit. They began unloading the truck, but they tired quickly. It was amusing to watch. There were some kids in the street, and they began hiring the kids to help them unload the truck. They were moving all the television sets into the store.

When at last the truck was empty and the drugstore full, they went across the street into the diner and ordered coffee. While they were drinking it, a man in street clothes came walking up the street. The detectives watched him from the window. They made him as a cop at once, and they watched with a kind of horrified fascination to see what he would do.

Obviously he wanted to get a pack of cigarettes or something from the drugstore. He tried the door, but it was locked. It was the middle of the afternoon, and he couldn't get into the store. He looked around and saw the truck parked out front. He peered in through the drugstore window. It was a drugstore, but he saw television sets stacked up and down the aisles. Every place he looked was television sets. There were television sets up to the ceiling.

The plainclothes cop turned away from the window,

crossed the street to the diner where the six hoods were drinking coffee, and called in a ten-thirteen on himself: assist patrolman. About thirty seconds later one could hear the sirens. There were police cars coming from all over. The hoods must have been aghast, but their faces showed nothing. They simply paid their checks and vanished.

Within ten minutes there were fifty cops in the drugstore. The first arrivals broke the door down, went in, and found men in there from whom they demanded bills of lading for the TV sets. When these were not produced, the men were arrested—cops came out of the store dragging them in handcuffs.

After that more cars began to pull up. Not police cars, but Volkswagens, station wagons. Nearly every cop in the precinct pulled up in his own car, and they started lugging television sets out of the store. They were tying television sets onto the roofs of the Volkswagens, they were shoving television sets into the station wagons. Up and down the street television sets were being carried to their cars. There must have been fifteen private cars with cops in uniform behind the wheel. They were waiting in line to get the television sets.

Worse was to come. The detectives hurried around the corner to their wiretap plant, turned their tape machine to playback and listened horrified as one cop after another spoke into Acervedo's tapped telephone. They were spreading the word about the TV sets. A squad commander called his division commander: "Hey, I've got a television set for the office." There were twenty or more calls on the tape of cops phoning friends and relatives: "Get over here fast. I got a television set for you."

After turning off the machine, the detectives sat in stunned silence. All realized the implications. This tape was evidence, and would be presented in court whenever either the hijacking or narcotics case came to trial, at which time it figured to convict twenty-five or so cops of stealing television sets. Of course part of the tape could be erased, but what was left still would indicate that 300 television sets had been delivered to the discount drugstore, and that about half had subsequently been stolen by someone.

Their tape would be enough to start a big investigation. As evidence, it would convict cops. They had best get over to the station house immediately, and warn the commander. The commander would have to get those 150 sets back, and voucher them all. Most of all, he should keep the rest of his cops away from the remaining television sets and off the tapped phone.

But as the four detectives drove to the station house, they once again became concerned about their narcotics case. If they mentioned their wiretap in the station house, this information surely would get back to Acervedo.

"Let me handle it," said Mandato, and he strode into the station house.

But the commander was not there. In a few minutes, Mandato came out muttering angrily. "I had a conversation with the lieutenant on the desk," he reported to his partners. "A big Irish fucking jerk. I said to him, 'Get those TV sets back. The walls have ears in that place,' and he starts screaming at me. Where was I from? Who was I? I told him I was from Narcotics and that the walls have ears."

"This guy doesn't know that the walls have ears," said Wolff. "He's a desk officer. Let me handle it."

Wolff went into the station house. Presently he came out and got into the car. "He understands," said Wolff.

But apparently the lieutenant did not understand at all, for no sooner were they back at their plant and clustered around their tape recorder than the tapped phone was in use again. Another cop was in the store. After identifying himself, the cop said, "How much do you think a twenty-inch RCA is worth? What if I can get you one for a hundred dollars?"

Leuci cried angrily, "Didn't anybody in the station house tell these guys?"

Cody said, "Let's go back to the station house, and speak to that lieutenant again."

This time Cody entered the station house. He and the

lieutenant were the same age, and the lieutenant listened to him. When Cody came out he looked satisfied. "I drew him a picture," Cody said. "I told him to get those TV sets back. I told him the goddamn phone was tapped. I told him enough. Don't use the phone. We are watching the place, lieutenant. Keep your cops out of there and don't use the phone there."

A single patrolman was sent to stand guard at the drugstore. It was now early evening. Upstairs the tailor and his wife were at dinner, and so the detectives decided to discontinue surveillance from there—there was nothing further to see anyway, except a bored cop across the street in the doorway.

So they returned to their basement plant, and tried to decide what to do with their narcotics case against Acervedo, and with this new hijacking case that had just fallen full-blown into their laps. The hijacking case was very strong—they actually had photos of the conspirators unloading the truck into the drugstore, and they had the voice of one of them on tape.

Very carefully they erased from their tape all the voices of cops stealing TV sets. After that they continued to wait in the basement room. They were waiting for Acervedo.

Outside in the streets darkness fell. The hours began to pass. The four detectives munched sandwiches, and waited. It seemed logical to expect Acervedo. He had not been there all day. He would want to look over his store. He would want to see how the hijackers had stacked the TV sets. When he found the cop on guard, perhaps he would phone someone, speak a guarded warning of some kind. This would tie him further into the hijacking conspiracy. With leverage like that, maybe they could get him to talk about his narcotics connections.

Suddenly the detectives were listening to still another outgoing call on the tapped line. The cop on guard was phoning the station house. He wanted to speak to the clerical man, he told the switchboard operator.

The clerical man, from his voice, was an old-time cop. From the conversation that ensued, the eavesdropping detectives judged that he was this young cop's mentor.

The kid wanted advice from his mentor, because in the desk in the store he had just found $2000.

The advice the old-timer gave him was to put it in his pocket.

But the patrolman was a rookie still on probation, and he pointed this out to his mentor. He didn't want any trouble, he said.

"That money is your money," the old-timer interrupted harshly, and for the next few minutes he pressured the rookie to steal it. "Nobody will know you took it. Any of the people who work in the store could have taken it. There were narcotics cops in the place today, weren't there?"

"Yes," whispered the rookie. This was true. Mandato and Wolff at one point had walked across the street and watched in amazement as the television sets went past them.

The old-timer said, "The narcotics guys took the money. Those are the fucking guys who took it. Put it in your pocket. Is it in your pocket yet?"

"Okay, it's in my pocket, but—"

Rushing to the drugstore, Leuci and Mandato rapped on the glass door. The tapped phone was on the wall close to the door. They could see the cop through the glass. He was still talking to his mentor on the phone. He had his overcoat off. He was wearing his gun belt, peering out at them.

Leuci held his shield up against the glass.

The rookie cop hung up the phone, and opened the door.

Leuci and Mandato strode into the store. "I'm Sergeant Russo from Internal Affairs," Leuci said. "What do you have in your pocket?"

The rookie cop wet his pants immediately. Everything went. He stepped backwards out of the puddle. He grabbed at his hair. Weeping and blubbering, he begged them not to arrest him.

"The owner of this store has been paying cops for years," Leuci said. "We have his phone tapped. Every word you just said was recorded. You fucking moron."

The rookie cop, tears streaming down his face, begged them to give him a break.

It was Mandato who took pity first.

"Listen, kid," he said. "We're not from Internal Affairs, we're from Narcotics. But that phone is tapped and there is a district attorney who is going to listen to our tapes. How many times do we have to tell you fucking guys? Now take that money and put it back in the desk."

For the third time that day, the four detectives drove to the station house.

Behind the desk was the same lieutenant. "You know, lieutenant," Mandato said in an icy voice, "I told you this afternoon we were watching the place."

The lieutenant's tour of duty had ended hours earlier. He was still in the station house because he had packed a television set and was waiting for transportation to take it away.

"You don't have to tell me my business," he screamed. "Who do you think you're talking to?"

Mandato said, "I'll tell you something." He turned around so that his glance included every cop in the muster room. "I'm going to say it loud enough for all you guys to hear. If we had a pair of handcuffs big enough to put around this whole fucking station house, we'd take the whole bunch of you. You know we are watching that place, we're taking pictures, we've got a wiretap on the phone. I suppose you never heard of wiretaps? It never occurred to any of you that the phone was wired? Everyone of you jerkos used that phone. Now I want to know who was the clerical guy that this young kid was just talking to?"

No one spoke.

Leuci said, "You guys are a disgrace. You guys are so fucking bad. You should all go to jail."

The lieutenant began to apologize, but Leuci cut him off. "And get all those television sets back. How many did you voucher, a hundred twenty-five? It's on the tape how many sets there were."

The lieutenant said, "We'll never get them back."

"You better get them back. Someday somebody is

going to play that tape. They are going to hear about three hundred television sets."

The lieutenant said, "We'll try to get them all back."

Now it was two years later, and the four former partners sat in the small office discussing the case. Four of the six men in their photos had turned out to be major Mafia figures. One of the four had been matched by his voice to the tapped telephone. It was these four who were about to go on trial.

By now the four detectives had been, in effect, talking about old times an hour or more, and suspicion of Leuci had evaporated. Caution was gone. These were four very close friends who, until a year ago, had virtually lived together, had risked their lives together.

They recalled that, finally, only about 170 television sets had been vouchered. The missing sets had not been noticed; no investigation had ever been done. The whole case was really rather funny—though serious too, for they were about to put four Mafia hoods in jail.

Just then Assistant D.A. Bornstein reentered the office, and he began to talk to them about their wiretap, and about the tape-recorded conversations off Acervedo's phone that formed part of the evidence.

"There is something I want you to hear," Bornstein said. "You guys are experts on wiretaps, right?"

The four detectives, suddenly aware of what was coming, gazed attentively at Bornstein, trying to look innocent. Bornstein played the tape. They listened to the sound of an incoming call. There was a short conversation, after which both parties hung up.

There had been an underlying subsidiary sound on the tape also. They all heard it. Bornstein played this section several times, then said, "What the hell is that? There is something strange on the tape. Let me play it a little further."

They listened to another incoming call, under which was the sound of a slight hissing.

Leuci turned to Mandato. "What the hell do you think that is, Frank?"

Mandato said, "Defect in the machine."

Bornstein looked at him.

Dave Cody jumped to his feet and said, "I have to go to the bathroom."

As soon as Cody had slouched out of the room, Wolff said to Bornstein, "Dave was taking care of the machine that day. Once in a while he gets a little nervous, and he probably screwed up on this particular afternoon."

Bornstein said, "The defense attorney has listened to this tape, and he said that it sounded like an erasure to him. I have a problem with it. Because it sounds like an erasure to me, too."

"What the hell are we going to erase?" Leuci protested. "It doesn't make any sense that we would erase anything."

Bornstein pointed out that on the following day they would be asked to swear in court under oath that the tape had not been tampered with. "Are you all willing to do that?"

They said they were.

Later they talked it over, but only briefly. The erasure had to do with protecting the precinct cops only. Tomorrow they would deny the erasure under oath. This was perjury, but it was irrelevant to the case of the four hijackers. It was the type of perjury that detectives—especially SIU detectives—committed all the time in the interest of putting bad people in jail.

End of discussion. There was no way that Leuci could dissent from this group decision short of announcing that he was now bound by stricter rules than in the past.

And so they went out of the courthouse and across to a bar where they had some drinks, and all of the old warmth and comradeship was there for an hour or so. Then Leuci left them and went back downtown to report to Scoppetta and Shaw.

In Shaw's apartment he told them what had happened. He told them about the hijackers, about the stolen TV sets, about tomorrow's courtroom testimony. His hand on his chin, Scoppetta listened to Leuci's story. Sometimes he laughed. Sometimes he said, "I just don't believe it."

But it wasn't a funny story and he and Shaw were grim-faced before it ended. Because tomorrow Leuci would testify under oath.

"If you testify," Shaw said, "you're going to commit perjury. We can't allow you to do that."

The two prosecutors talked it over. They would have to begin an investigation into the stolen TV sets, that was clear, even though the case was two years old and might jeopardize Leuci's cover. Above all, Leuci must be kept off the stand tomorrow—and the other three detectives must be prevented from perjuring themselves also.

How were they to do this? At the close of the business day, they decided, they would drive to the Bronx to talk to District Attorney Burton Roberts. Roberts would have to be sworn to secrecy, of course. For maximum weight they ought to bring U.S. Attorney Seymour with them.

This was done. Their story, when they had told it, was followed by a stream of violent curses by Roberts. But after a time he calmed down, and it was he who worked out the only way possible to keep Leuci and the other three detectives off the stand.

"We're going to give these four hoodlums a misdemeanor plea," Roberts said disgustedly. "They've been after a plea for a long time. But we had them cold. Now we'll have to give it to them. That's it. We get a conviction on the books, and they walk."

The next morning the four detectives were waiting in a witness room when Bornstein entered and announced that the case was over. The people had decided to accept a misdemeanor plea.

Bornstein was not at ease. He seemed to look calculatingly at each face in turn. Apparently he had been told that a big investigation was going on, that one of these four men was involved in it, and so could not testify. Now he was asking himself: which one?

So the four detectives left the courthouse, and went out and had lunch together. In the restaurant Mandato never stopped watching Leuci. He sensed something that Wolff and Cody sensed also. During the meal, though all four men talked a good deal about the old days, the old

warmth was not really there, and there were moments
when the other men seemed to take a step back from
Leuci, as if to say: We're not sure of you any more.

Lunch ended. Out on the sidewalk they all shook hands
and called out, "Let's stay in touch."

Leuci drove away. The others watched him go. After a
moment they too went off in separate directions.

11

AFTER DINNER in his Brooklyn Heights apartment, Shaw brought out a folder, and showed the photos of two enormously fat individuals whom he identified as bail bondsmen. Did Leuci recognize these men?

The detective responded cautiously that one seemed familiar. Actually, Leuci had recognized both photos. But he was watching Shaw carefully.

Shaw began to explain that these bondsmen, together with a third one, were reputed to be case fixers. They worked almost as a team, and they were part of what had become known to law enforcement as the Baxter Street Crew. Baxter Street ran behind the courthouse. It had one or two bars usually filled with cops waiting to testify, and above the bars were the offices of lawyers and bail bondsmen. Lawyers who worked out of Baxter Street were called the Baxter Street Bar. Many were ambulance chasers. Others, it was rumored, regularly bribed cops and other witnesses to change testimony. It was often said that the worst of the legal profession kept offices on Baxter Street.

According to Shaw, a South American drug dealer named Felix Martinez, who was in jail, had denounced these bail bondsmen. Martinez had been arrested by four SIU detectives, and his narcotics seized, and one of the bail bondsmen had come to him in prison. If Martinez would pay $110,000, his seized narcotics would come back from the police lab marked "no narcotics."

Martinez remained two days in jail while his wife scraped up $90,000 and turned it over to the bail bondsman. The following day Martinez was called into court and his case dismissed on the grounds that the physical evidence against him had proven to be not narcotics at all.

As soon as he was on the street again Martinez received a visit from the same bail bondsman who informed him that he still owed $20,000. Martinez protested that he had no more money, that his wife had borrowed from every relative, had scraped up every last cent.

The bail bondsman suggested that Martinez go back to pushing dope in order to come up with the missing money. Martinez had done so, and promptly been caught again by a different team of detectives. He was now back in jail awaiting trial.

Martinez's allegations against this bail bondsman were of little legal value, Shaw told Leuci, because they were the unsupported statements of a co-conspirator. Additional evidence would be necessary before law enforcement could move against this one bail bondsman, and it would be nice at the same time to move against all three.

Was there any way, Shaw asked Detective Leuci, was there even a one-in-a-million chance that Leuci could get inside this Baxter Street Crew, could expose and clean up the whole mess?

"Any chance at all?" inquired Shaw hopefully.

Leuci studied the two mug faces again. One, Nick DeStefano, was especially familiar, and he realized now that he had often seen him in the company of a detective named Nick Lamattina. It seemed to Leuci that Lamattina could be his entrée to DeStefano, and that DeStefano could be his entrée to the Baxter Street gang.

But he said nothing to Shaw or to Scoppetta, both of whom were watching him anxiously. Instead he promised to think about it, and to give his answer tomorrow.

The next morning Leuci sat at his desk at the SIU office and brooded about Detective Lamattina, who was not a SIU detective. In the past, any detective who had arrested a South American would sometimes find a note in his box saying: *Please call Nick Lamattina.* This had happened to Leuci only once. Subsequently he had met with Lamattina, who had said, "I know some people that are interested in this case. Do you want to sell the case?"

Leuci had considered Lamattina's blunt approach both stupid and insensitive. How did Lamattina know what kind of case it was, or how the arresting detective, Leuci, felt about it? Lamattina had never even sounded Leuci out. Just, "Do you want to sell the case?"

"I can sell my own cases," Leuci had answered with annoyance. "I don't need you to do that."

Now Leuci continued to brood about Lamattina, who was a friend of DeStefano, and about DeStefano, who was in tight with every corrupt lawyer and bail bondsman on Baxter Street. Studying a case folder at a nearby desk sat Carl Aguiluz, most of whose cases had involved South Americans. Had Carl ever had a note like that from Lamattina? Leuci wondered. Could Aguiluz tell him anything about either Lamattina or DeStefano?

Contrary to what outsiders seemed to think detectives never sat around recounting old scores, and in fact would recoil in suspicion from certain types of direct questioning even by partners. So Leuci, who had never worked a case with Aguiluz, knew of no specific past act of misconduct by the Honduras-born detective. He simply sensed that there had been some—no, many—such acts. It was an instinctive conviction based on small, scarcely perceived details, but it was so strong as to constitute knowledge— knowledge one could act on. If asked, Leuci would have been hard put to explain his conviction: it was based not so much on Aguiluz's nice clothes as on the way he talked, the way he walked. He moved with the assurance of a man with money in his pockets. Although there was a handful of honest detectives in SIU, Leuci was certain Aguiluz was not one of them.

"Carl, did you ever do anything with Lamattina?" The SIU euphemism, "anything."

Leuci was standing in front of Aguiluz's desk. He had decided to ask his question outright, and as he did so he was confident that Aguiluz would answer, for this was the type of question one detective could ask of another. It was a legitimate question. There was a reason for asking it.

Aguiluz glanced up sharply. Then thirty-six years old, he had been a cop for only seven years, but, because of his one astounding seizure, he had gained enormous fame. Before the seizure he had not even had a desk of his own, or else he had had to work at a desk in the hall. After it he was a star, and other detectives were eager to join his team. In SIU the detectives were always talking about "The Door." One day, all liked to boast, they would go through "The Door," and their lives and careers would be made. They would never have to worry again.

Aguiluz, almost alone among them, had actually been through "The Door."

For a moment Aguiluz studied Leuci, as if deciding how much to say. The two men were built somewhat alike—Aguiluz, who stood only five feet nine, weighed 190 pounds—and they even looked somewhat alike: black hair and eyes, dark skin. Leuci had a Sicilian cast to his face, whereas Aguiluz looked Central American, almost Indian, as if there were a faint admixture of Mayan or Aztec blood in his past.

"Stay away from Lamattina," Aguiluz advised Leuci now. "Him and Nick the Bondsman are unbelievable guys to deal with. Don't trust them. Do it any other way. Everybody that deals with them winds up getting allegations, because they are shaking people down after you have done your contract. They go back and ask for additional money."

Leuci was encouraged. He felt free to go after Detective Lamattina, a fellow cop.

"Thanks, Carl," Leuci said, and he meant it.

Aguiluz did not inquire why Leuci had wanted or needed information about Lamattina. In SIU a rigid code applied: no unnecessary questions were asked.

Without advising either Scoppetta or Shaw, Leuci phoned Lamattina and told him a concocted story, half of it true, half false: the drug dealer, Martinez, was cooperating with the prosecutors. A bail bondsman was involved. His information, Leuci said, came from a friend who was a corrupt agent working inside the federal attorney's office. Lamattina sounded eager, and agreed to meet him the following day.

So Leuci went back to Scoppetta and Shaw, and told them what he had done. The case was under way. Through Lamattina he would try to get close to the Baxter Street bondsmen.

"I told him there was a corrupt agent inside your office who wants to sell the case," Leuci added.

This amused Shaw. "That doesn't make us look good."

"I'm not worried about you guys looking good," said Leuci.

Scoppetta studied Leuci with a worried frown. He was always worried when Leuci made moves on his own, for this threatened Scoppetta's control of the investigation. In addition he had begun to worry about Leuci's safety, for the detective had been searched, or threatened with a search, several times already. Always, so far, he had managed to talk his way out of trouble.

Once he had gone to the Mafia hoodlums Louis Tolentino Sr. and Jr. He had arrested Junior the year before, and the case was now coming to trial. The Tolentinos were trying to bribe him through their lawyer. Suddenly Junior Tolentino had broken off the conversation with Leuci saying, "You're not wearing one of those things, are you? I'm going to search you."

This was in the street in the Bronx in front of the private garbage company the Tolentinos owned. As Junior's searching hand neared the microphone taped to the detective's chest, Leuci grabbed it saying, "That's not where you look. If you are searching a guy for a microphone, you grab him by the balls, because that's where he is going to hide it. He knows you are not going to pat him there."

So saying, Leuci guided Junior's hand toward his groin.

The drug dealer jerked his hand back, saying, "If you got it there you can keep it."

Scoppetta, listening to this dialogue on the tape later, had been profoundly sobered. How long could such luck last? And it had frightened Scoppetta when he looked across at Leuci and found the detective grinning with pride in himself. He was almost laughing. Now Leuci, wired for sound, wanted to walk in on the Baxter Street Crew, men who were considered extremely dangerous. Certainly they would, Scoppetta felt, want to search Leuci before talking to him.

Scoppetta had recently spoken with Bell and Howell.

New equipment was available, he told Leuci now. It was possible to fit a microphone into the heel of a shoe. There was a fake .45 caliber automatic with a transmitter in the handle where the bullet clip should be.

But Leuci objected. He preferred to leave his gun in his attaché case, he said, or in the trunk of his car. He preferred to walk about unarmed most of the time. He had no intention of carrying a .45, nor of sticking his foot in the mouth of somebody who was talking. He was happy with the transmitter he had been wearing. He had been able to talk his way out of every tight spot so far, had he not? What was there to worry about?

"That's what it's all about, Nick," said Leuci. "Anything that comes easy isn't going to be worthwhile."

The following day, Leuci met Lamattina as agreed at the information booth at the courthouse. It was noon, and crowds of people moved through the vast lobby.

Leuci's backup agent today was John Buckley, another IRS man. Buckley, newly assigned to Scoppetta, was a rumpled little man, only about five feet six inches tall, and over fifty years old. He had had a partial stroke, and was crippled in one arm, and his principal value was his inconspicuousness. Carrying his recording gear in an attaché case or gift-wrapped box, he could move in close. To any cop, bail bondsman, or lawyer who might notice him it would seem inconceivable that this little fellow could be The Man.

Lamattina and Leuci walked out into the street. It was lunch hour on a bright sunny day, and hundreds of people moved by them.

Up the street the two detectives entered a Chinese restaurant. It was empty. Leuci had expected crowded tables and considerable noise. When Buckley came in he would be conspicuous. The new investigation was not yet twenty minutes old, and Leuci had lost control of it.

A great fat man came into the restaurant and approached their table. Lamattina introduced him: Nick DeStefano.

Leuci and DeStefano shook hands. All three men then sat down, studied their menus, and ordered. When these details were taken care of Leuci repeated the tale he had already told Lamattina: that he had learned from a friend in the courthouse that the drug dealer was squealing. DeStefano himself was threatened.

DeStefano listened intently. Only when Leuci's narrative ended did he start to speak, but he was interrupted by the waiter setting dishes before them. Even before the waiter had gone, the fat man began to eat. He ate avidly, singlemindedly, and with considerable noise.

At the next table John Buckley was trying to consume four courses of Chinese food. The little man had his gift-wrapped box on the table. He wore grandma glasses, and every once in a while he would peer at Leuci.

Eventually DeStefano could eat no more. Turning to Lamattina, he said, "Maybe this guy can help us with the other thing."

The two men nodded at each other. Then Lamattina addressed Leuci.

"Look, there's something else we got going. It's very important."

He began to outline a narcotics case in which Leuci could earn immediately, if he would take part. If he would register a certain drug dealer as an informant and predate this registration by several months, he would be paid $6000. Two lawyers, the assistant district attorney, and the presiding judge in the case were also being bribed to see to it that the dealer went free.

"I'm going to tell you something that's even more important than these two cases we've discussed so far," said DeStefano. "Did you ever hear of a guy named Eddie Rosner?"

"Yeah," said Leuci, who had no idea who Rosner was. "I heard he's a fucking creep."

"Why did you say that? I know he has a bad reputation, but he's a good guy."

There was a case pending against Rosner for subornation of perjury, DeStefano explained. Subornation means to cause perjury to be committed. Rosner, a lawyer who often defended major dope dealers, would pay plenty to find out what was going on in his case, DeStefano added.

Leuci said he would talk to his friend in the courthouse.

"If I can help you and Rosner I'll be glad to do it."

In a state of considerable elation Leuci hurried away from the restaurant. It was an incredible beginning for any investigation, and he knew it. Everything anyone had ever thought about the Baxter Street Crew had been detailed in this first meeting. These people could get to judges, district attorneys, lawyers, cops.

Leuci did not realize then that the most important name dropped that night was Edmund Rosner. Rosner was the defense attorney who stuck in every prosecutor's craw. "Every era has a public enemy number one among lawyers," said an assistant U.S. attorney about this time, "and Rosner is ours."

Rosner was then thirty-five years old, and he was rich and successful. His specialty was taking heroin dealers that the government had cold—and then winning them acquittal. Rosner won case after case. He won many of them the same way—by bringing in alibi witnesses who swore that the defendant had actually been with them in some other place. Each time this happened the government screamed perjury, but no perjury could be proved. The defendant walked free. Rosner banked his big fee. And government lawyers huddled to see if they could not somehow prosecute Rosner for making a mockery of the law, of judicial procedure, and of themselves.

He was a large, somewhat overweight young man, with a slightly pockmarked face. His manner was arrogant. In court he strutted, he postured, he was loud—and he carried this performance to such lengths that his opponents conceived for him a physical distaste as well as a legal one. They called him obnoxious, a man (according to one assistant U.S. attorney) with a detestable face.

They saw him as standing constantly on the fringe of cases where witnesses appeared to have been bribed, where perjured testimony was apparently given. Other times witnesses had simply disappeared and at least one was believed by prosecutors to have been murdered to prevent his testifying.

Rosner was an affront to all they stood for.

The Hernandez case was, to them, typical. A federal

agent had made a direct undercover narcotics buy from Hernandez, a Cuban. Hernandez retained Rosner as his attorney. The case went to trial. It seemed open and shut, and at the end of a single day the government rested.

Rosner then called three defense witnesses. All three testified that Hernandez could not have committed any narcotics sale in New York that day for he had been with them in Florida planning a secret mission to Communist Cuba for the Central Intelligence Agency.

Shocked, the government attorneys requested a recess while they checked with the C.I.A. One of the three alibi witnesses was, in fact, a paid operative in the Miami area. All three of these alibi witnesses were lying, the prosecutors believed, but the case seemed ruined— Rosner was about to beat them once again, and they were enraged.

But Hernandez had got married around the time of the sale, and now one of the prosecutors, Dan Murdock, went down to the marriage license bureau, thumbed through hundreds of records and found that, on the day of the sale, Hernandez was not in Miami at all, but in New York getting a blood test to get married.

Murdock hurried into court and blew Hernandez's alibi to pieces. The dealer was promptly convicted. All three alibi witnesses were then put before a grand jury. All retained Rosner as counsel, and all refused to admit perjury or talk about Rosner.

Meanwhile, Hernandez was in jail, and he did not like it there. He retained Rosner to appeal his conviction for a fee estimated at $10,000. Time went by. Hernandez heard nothing about his appeal, and then he came to the conclusion that Rosner had never bothered to file it. Furious, Hernandez wrote a letter about Rosner to the presiding judge.

After interviewing Hernandez in jail, drug enforcement agents went to Miami, where they found witnesses willing to testify against not only Rosner but also against Nick DeStefano and Nick Russo, both of them New York bail bondsmen. According to this testimony, Rosner had sent DeStefano and Russo to Miami to bribe the Cubans to give the perjured testimony that was supposed to have acquitted Hernandez.

At last a case against Rosner. He was indicted for subornation of perjury, and Hernandez was released from jail on parole. The government appeared to have a strong case against Rosner, for not only would Hernandez testify against him, but so would Gilberto Pulido, one of the other Cubans.

But the trial was repeatedly adjourned at Rosner's request. Hernandez began to complain to the prosecutors that he feared for his life. He was terrified of Rosner, he said. Pulido was put into protective custody in time, but not Hernandez, who one day disappeared without a trace.

Immediately Rosner moved to go on trial at once, and now it was the government who was obliged to request one adjournment after another. Without Hernandez, a prosecutable case against Rosner simply did not exist—unless Leuci was about to develop a new one now.

When Shaw had heard Buckley's tape, he ran over to Leuci, and grabbed his hand. Leuci looked across at Scoppetta, then up into Shaw's intense face. The six-foot-five-inch Shaw said, "Bob, if nothing else happens except that we get evidence of what Eddie Rosner has been doing, we'll be happy." And he began to describe Rosner with some heat.

Scoppetta then switched the conversation. He wanted to know if Leuci had been searched.

"Lamattina didn't search me," Leuci said. He looked and sounded cocky. No one was suspicious and Scoppetta was foolish to worry.

However, when he lay in bed later, Leuci found himself brooding about the prosecutor's warnings, and he continued to brood about them, off and on, all the following day.

When night came he went to meet Lamattina. The meeting place was a bar in Brooklyn. Leuci stood out on the sidewalk waiting. At last the other detective came walking up. They greeted each other like old friends—which they were not—after which Lamattina gave a kind of embarrassed cough.

"DeStefano called some people," Lamattina said apologetically. "They said they didn't know if you could be trusted or not. I told him it was all bullshit, but he wants me to search you."

Leuci stared at him.

"I told Nick it was all bullshit," repeated Lamattina apologetically.

Leuci, thinking fast, supposed that once they were inside the bar, he would be invited into the men's room and told to open his shirt. This would take only a moment, and it would of course reveal any wires taped to his torso.

"Where is the sonuva bitch?" said Leuci.

"He's waiting inside."

They walked into the barroom. It was crowded. They walked down the bar. There were tables in the back. DeStefano sat at one of them. Looking like a fat, gloating Buddha, he watched the other two men approach. Behind his back were the doors to the rest rooms.

Leuci stopped in his tracks. He looked hard at Lamattina. "Go ahead and search me," he said coldly. "Search me right in front of him. I want to look at him, and when you don't find anything I'll knock him on his fucking ass."

"Don't get excited, don't get excited," pleaded Lamattina. "That will ruin the whole thing."

Leuci had one advantage and one only: body searches were an embarrassment on both sides.

"I'm supposed to search you without you knowing it," said Lamattina lamely.

Leuci gave him another icy glare. "How are you going to do that?"

"I know how to search somebody for a wire. Do you think I'm a jerk?"

At his table sat the fat bail bondsman, watching. On his face was an expression that could only be described as a smirk.

A few feet from the table Lamattina suddenly grabbed Leuci by the back of the head, as if with rough affection. He then—mimicking affection still—rubbed his hand across Leuci's shoulders and down his back, and then whacked him on the ass.

Still smirking, DeStefano looked at Lamattina and said, "Well?"

"The guy's not wired."

Leuci said, "If that's what you're worried about, let's skip it. I'll see you around." He started for the door.

But the other two men pulled him down into a chair. "I heard some stories," the fat man said. "People wonder about you. This whole situation you bring me seems too good to be true." His jowls moved. His head nodded up and down. "Too good to be true," he repeated.

Leuci shrugged, concealing his admiration for DeStefano's instincts. These instincts had been nurtured in dozens of shady deals. But DeStefano failed to heed them now.

"Okay," he said, and his voice changed cadence, "I've talked to Rosner. Here's what we want. We want the grand jury minutes of the rat who testified against him. And we want the thirty-five-hundred material."

"What the hell is thirty-five-hundred material?"

"That's witnesses' statements."

"I never heard of it."

"Well, that's what we want."

By law grand jury minutes were secret. So was thirty-five-hundred material.

"I don't know," said Leuci, "I'll ask my friend."

Lamattina glowed. He had brought DeStefano and Leuci together, and he was a part of it, and there was going to be money paid.

"Eddie wants to meet you," DeStefano said. He leaned forward, his great bulk pressing against the edge of the table, and in an instant he became no longer Rosner's partner, but Leuci's. "This is worth plenty to Rosner. It's important that you and I get together and lean on him. Eddie's got a lot of money. He'll pay a lot of money. You got the drift?"

Leuci returned late to Shaw's apartment, and made his report. Margaret was already in bed. Scoppetta sat there in a business suit. Shaw was wearing chino pants and a

T-shirt, and Leuci's report enraged both men. "This guy DeStefano is bad enough," said Shaw, "but Rosner is a cancer. It's unbelievable that a lawyer could behave that way. You've got to make this case, Bob."

But there had been no recording of tonight's conversations.

"Why weren't you wearing a wire tonight?" asked Scoppetta.

"Because I was searched tonight," Leuci retorted. "He could have found it easily enough. Look, I don't want you to tell me when I should or should not wear a wire. I can tell when I can wear one, and when I can't."

The next meeting took place in an Italian restaurant in Brooklyn. John Buckley sat at the table opposite with his attaché case on the floor. Leuci avoided looking at him, and never once did Lamattina or DeStefano even glance in his direction.

"I got another proposition for you," said DeStefano. He plucked a squid out of a dish, held it aloft on a fork, then plunged it as if for punctuation into his mouth.

That night five different corrupt situations were outlined—Leuci was asked to reach and pay off five different teams of detectives. DeStefano had commitments from defendants, all of them South American drug dealers, in all five cases, he said. More than $150,000 was involved. Principally DeStefano wanted testimony changed. But in other cases, just to be safe, he planned also to pay off the assistant D.A. prosecuting the case, or the judge presiding so as to get the case thrown out.

The fat bail bondsman thought of himself as serving the public good, he said. He was aiding South Americans who could hardly speak English. He would help such men. He would help them solve their problems.

The dinner meetings between Leuci, Lamattina, and DeStefano continued for most of a month. The three Italian-Americans gorged themselves on Italian delicacies, mostly pasta afloat in seafood. They mopped up sauces with bread, they swilled Italian wine. Night after night John Buckley took up position at the table opposite, or even at the adjoining table.

12

AT LAST to one of the Italian-American dinner meetings came Lawyer Edmund Rosner in person. Sitting down beside Detective Leuci in Ruggerio's restaurant in Brooklyn, he attempted to discern exactly how well connected Leuci might be—and once the lawyer became convinced that Leuci was very well connected indeed, he reiterated that he would pay good money for any secret material Leuci could get.

Rosner now relaxed, and as he sat at dinner with the other men he talked easily and fluently on a variety of subjects. Though not much older than Leuci himself, he was well dressed, well educated, obviously successful and prosperous. From time to time, when the conversation leaned in that direction, Rosner would berate the government, accusing prosecutors of abusing their privileges to execute the law. Rosner felt that he had every right to use any tactic available to him to defend his clients. He spoke aggressively, like a street fighter, but also with a good deal of charm. He even spoke of Hernandez, the missing witness in the case against himself.

"The government thinks I killed him," he said. "I didn't kill him. He's just hiding out."

As the conspirators consumed dish after dish of Italian specialties, and bottle after bottle of red wine, the conversation turned to Rosner's current big case, which involved one Alvin Bynham, whom the police believed to be the biggest black narcotics dealer in the country. This was a conspiracy case, and there were a number of high-ranking Mafia figures involved with Bynham. According to the indictment, the Mafia was the supplier, and Bynham the buyer, of vast quantities of heroin.

The case would soon come to trial, at which time the

government, Rosner had learned, would spring a secret witness on him. This witness's testimony would perhaps be devastating to Bynham. Rosner supposed it was a man by the name of Jack Stewart. Could Leuci find out who the secret witness was?

Probably, the detective replied. Then he added, "But you have to guarantee that he isn't going to get hurt."

Rosner got up from the table and walked some distance away. DeStefano glanced toward Rosner, and then at Leuci, and said, "Hey, there's no way we can guarantee you that."

Leuci muttered that he was not going to be responsible for getting someone killed.

The fat man's face grew dark. "The guy's an informant. He's a rat. He deserves to be dead."

Around midnight they came out of the restaurant onto the sidewalk. They were sated with food, good wine, and three hours of apparent conviviality. Negotiations were over. The deal was sealed. On the sidewalk there was handshaking, backslapping, and friendly laughter. When the other men had driven off into the night Leuci, trailed by Buckley, drove to Shaw's apartment.

Ripping the paper off his gift-wrapped box, Buckley set up the spools, and the men leaned forward, trying to separate the voices, trying to decipher the words, trying to hear Rosner offering the bribe to Leuci. There was Italian music in the background, people laughing, dishes clacking. The men were listening hard. "There—" Leuci said. "Hear it?"

But Shaw had heard nothing. The machine was stopped, and the same section played again—and then still again. Shaw listened and didn't hear it, and listened and didn't hear it. Six times Leuci played the incriminating words. "I hear it," Shaw shouted. "That time I heard it. That's his voice. That's him. It's there, it's there."

No money had changed hands. Legally this wasn't necessary. The offer alone was enough. There was evidence on this tape sufficient to convict Rosner of bribery.

Shaw moved about the room clapping his hands, grinning. "We got the son of a bitch." He slapped Leuci on the back. "You have done a fantastic service for your government tonight."

Perhaps a jury would not be impressed. It was best to reinforce the evidence, if possible.

So Leuci continued to meet with Rosner and DeStefano, usually at the same restaurant. At each meeting Rosner probed for secret information: witness identities, locations where witnesses were kept under guard, secret testimony against the dope dealers he represented. Also, he was trying to beat down Leuci's price for the secret documents in the government's case against himself. At one of these dinner parties Leuci handed over these documents. At others he was paid money—$2850 in all.

Also the detective was searched many times, by both sides. If it was expected that bribe money might change hands that night, then Leuci would be searched by one of the IRS agents, and the contents of his pockets noted, before he set out to meet Rosner. He would be searched again after leaving Rosner, and the extra money he now carried would be vouchered, and a memo made for later presentation in court.

Regularly Leuci was searched also by Lamattina, who was taking his orders from DeStefano. DeStefano continued to sense that there was something wrong with Leuci. At every meeting, the hair on the back of his neck would rise up. But he did not know what to do about it, other than to order Lamattina to pat Leuci down.

Leuci seemed able to guess in advance which nights he would be searched, and when Scoppetta or one of the IRS agents came forward with the equipment, he would hesitate a moment, then refuse it. It was as if he could measure from across the city the intensity of DeStefano's instincts. Later, in a barroom or restaurant, he would stand docilely while Lamattina quickly patted him down.

Lamattina was always surprised, at the conclusion of each search, to find that Leuci was unarmed.

"Where is your gun?" It was a cop's question. Lamattina asked it repeatedly. Cops came to feel naked without a gun's weight on their hips.

But Leuci's gun was in his attaché case locked in the trunk of his car. "If I'm working, I carry it. If I'm meeting guys for dinner, I don't. Besides, you have a gun. What do I need one for?"

This answer failed to satisfy Lamattina, or DeStefano either. It seemed further proof that Leuci was "strange."

Leuci decided to play on DeStefano's fear in an attempt to relax him.

"Let's not sit next to the jukebox tonight, because I am not getting any kind of recording."

"That's not funny," said DeStefano.

Leuci began to brag that he was indeed working for the government, and so was that barmaid across the room, whose transmitter was stuffed in her—

They all laughed, but DeStefano's laugh was dry.

To Shaw and Scoppetta, DeStefano's suspicions had become so intense they were almost visible. DeStefano was a sinister man. How soon before he ordered Leuci stripped, and found the transmitter?

Once he found it, what would he do next? Leuci wouldn't be able to defend himself because he didn't carry his gun. The two prosecutors had long since realized the awful responsibility they bore for whatever might happen to Leuci.

"Will you please carry your gun," Shaw begged. New York cops were obliged to wear their guns at all times, on or off duty. To be unarmed was a breach of regulations and it was also, in Leuci's case, extremely dangerous. "Carry it, please," said Scoppetta.

But Leuci continued to refuse, until Scoppetta began to believe that this refusal was part of the ambivalence Leuci felt toward his role. If he was found out by DeStefano—or any other subject—and if his duplicity was felt to be so heinous that the verdict was to kill him, then he chose in advance not to be able to defend himself.

DeStefano, never able to quiet his suspicions, kept calling people around the city, people he trusted: Do you hear anything about Leuci? Do you know anything about Leuci?

It was now October 1971. The Knapp Commission was

about to begin televised hearings. It was known that a number of cops, their identities still secret, would testify. Rumors began to circulate that one of these witnesses was Leuci. Once the rumor started, it began to acquire weight, for it sounded reasonable. Leuci was acting funny. He was avoiding friends from his past. He was seen in odd parts of the city at odd hours.

Leuci knew he was hot. In an attempt to negate the rumors, he began to make jokes about them. When the Knapp Commission hearings started, everyone was going to know who the rats were, he told people. The rats were going to come out from the woodwork. He himself was going to be the star rat, and he was planning to buy a new suit, and get his hair cut for his television appearance.

Scoppetta and Shaw had become extremely nervous. They wanted Leuci to drop out of sight until the Knapp Commission hearings were over and the heat had died down. They again insisted that he start carrying his gun. But Leuci, growing cockier, laughed at their fears. "We have this thing going now," he said. "Let's keep it going."

DeStefano, meanwhile, continued to place calls, continued to ask questions, and in this way he learned that a mystery witness would testify before the Knapp Commission, and would blow the lid off narcotics. The name of the mystery witness began with the letter B.

To DeStefano this information constituted solid proof. The mystery witness must be Leuci, and he should have paid attention sooner to the hairs crawling on the back of his neck. But it was perhaps not too late. He phoned Lamattina, and they set up a meeting with Leuci. Leuci should wear a suit, they told him. They would go to a nice restaurant and then maybe meet some ladies. They would meet on a street corner near Little Italy.

Leuci alerted his IRS backup team and also Shaw, taped his wires into place, and drove toward this meeting. He suspected nothing.

13

AFTER parking his car some distance off, Leuci approached the street corner on foot. DeStefano and Lamattina were already there. They looked agitated about something. They were circling each other. De-Stefano's finger waved in the air. Lamattina's head was down, and he was shaking it back and forth.

As Leuci greeted them, he realized that for him this was a dangerous area of the city. It was a neighborhood full of brick-strewn alleys and empty loft buildings.

Immediately Lamattina put his hand on Leuci's back and began to rub in a circle, obviously searching for the wires. The dialogue that follows was recorded in the backup car, and is from the transcript.

Leuci said, "Are you guys all right? What's the matter?"

DeStefano said, "Bad. We're doing, we're doing bad."

"Bad? What's the matter?"

"Everything's wrong," said Lamattina. "Walk."

"What's wrong with you two guys?"

"Walk." Lamattina grabbed Leuci's arm, and turned him down Crosby Street.

"Walk," DeStefano said. "We've got to clip this guy."

"What's wrong with you two guys?"

Leuci shook loose from Lamattina. Recognizing DeStefano's panic, and his own peril, he began to glance around for his backup team. But he was being marched down Crosby Street against the traffic, and the backup car, unable to follow, had already lost visual contact.

To right and left passed warehouses, abandoned tenements, lofts. Leuci was not yet worried about being killed, only about being searched. They could drag him into one of these empty places, search him, and find the wire.

Scoppetta had been right. This was incredibly

dangerous. Why had he not listened? Why had he chosen to wear the wire today?

DeStefano said, "You know what we heard a little while ago?"

"What?"

"That you are a rat, and you are going to testify tomorrow."

"Yeah, right. Let me tell you something. I've been telling that to everybody in the office. I'm fucking them around. You got the same kind of fucking attitude as those guys in the office, understand. Leave me alone now. Wanna leave me alone?"

Leuci was trying to remain calm, but DeStefano's fear seemed contagious.

"Wait until after next week, if that's the way you feel about it," Leuci said. "This thing was a big fucking joke. These guys in this office are unbelievable. Forget it. Forget it."

DeStefano said, "Who you tell it to?"

"Everybody."

"Who's everybody?"

"I was in the office yesterday. There was seventeen guys in the office. Everybody says, hey tomorrow you gonna testify before the Knapp Commission, right? I said, yeah, that's right. Hey, hey, Nickie, you wanna do something? Just call up my office and talk to the trainee there. There were twenty people in there and I'm saying I'm gonna be the next guy to testify at the Knapp commission."

They had him by both arms. As they marched him along he realized that until now he hadn't seen the danger at all. How could he not have seen it?

Lamattina pushed him against a wall and searched him up and down, hands moving underneath the arms, around the chest. Before Lamattina's hands got inside his jacket, Leuci pushed him off. Lamattina said, "Where's your fucking gun, Bob?"

"You all may think it was a joke. I don't wear a gun."

"Where's your gun?"

"It's in my trunk, do you want to go get it?"

"No," Lamattina said.

"I never wear the fucking thing. I only wear it when I'm

working. All kidding aside, you really gonna give me a fucking attitude. I ain't kidding you, Nick."

They were holding him tight by both arms.

"I'm—I'm—really—no fucking joke. This bullshit, playing fucking games."

DeStefano stuck his finger in Leuci's face. "We're not fucking playing games here."

The two IRS agents, frantically trying to find Leuci, were moving further and further out of range. From time to time their receiver lost his voice entirely. There were gaps in the transmission of thirty-one seconds, eighteen seconds, twenty-four seconds. They were driving in circles, looking for him. The transmission gaps became longer: a minute and five seconds, four minutes fifty-seven seconds, seven minutes fifty-three seconds.

Leuci began to protest that, because he was due at any moment in court, he had to phone the SIU office, get someone to phone and get the case adjourned. This was the last time the case was on. If he didn't show up, the case would be thrown out, and he would get in trouble.

But Lamattina and DeStefano continued to walk him fast along the sidewalk and they were carefully looking over each tenement and loft they passed. It was broad daylight, and incredible, Leuci thought, that this could be happening to him. The streets were full of people but these two thugs were looking for a place to kill him and dump the body. But he was still a cop. They would have to kill a cop. They were not sure yet.

Leuci insisted that he had to phone about his court case. It was an argument which, to the bail bondsman DeStefano and to the detective Lamattina, had great weight. Besides, they needed a moment to talk to each other, and so Leuci was allowed to step into a grocery store to phone SIU. They stood close while he attempted to force a dime into the pay phone. At first he could not get the dime in. It was his intention to phone Shaw. There was no one at SIU he could turn to, or so he imagined, and Shaw was more likely to be in his office than Scoppetta. He would speak in code. He would tell Shaw that these two thugs were going to kill him. Shaw would save him.

But he misdialed, or else the phone was out of order.

He could not make it work. He tried again.

This time Shaw's secretary came on the line. "Mr. Shaw is out," she said curtly.

"It's Bob Leuci. This is very important."

"Who?"

"Detective Leuci. Sonny." Sonny was Leuci's code name.

"Mr. Shaw is out. How many times do I have to tell you? Don't you understand English?" She hung up.

Outside the grocery store, DeStefano and Lamattina again had Leuci by the arms, again marched him along. They had had a conference, and their indecision was over. That was the frightening thing. They knew what they were going to do, and where they would do it.

Leuci, talking fast, began embroidering on past stories, and inventing new ones. He realized he was groveling in front of Lamattina and DeStefano. Scared as he was, he was furious with himself for groveling, furious with himself for not having his gun. He wanted to blow his cover, tell them who he was, arrest both of them. Most of all, he wanted to live. He remembered something Mikey Coco had said to him one time, "Bobby, everybody cries before he dies."

In a moment he believed he would beg them to spare him. They were a couple of shits. Nonetheless, when they dragged him off the street into some alley, he would beg for his life. He glanced up at street signs, searching for something to save him. They had come into Little Italy now, and there on the corner of Elizabeth Street stood Alphonse Indelicata, the Mafia killer known as Sonny Red.

"Look," Leuci said. "Go talk to that guy. If he don't vouch for me a thousand percent, I'll go some place and you can pull the fucking trigger then."

"Don't go down asking for that," DeStefano said.

DeStefano and Lamattina eyed each other. Then, while Lamattina held Leuci tightly by the arm, DeStefano strode across the street and conversed with Sonny Red.

Sonny Red had been a contract hit man. In prison for first-degree murder, he had once hung suspended in handcuffs for two days rather than tell his guards the name of whoever had supplied him with sandwiches. There was testimony on record that he had once killed a man by driving an ice pick so hard through the victim's chest and into the floor that the body had to be pried up with tire irons.

Sonny Red and John Lusterino had been in prison together. Leuci had met him and done him a favor once. Did Sonny Red remember?

Leuci peered across the street. Sonny Red, his head down, stared at the sidewalk. DeStefano stood close to him, belly almost touching, talking urgently.

Leuci saw Sonny Red's head come up. The killer's eyes flicked toward him across the street. After a moment a grin came onto Sonny Red's face. That grin could mean anything. It's a nice kind of grin, Leuci told himself. At least a sign of recognition. Leuci saw Sonny Red nod to DeStefano, and then walk slowly away.

DeStefano waited for a break in the traffic, then waddled quickly across the street toward Leuci and Lamattina.

"I said to him, we think he's a rat, we think we should kill him," DeStefano reported. "He tells me, if you think he's a rat, then you should kill him, but if you kill him you better be sure he's a rat, because he's a friend of ours."

On Leuci's arm Detective Lamattina's grip softened.

The fat bail bondsman smiled warmly. "No hard feelings," he said.

They let Leuci go. He made it to a phone booth. The good guys wanted to kill me, he told himself. The bad guy saved my life.

He dialed Shaw's office a second time. The same secretary came on the line. He said, "You tell him that Sonny called and I'm going to be at his fucking house. Tell him I'm pissed, really really pissed. Tell him just like that."

"Mr. Leuci, Mr. Sonny—"

"Tell him. Tell him just like that."

Leuci got to his car. He drove across the Brooklyn Bridge, across the sparkling New York harbor. Outside Shaw's apartment he paced the promenade along Columbia Heights Street. He could see lower Manhattan, and most of the East River.

When he turned around he was looking at the third button of Mike Shaw's shirt.

"Mike, you are a fuck."

"I'm really sorry," Shaw said. "I'm really, really sorry."

"Those fucking guys nearly knocked me off. All you had to do was be there. Who did you go out to see, and how important was it? I nearly got killed."

Tears welled up in Shaw's eyes.

"Mike, you don't give a shit about me."

"Don't ever say that to me again," said Shaw. "I give you my word that this will never happen again. Whenever you need me, I'll be there. From now on. I'm so sorry. I'm so sorry."

A taxi pulled up, and out jumped Scoppetta. "Bob, are you okay?"

The three men went up to Shaw's apartment. "I want New York City cops with me from now on," Leuci said. "I was walking along the street with these two jerks, and those IRS agents didn't understand what the hell was going on. A cop would have seen it. A cop would have known what to do. I want New York City cops. These IRS agents are only worried about blowing the investigation. Cops would be worried about me. I want cops."

They were trying to calm him down. Shaw handed him a shot of liquor.

"DeStefano said to me that it was a good thing I showed up," Leuci babbled, "because they were on their way out to my house. My wife, my kids are out there alone. For all we know these sons of bitches have sent somebody out to my house already. I want New York City cops. I want this cop that lives across the street from me involved. I want some cops who know the streets."

The fear that he had controlled earlier he could control no longer. He burst into tears.

"I think it's over," Shaw said. "I think we ought to end it. You're too hot. It's too dangerous for you."

But Leuci immediately began to protest, "Let this Knapp Commission thing die down. The public hearings will be over, and I won't have been on them. Everything will be fine after that."

"You need a vacation," Shaw said. "We need one, too. I want you to take your wife and kids and go away for a couple of days."

"Where am I going to go?" Leuci said. "We never had a vacation. We wouldn't know where to go."

Shaw said he'd make arrangements. The cost would be on the government.

Scoppetta phoned Gina Leuci. In a soothing voice he assured her that everything was all right, but that her husband needed a rest. "We want you two to go away for a couple of days. We want you to make sure he goes. We want you to go at once."

This message terrified Gina. Close up the house and go. Take the kids and go. Immediately. Go.

Leuci left there and from the nearby Seventy-sixth Precinct telephoned SIU to check in with his boss, Sergeant Cohen—corrupt Sergeant Cohen whom he believed he despised.

He was not prepared for Sergeant Cohen's frantic voice. "We were afraid you'd been hurt," cried Cohen. "You didn't go to court. You didn't call in. Some cops saw you in the street with some rough-looking guys."

"I did have some problems with some fucking guys," Leuci admitted.

"Are you okay?" Cohen demanded. "Stay right there. Maybe those guys are still around. I'm going to bring help. Sheridan and I will be right there. Stay where you are. We're coming right away."

A few minutes later a car pulled up. Out jumped Cohen and Sheridan. When Leuci told them what had happened, that Lamattina and DeStefano had threatened to kill him because they thought he was going to testify at the Knapp Commission, Sheridan flew into a rage. He wanted to go after Lamattina and DeStefano. "I'll find those two sons of bitches and—"

"You're always kidding around like that," said Cohen to Leuci. "That's a serious thing. You've got the guys in the office upset. I know you are not going to testify. Jim knows you are not going to testify. But you shouldn't kid about it."

Driving home, Leuci thought about Sheridan and

Cohen, who were on their way to jail but didn't yet know it, and about how much he wanted to dislike both of them. But it was impossible to dislike them, especially Sheridan. Sheridan was so strong, and being with him made Leuci feel so strong. He was a big, physically strong man, an intimidating man, and it was an awful thing to betray him this way. And Cohen. How could he hate a man so willing to rush to his defense when needed?

By the time he got home, Gina had the kids dressed and the bags packed. She was ashen. It was then about six o'clock at night. She knew something was wrong.

They drove out to Montauk Point. Shaw had arranged for them to live in a kind of chalet on the beach overlooking the ocean. In front of the window was a sweep of sand dunes, and then the waves. Both found the scenery absolutely breathtaking. It wasn't summer anymore, and there was no one else on the beach. For hours they walked up and down the beach, and talked about their life, and about where Leuci's path would lead them. Once Gina said, "You got caught doing something, didn't you? That's why you are doing this thing."

Leuci shook his head. No, he hadn't been caught.

After a moment Gina said, "The most horrible thing that could happen is that I lose you. If I lose you like this, there is no honor in it for you." They stood on the beach gazing out to sea. "I know how you watch those inspectors' funerals on TV," Gina said, "and how carried away you get with it all. If those two men had killed you, there would be no inspector's funeral for you. You would have been described as a corrupt cop who was caught in a bad situation."

Leuci thought about it. "That's not true. They would have had an inspector's funeral for me."

"No. How could they have an inspector's funeral if you were killed by another cop? They wouldn't do anything. The politicians would be explaining you for three weeks."

Leuci thought about this. It was perhaps true. "What makes you think it's important for me to be buried in an inspector's funeral?" he asked Gina.

"I know you so well. You look forward to your death,

and this whole business of having that kind of funeral. But I don't look forward to it."

Once long ago he had told her that if he had to die young, he wanted to be killed in the line of duty. He didn't want to be killed in an automobile accident, or a plane crash, or fall off a goddamn sailboat and drown. If it was meant for him to die young, then he wanted to die among his friends. He had said that to her never thinking she would remember.

They talked about what they would do when this job was over. Leuci told her then something of what he felt, even though he still had not been able to explain it very well even to himself. But he wanted to feel clean again. He wanted his former innocence back. He wanted to feel about being a cop the way he had felt at twenty-one when he first came out onto the street wearing his blue uniform.

He told his wife that he was totally committed to this road he had taken, and by the end of the weekend Gina was very much in his corner. By then, romping on the beach with the children, Leuci was relaxed enough to laugh, to fool with the little ones, to do impromptu dances on the sand with his wife. Once Gina said, "The Bob Leuci I knew is gone. We haven't laughed and kidded with the children like that for months and months and months. I want you to see this whole thing through and be proud of yourself again. Then you can laugh again all the time the way you used to."

This was the first time Leuci realized how grim he—like his life itself—had become.

On television they watched the Knapp Commission hearings. The secret witness was indeed a corrupt cop whose name began with B: Patrolman Bill Phillips.

The hearings ended. The Leucis' days at Montauk Point ended also, and they drove home. It had been a super weekend for them both, and for their marriage, and it was also a super weekend for the investigation because the Knapp Commission hearings had taken place and Detective Bob Leuci had not appeared to testify. When he reported to the SIU offices the following morning, everyone was glad to see him again, and the heat was off.

14

FOR THE REST of the year Leuci went on working full time at SIU. He was still team leader. It was his job to select the targets his team would zero in on—a steady succession of targets—and now he selected a man named Peter Corso.

As with most SIU targets, the selection of Corso was accidental, almost arbitrary, but from the moment that selection was made, Corso became a man with problems. He had three highly skilled detectives after him. They intended to pin something on him, narcotics if possible; otherwise—anything. His chances of escaping were slim.

Some months previously a convict serving a long sentence on narcotics charges had asked for an interview with Leuci. The convict had wanted to trade information on his former colleagues. He wanted a reduced sentence, and he had mentioned Peter Corso. Corso, the convict said, regularly moved big packages. Leuci, who was not even in SIU at the time, had done nothing with this information. Leaving the convict to rot, he had merely filed away the name. Now, needing a target, he brought it out.

Where to find this Corso? A check of SIU records showed he had been in jail, but was out now. The state parole board said he had not reported for months. The parole board, supposedly, was looking for him. They provided Leuci with a recent picture, and with Corso's last known address, a brownstone house in Brooklyn.

The thing to do then was to begin surveillance on Corso's house, where his wife and children still lived. The team, Leuci decided, would watch the house for a full week, ten hours a day. It was Leuci's hope that, in the course of a week, Corso might return to visit his family.

Sitting in a parked car opposite Corso's house and some distance up the street, the three detectives—Leuci, Sheridan, and a new man named Stanley Glazer—began their watch. The hours began to pass, and then the days. They relayed each other. Sometimes two men sat in the parked car, sometimes only one.

It mattered little if the presence of the detectives was noted and caused talk in the neighborhood—the subject, after all, lived elsewhere. Still, basic precautions were taken. If a detective watched alone he sat on the passenger side of the car, as if waiting for the driver to return. Two detectives would sit one in the passenger seat and one in the back. Same thing.

Six days passed. Around noon on Sunday morning a car pulled up; and a man climbed out carrying what looked like a box of Italian pastries. He was well dressed, and he walked without hesitation straight into Mrs. Corso's brownstone.

The detectives on watch were immediately excited. Although stationed too far away to see the man's face, they were sure this was Corso. They waited outside for four hours. When Corso at last came out of the building, they tailed his car across the bridge into Manhattan. Once they pulled almost alongside—close enough to match his face to the picture they had. Peter Corso. There was a good resemblance. It was probably the same man.

They tailed him to a building on East Seventh Street. He got out of his car, locked it, and entered the building. Five minutes later Leuci sauntered into the lobby. His eye ran down the names on the mailboxes. He didn't expect to find the name Corso. He did expect something close. One name stood out—Peter Carbone. People living under aliases almost always chose something close.

One week had already gone into this surveillance. Now they decided to invest another in tailing the subject through the streets.

But during that week, nothing happened. They took Corso-Carbone to a few bars on the East Side, and to a particular bar near his house. They watched him smoke some pot. He was an older man—close to 60—but was behaving like a kind of hippie. Usually he was in the company of a very beautiful girl, and he seemed to be trying to pretend he was her age. The detectives recognized the pattern—Corso had been in jail for a long time and now, in the street again, he wanted to be part of the new scene. His behavior was ridiculous, but also sad.

The second week ended. Corso had talked to people in bars, but there had been no furtive meetings that might have been drug transactions. He had met no one who gave the appearance of being a big-time drug dealer.

After a conference with Sergeant Cohen, the decision was again made to put in an illegal wiretap. The reason was the same—it was the only quick, simple way to see if Corso was doing any narcotics business. Leuci, Sheridan, and Glazer went down into the basement of the building on Seventh Street. Leuci found and branched into Corso's wires, hid the self-starting tape recorder in a closet, and they went back up to the street.

Now the surveillance of Corso was considerably easier, for the tapped line informed them of his movements in advance. The man kept strange hours: he was out most nights till dawn, and then slept all day. The three men stalking him arranged their schedule around him.

Corso's beautiful girl friend, called Poopsy, had moved in with him. It was Poopsy's habit to get on the telephone and talk for hours. The detectives considered her a total moron, but they learned more information from her rambling conversations with girl friends than from calls Corso made. Corso was an old-time Italian hoodlum. On the phone he was guarded. Whereas Poopsy would tell everybody where they had gone the night before, whom they had seen, and where they planned to go next.

A good deal of telephone conversation concerned Corso's son-in-law, a man known as Jack. We saw Jack last night at the Copa. Jack looks terrific. We were with Jack last night—Jack seemed increasingly interesting, but the eavesdropping detectives couldn't identify him.

From these same phone conversations the detectives gathered that Corso had two daughters. They would occasionally phone their father. It was Frances who was married to Jack. The detectives were puzzled. They decided that the missing ingredient must be the son-in-law, Jack.

One day Frances made a collect call to her father's house. She identified herself as Frances Bless. The name rang a bell with Leuci, who had by now been a narcotics detective for most of eight years. He looked up Jack Bless in the SIU files, and cross-checked with the Federal Narcotics Bureau.

The first name was spelled Jacques. Jacques Bless was listed in both places as a major narcotics dealer and as a close associate of Spanish Raymond and Anthony Angeletti, major dealers from East Harlem. His French first name was an affectation. Bless was of Hispanic origin. He was alleged, in police circles, to have ordered and/or participated in a number of killings. He had been marked "extremely dangerous."

The case, now in its fourth week, was starting to come together, and the three detectives were extremely excited. However, they still had overheard no conversation involving narcotics nor had Corso made contact with Bless.

But one night the following cryptic telephone call came in:

"This is Johnny from Brooklyn. Hey, I ran into somebody. It sounds like something very nice. These people have a lot of money."

"We'll meet tonight," said Peter Corso.

An address was specified, but as old Peter Corso left his house that evening, Leuci decided not to tail him. "This looks really good, whatever it is," he said. "I don't want to take a chance on blowing it. Let's wait right here."

Some hours later Peter Corso returned. The three detectives gave him time to get upstairs, then hurried down into his cellar. Corso made just one telephone call—to his son-in-law, Bless. The three detectives listened as he made it.

"This is your father-in-law calling."

"If you got something to talk to me about," said Bless, "come up to my house. We'll talk about it."

Corso left his house, got into his car and, tailed by the three detectives, drove to an elegant apartment building on the Upper East Side. As the doorman took Corso upstairs in the elevator, Leuci checked the bells and found the name he was looking for: Jacques Bless.

In their own car, the detectives talked it over. They had identified Bless's address. They had Corso meeting Bless. There was apparently some kind of a deal going down.

The following day, crouched over their tape deck in Corso's basement, they listened to Corso talking to Bless, and heard Corso order "three shirts." As far as the detectives were concerned, this meant three kilos of heroin. They were as eager as rookies. What else could it be? Three ounces? Three-eighths of a kilo? No, it was three kilos. Jacques Bless was not going to get involved with anything less.

So they hurried to court, where they applied for and were accorded search warrants for Corso's house and Bless's house both. Before executing the warrants, they made a final check on the tape recorder in Corso's basement. There was only one brief conversation on the tape: Corso and Bless would meet in a few minutes at Jack's Barbershop on Sixty-ninth Street and Madison Avenue.

With the three kilos? Without? And what did "in a few minutes" mean?

The detectives had no notion of how old this conversation might be, and so they sped hurriedly uptown toward Jack's Barbershop. There, however, they found no one except barbers. No Corso. No Bless. Nobody waiting on the corner. And no heroin.

It was noon.

Back to Corso's apartment. Three o'clock passed. Four. Repeated checks were made on the tape in the basement, but no new calls were registered. The detectives sat hunched and despondent in their car. Dusk fell, and then it was night. There was no sign of Corso, and no conversation on the phone. At last two calls did come in. They were widely spaced. Both were from Jacques Bless to Corso's girl friend, Poopsy: Have you heard from Pete?

But no one had heard from Pete.

At midnight the detectives were still there, waiting. And they were ducking into the cellar with ever greater frequency. At last a call came in. "Are you sitting down, Poopsy?" asked a woman's voice. "I have some bad news."

Poopsy began screaming, "They have killed my Pete!"

"No, no, it's worse. He's been locked up. So has my Ralphie."

"No, no! Pete's on parole. I'll lose him forever."

The three detectives were first shocked, then terribly disappointed. Who had arrested Peter Corso? The cops? The feds?

They trooped disconsolately back to the SIU office, where their first job was to find out who had arrested Peter Corso. They phoned around. The answer turned out to be the Joint Task Force, and the arresting officer had been Detective Joe Nunziata.

The Joint Narcotics Task Force of detectives and federal agents was a small elite unit that had been conceived as a kind of super SIU. It fed arrested dope dealers into federal courts, where they were tried promptly under the strict, new federal laws. The Task Force was heavily funded, and one of the first SIU detectives assigned to it had been Joe Nunziata.

At one o'clock in the morning, Nunziata and Leuci sat opposite each other in a diner on West Street. Nunziata, who was then thirty-nine, wore a suit and a topcoat, and with his graying hair he looked like a prosperous business man. Both men had been working now all day, but Nunziata appeared fresh, whereas Leuci was bleary eyed. The two men ordered coffee.

Leuci was there to worm information, if he could, out of Nunziata. Leuci and his team had just lost Corso to Nunziata, plus what had turned out to be three kilos of pure heroin. But Bless was still at large. Leuci wanted to know if Nunziata was onto Bless too. The difficulty would be to find this out without having to give up Bless's name.

"We were on Corso," Leuci began. He stirred his coffee. "We were wondering how you happened to get on him?"

Nunziata, grinning expansively sat back and blandly

announced that Corso's heroin had come straight from
Little Italy—"from The General and Sonny Meatballs."

Leuci, knowing it had come straight from Jacques
Bless, nodded. "That's what we thought too."

At one time Nunziata, who was eight years older, had
been Leuci's mentor and almost, in a Police Department
sense, his father. The relationship between them was still
very close—affection on Nunziata's side, admiration on
Leuci's. But as they sipped their coffee in a cheap diner in
the middle of the night, they went on sparring with each
other.

They had first met eight years previously, when a mass
of demonstrators had converged on a precinct station
house being guarded by a single patrolman, Robert Leuci,
aged twenty-three. One moment Leuci had stood between
the mob and the station house door, and the next he was
on his back in the doorway, and they were trampling him.
One demonstrator had Leuci by the neck and was banging
his head against the floor.

Just then about twenty cops on horseback came
galloping down the street. The demonstrator pummeling
Leuci let out a scream, went flying backwards into the
wall of the station house, and remained pinned there by
the butt of a police horse. The horse was halfway up the
station house steps, and the cop in the saddle, Patrolman
Joe Nunziata, looked down on Leuci with an enormous
grin, saying, "Are you okay? Are you going to take this
collar?"

"He's my collar," Leuci said. "I want him."

"Let me just take some of the wind out of him first,"
said Nunziata, and he pulled back on his horse. The
demonstrator let out a muffled scream and collapsed to
the ground. "I'll see you around," said Nunziata,
grinning, and he galloped away.

Once both were in Narcotics they worked cases
together, made arrests together, dined and drank
together, and Leuci fell somewhat in awe of the older
detective's style and skill. They were not partners.
Nunziata had a steady partner, and Leuci's was Frank
Mandato. Later, when Leuci moved up into SIU,

Nunziata, who was already there, asked him to join his team. But Leuci refused because he wanted to be a team leader himself. As the years passed, the two men had become even closer friends.

But rivals, too.

Leuci now stirred his coffee. "Do you know who Corso's connection is, Joe?"

"Yes. Do you?"

"Yes."

Nunziata was grinning fondly at his former protégé. "Are you going to tell me who it is?"

"No. Are you going to tell me?"

"I don't think so," said Nunziata affectionately.

Leuci left the diner convinced that Nunziata knew nothing about Jacques Bless, that he had been investigating someone else and had dropped Corso almost by accident; and this is what he reported to Sergeant Cohen and to Sheridan and Glazer a few minutes later. Though they had lost Corso and three kilos of heroin, they might still make a case against Bless.

They still had their search warrant, but they couldn't decide whether to serve it now in the middle of the night or not. Sheridan wanted to ride uptown and kick Bless's door in. They would find whatever they might find. To this plan the others presently agreed.

An hour later all four men were parked across the street from Bless's apartment building. They could see the doorman in his uniform standing behind the glass doors. They were calmer now and were having second thoughts about kicking Bless's door in. It was unlikely that a man like Bless would keep any heroin in his house. If he had stayed untouchable until now, it was because he never handled narcotics himself.

So what was the best thing to do?

"I think," said Sergeant Cohen, "that Bless would be interested in buying our tapes of him talking to Corso."

This produced excited conversation inside the car. Bless didn't know the wiretap was illegal, all agreed. He would think the tapes put him in the middle of the conspiracy. They could threaten to turn the tapes over to

Nunziata and the Task Force unless he paid them. Cohen paused a moment, then added, "Now we are talking about big money."

Sitting in their parked car, watching the doorman through glass across the street, the detectives talked about money. It seemed to them that Bless might be willing to pay up to $50,000 to have the tapes destroyed.

That was the price decided upon: $50,000. The other three appointed Detective Leuci to sell the tapes to Bless on their behalf. Leuci was the most experienced and also the most devious among them, and surely he would be able to work out a way to contact Bless and to complete the sale.

And so, the long day ended. They put away their search warrant, turned from Bless's house, and went home to bed.

Leuci reported all this to Scoppetta and Shaw the next morning. The story excited them, and they ordered him to go through with the sale. There seemed, they said, a real opportunity here to nail Bless for bribery—which was important, because the man had proven immune to the narcotics laws. And to nail Leuci's three partners for bribe receiving, of course.

Fifty thousand dollars. The case was so important that five men—Scoppetta and Shaw on one side, and Cohen, Sheridan, and Glazer on the other—began to press Leuci every day: Have you managed to contact Bless yet? How soon will he come up with the money? But contacting Bless proved not so easy to do.

15

IT WAS NOW Christmas 1971. Ten months had passed since Leuci's first conversations with Scoppetta.

One night when Leuci appeared for dinner at Shaw's Brooklyn Heights apartment, a man he didn't know was already there, sitting on Shaw's sofa with his shoes off and his feet up. He introduced himself as Andrew Tartaglino.

The Leuci investigation was about to move onto a new and higher plane.

"I've heard all good things about you," Tartaglino said to Leuci. "The bad things that I've heard over the years I think I'm going to forget about. I like to hear these new good things."

Tartaglino was a small man. There was something careful and immaculate about him. He spoke softly, almost monotonously. Hardly anyone, meeting him for the first time, suspected the force that drove him, and he did not seem a man to fear. Most of the people he had put in jail had not feared him until it was too late. Certainly Leuci, who had never heard of him before, did not fear him now.

Tartaglino was Number Two man in the Federal Bureau of Narcotics and Dangerous Drugs. His specialty was integrity. He was often called the finest integrity agent the United States had ever produced. Those who hated Tartaglino, and they were many, accused him of being obsessed with corruption. When he found it he would crush it, and the people involved in it, too, according them no sympathy, no understanding, and no quarter.

Tartaglino, then forty-six years old, had graduated from Georgetown, had served as a U.S. Navy lieutenant, and had then become a narcotics agent. After four years assigned to New York, he had spent five years in Italy and France—he spoke Italian fluently—attempting to crush the New York drug trade at its various sources. Returning to the United States, he had moved quickly upward in rank.

Four years previously he had heard Leuci's name for the first time. An integrity unit under Tartaglino had been sent into New York to root out corruption among federal narcotics agents. The investigation was so sensitive that only senior people were chosen to work under Tartaglino.

There was a direct relationship between the rise of the drug traffic and failure to combat corruption, Tartaglino believed: "I could map you a graph showing the direct parallel between the rising heroin traffic in the nineteen-sixties and the lack of effort to fight corruption. New York City was the hub of it all."

In New York in 1967 Tartaglino began arresting men he knew intimately, men whom he had gone through treasury school with. It was said that, in a cold-blooded business, Andrew Tartaglino was the most cold-blooded of all.

Technically, Tartaglino was investigating corrupt federal narcotics agents only, but one case led him directly to Detective Frank Mandato, and from there to Mandato's partner, Leuci. Tartaglino cut the case in half, as was the policy at that time, and turned his Leuci-Mandato material over to the Police Department, where it was vaguely investigated, then dropped.

Leuci had been just a name to Tartaglino. He never met him. But it was a name that recurred, and the name Babyface recurred also. There may have been more than one Babyface, but Tartaglino did not think so. Anyway, prior to tonight's meeting he had refreshed his memory by reading through the Leuci file. He was aware that Leuci, in admitting to Scoppetta two or three acts of minor misconduct, had vehemently denied participation in the drug traffic itself; he said he had never bought or sold drugs. But Tartaglino's intelligence file—and his memory as well—indicated otherwise. Tartaglino had no proof. He did have solid suspicions.

Tartaglino, sitting at dinner in Shaw's house, had chosen not to reveal to Scoppetta and Shaw that he believed Leuci to be a villain, because, in a world of trade-offs, the villain, now, could be extremely useful to him. Tartaglino was considering taking over the funding and staffing of the Leuci investigation, and directing it himself. The purpose of tonight's meeting was to get a feeling both for Leuci and for the new directions in which Tartaglino might point him.

A few days later Shaw handed Leuci a government travel voucher and told him to fly to Washington to see Tartaglino a second time. The experienced detective was immediately fearful. He had never been to Washington before. Why was he being summoned?

In Washington he was ushered into Tartaglino's office, and it impressed him tremendously. Tartaglino, who was on the phone with a senator, gestured Leuci toward an armchair. Leuci gazed about him wide-eyed. Machines standing against the wall provided direct link-ups to many of the major cities of the world. Tartaglino's desk and filing cabinets were in the next room—this room contained only a couch, armchairs, a sideboard, a television set. Leuci had never before known a man who occupied not an office, but a suite. This guy is not a nobody, he told himself. This guy is an important guy.

Tartaglino took his shoes off, sat on the couch with his feet up, and began to explain that he had agreed to commit men and funds to Leuci's investigation. He would bring in an agent from Saigon, he said, and another from Dallas. He would bring other good agents in from elsewhere. Leuci, henceforth, would not be alone. He would be surrounded by many of Tartaglino's best men. Tartaglino himself planned to spend a good deal of time in New York.

"We also have an undercover guy," Tartaglino said, watching Leuci carefully. "We would like to put him with you as soon as possible."

There was a heavy silence. They're going to push me out, Leuci thought, and bring in their own undercover guy.

Even before he could articulate his thought, Tartaglino said, "Don't think what you're thinking. You're the guy that knows this setup. We may bring in another undercover guy, if you agree, just to help you in a couple of situations. He's an Italian." The two Italian-Americans nodded at each other. "He's very bright. He's stationed in France right now, but we would like to bring him in, if you'll agree."

Tartaglino put his arm around Leuci. "Let me drive you back to the airport."

But the detective, unwilling to take up the time of such an important man, declined. He would take a cab. On the plane back to New York Leuci brooded. Tartaglino was bringing in agents. The investigation had moved out of New York. The federal government was running it now. Henceforth, Tartaglino had assured him, he would be flying to Washington frequently. It was still his investigation, though. It had merely gotten bigger. He felt extremely heady. He felt like James Bond.

When he got home he recounted the entire experience to Gina. He was filled with excitement, but Gina began shaking her head.

"This started off small," she said. "Now it is growing into something very big, very important. The more important this investigation gets—don't you realize—the more important you are going to be. The more important it will be, maybe, to hurt you."

"Who's going to hurt me? No one is going to hurt me. Why should anyone want to hurt me?"

Tartaglino wanted to know everything Leuci was doing, and he began to study each segment separately, and then he began to bring in his own agents, one from Tokyo, others from Europe. He moved in some female agents to take over surveillances. He provided the investigation with new cars, new wire transmitters and recorders, and two cover apartments, one in the Stanhope Hotel and the other in a private apartment house on Sutton Place. These were fancy luxury apartments; when they were not being used for conferences and debriefings, Tartaglino's agents slept there. Tartaglino himself came often to New York, and he summoned Leuci regularly to Washington.

To Shaw and Scoppetta he seemed the most creative law enforcement man they had ever known. They were dazzled by him and by his ideas.

"I believe in testing people," Tartaglino told them. "If you have allegations against a certain agent or police officers, you can test that man. You can create a set of circumstances that are not real.

"For instance, suppose an officer told you that he participated in a raid with three other officers; they kicked the door in, and there was a lot of money, and a lot of drugs, and they cut the money up—I think you can test those other three officers. You can cause those officers to go through the same type of raid again, to see how they would react. You can set up an apartment with heroin and counterfeit money. You can put one-way mirrors in there, and wire the room up, and cause them to raid it—you can cause that to happen. Now the raid in question may also serve to exonerate them. You know exactly how much money was put in there, the quantity and purity of the drugs, and you can watch to see what ends up vouchered with the property clerk. You know what was in the room. You know whether these officers are honest or not."

"As an investigative technique, this one has been very, very successful in the past. It has been the basis for many prosecutions."

The more Tartaglino studied Leuci's operations so far, the more he focused in on a Queens sergeant named Peter Perrazzo.

Leuci, during the past several months had made a number of recordings with Perrazzo, for whom he had once worked. Perrazzo had bragged about being able to fix the Brooklyn district attorney's office, and also the Queens district attorney's office. But he could not be indicted or prosecuted, because it was all talk—so far. Leuci had waited for the conversations to turn into action, for Perrazzo to take him somewhere. But this had not happened.

It was Tartaglino's idea now to have Leuci move

someone else in with Perrazzo. It was not that he was dissatisfied with Leuci's performance, he said. Rather he wanted another agent moved in as a kind of insurance policy. And he wanted Leuci insulated from Sergeant Perrazzo.

The agent Tartaglino had in mind was Sandy Bario, whom he flew in from France, and he arranged for Bario and Leuci to meet. He himself did not attend this meeting. Afterward, Leuci met with Tartaglino, Shaw, and Scoppetta, and listened to the plan Tartaglino had concocted.

First of all, Tartaglino said, Leuci would go to Perrazzo. "You will tell him you have information about a narcotics courier, Bario, who is going to be at a motel at the airport, who can be ripped off."

Realizing that Tartaglino must have used this same plan many times in the past, Leuci interrupted. "Why don't I rip this guy off myself?"

"You can't. You're doing business with his people."

Leuci nodded.

Tartaglino continued, "You don't want Bario locked up, for the same reason. Perrazzo should simply rip him off, but you want your share in the score."

"That doesn't sound so bad, so far," Leuci said. "Is he going to have drugs?"

"He's not going to have drugs. What he is going to have is a phony passport. And he's going to have a lot of money. Tell Perrazzo about the phony passport. Perrazzo should threaten to arrest Bario because of the phony passport, and Bario will pay to avoid arrest."

Tartaglino gave his gentle, quiet smile. "Bario's going to be wired. The room is going to be wired. Perrazzo is going to rip him off, we hope. We don't know. Whatever money Perrazzo takes you have to share in, because we want some of our money back, and in addition the money he gives you will serve as evidence in court."

So Leuci went to Perrazzo, and retold this story. Perrazzo, who was a middle-aged man with twenty-five years in the Police Deparmment, was delighted. He had some detectives he could trust, he said. He and these detectives would be able to take care of this courier. No problem.

The next day Perrazzo and two detectives broke in on Bario, threatened him with arrest, and stole $8000. Perrazzo, when he met Leuci later, was exultant. "Every time this guy comes to town he's going to give me a couple of thousand," Perrazzo reported as he handed Leuci money. "You'll get your share, Bobby. I won't forget you for introducing me to this guy. We got a nice association going. We spoke to each other in Italian."

Leuci went to see Tartaglino.

"We now have a solid case against Perrazzo," Tartaglino told him. "And Bario is in solid with Perrazzo. That is only step one. We have a long way to go."

Tartaglino was thinking it out. "What we have to do now is plan our next step," he said. "How are we going to use Agent Bario and Sergeant Perrazzo together?" Tartaglino was studying Leuci carefully.

"What I would like to do," Tartaglino said presently, "is send someone else in to Perrazzo. Another agent. But we'll make this one too big for a sergeant. We'll make him a don from Detroit. We're going to figure out a way that Sergeant Perrazzo can move this guy directly into the Queens district attorney's office."

Presently Tartaglino put together a grandiose scheme, and Scoppetta and Shaw, when they heard it, were as awed by Tartaglino as Leuci was.

To Leuci, Sergeant Perrazzo had once bragged of his friendship with a high-ranking assistant district attorney in Queens. Tartaglino said, "We'll set up a situation in which the sergeant brings this Mafia don from Detroit directly to this assistant D.A. We know now that Sergeant Perrazzo is a corrupt cop. Our intelligence data says that the D.A. is not what he should be. The Mafia don will have plenty of money. Let's see what happens."

Again Leuci was employed as first actor in the drama. Meeting with Sergeant Perrazzo, he explained about the don from Detroit. He warned Perrazzo to be careful of how he talked to this man. This was a man who had to be treated with respect. He had a lot of money, and wanted to set up something out at the airport.

The meeting between Mike Paccini, federal narcotics agent, alias the don from Detroit, and Sergeant Peter Perrazzo took place in Tartaglino's cover apartment in the Stanhope Hotel. Agent Paccini, a big burly man, looked tough but was a consummate actor, and he played his role with a kind of quiet sensitivity. Without ever raising his voice, he communicated the Mafioso power Sergeant Perrazzo was looking for, and he explained that he wished to set up regular payoffs by organized crime to law enforcement personnel so that certain goods could move freely in and out of Kennedy Airport. To do this it was necessary to fix the Queens district attorney's office. It was Perrazzo's job to arrange a meeting between Paccini and the assistant D.A. in charge.

Sergeant Perrazzo seemed extremely impressed by the expensively dressed, scented don from Detroit, and a number of meetings between them followed. But Perrazzo was never able to bring the D.A. in person to any of these meetings. The D.A. was agreeable also. But, according to Perrazzo, he wanted Perrazzo to collect the money and bring it to him.

So that scheme of Tartaglino's fell through. Tartaglino was disappointed, Scoppetta was disappointed, Shaw was disappointed. Paccini and Leuci were disappointed also. "On to bigger and better things," said Tartaglino, and he began to concoct his most grandiose scheme yet.

16

FROM BOTH SIDES Leuci was being badgered about
the Jacques Bless case. Had he made contact with Bless
yet, asked Scoppetta. Would the $50,000 bribe go down
or not, demanded Sergeant Cohen. The incriminating
tapes were growing moss. What was Leuci waiting for?

Leuci was telling the same story to everyone. It had to
happen naturally or it wouldn't work. Bless was shrewd
and he was dangerous. If he was still untouched by the
law, this was because he insulated himself from every
transaction. Intermediaries went to jail, not him, and
anyone who broke through the insulation in a suspicious
manner risked getting knocked off.

If properly approached, Leuci kept saying, Bless would
pay the bribe. But "properly" did not mean head-on.
Detective Leuci could not ride the elevator up to Bless's
apartment and ring the bell. Bless had to be reached in
some devious manner that would seem to him natural.
The tapes, or Leuci, or both, had to come to him with
impeccable credentials. It had to be set up in some way,
and this took time.

What, then, were Leuci's plans? He had none, except to
wait. A hunter didn't stalk an animal, Leuci pointed out.
An animal's senses were too acute. Instead the hunter put
himself in a spot where the animal figured to pass by, and
he waited. A detective was a hunter, and did the same.

Meanwhile, Leuci became ever more emotionally
committed to Sheridan and Glazer. They were his
partners. He was with them every day. He didn't want to
know them or like them or hear their problems, but he
couldn't help himself. It was especially difficult with
Sheridan, who wanted so much to be friends, and couldn't
understand why Leuci held him off. "You would respect

me," the thirty-three-year-old Irishman said one day, "if only you would permit yourself to get to know me."

Leuci, each time he looked at Sheridan, thought: Every day is for you one less day of freedom.

It was Sheridan who warned Leuci about his so-called friends in SIU. These men were not truly his friends, he said, for they spoke against him behind his back. "You're too good, Bob," said Sheridan in his lilting brogue. "You don't see it. They really don't like you. They think that you were sent back into SIU for a reason. They are always talking bad things about you. I am more your friend than any of them. The bite of my tongue you will never hear."

One night, waiting for a case to be processed in night court, Leuci stood with Sheridan at a bar. When he glanced up, he saw DeStefano approaching.

"I'm glad those Knapp hearings are over," the fat bail bondsman said. "Jesus, you didn't testify much. Buy you a drink?" And smiling pleasantly, he added, "I still can't get over it," he said. "You never wear a fucking gun."

Sheridan, the veins standing out in his neck, put his face within inches of DeStefano's. Sheridan was a big rawboned man with heavy hands, clenched now into fists. "When he's with me," hissed Sheridan into DeStefano's face, "he needs no gun."

"Can't you guys take a fucking joke?" whined DeStefano.

"You're too good, Bob," said the Irishman, pushing DeStefano violently away. "I don't know why you deal with these greasy sons of bitches."

Leuci went to Scoppetta and began to plead in Sheridan's behalf. Sheridan was not really a bad man, he said. He didn't deserve the terrible things that were about to happen to him. Scoppetta had arranged for Hubert to be transferred to Intelligence. Why couldn't the same thing be done for Sheridan? Sheridan certainly wasn't the instigator of any of these corrupt deals. He was a tough, brave cop who went along with the others.

What about Stanley Glazer, Scoppetta replied. What about Sergeant Cohen? Was Leuci going to behave this way with everyone? Scoppetta's voice was full of sympathy: "Are you going to fall in love with each guy?"

Then he shook his head. There was nothing he could do. "We know you have this problem," he said. "We understand that it is only going to get worse. Please believe that we'll be with you. We'll stay with you till the end. We'll get you through it."

Leuci's other problem, making contact with Jacques Bless, was solved by Bless himself. Imagining himself possibly implicated in the Corso case, Bless sent a lawyer to DeStefano, and DeStefano came straight to Leuci. Could Leuci find out, DeStefano asked, if there was any heat on Jacques Bless?

"I have news for you," replied Leuci. "There's a lot of heat on Jacques Bless." And he began to describe the tapes he and his partners had made of Bless talking to Peter Corso. The tapes put Bless solidly into the conspiracy, Leuci said, but they were for sale for $50,000.

DeStefano nodded. Bless was a big-time guy and would pay that much money, he said, and he promised to send Lamattina back to the lawyer with Leuci's proposition. Lamattina had worked with the lawyer before and would know how to handle it.

And so Leuci once again began meeting regularly with Lamattina and DeStefano at Ruggerio's Restaurant in Brooklyn. They were convivial meetings. There was going to be money for everyone. Lamattina had met Bless's lawyer. If the tapes were for real, Lamattina said, the dope dealer was willing to pay $50,000 to have them.

At length Leuci agreed to gather his tape spools together and hand them over to Lamattina. Lamattina would listen to them to corroborate their validity. He would then turn them over to Bless's lawyer, and the money would be paid.

The next day Leuci and Lamattina met outside the Fourteenth Precinct station house, and the tapes were transferred from Leuci's car to Lamattina's. When Lamattina asked for something to put them in, Leuci plucked from his briefcase a brown manila envelope that seemed to be empty. Lamattina stuffed the tapes into the envelope and went home for the weekend.

In fact, the envelope was not empty. It had been given to Leuci by Scoppetta and still contained a memo from

Scoppetta to TPF-1 (Leuci's code name), requesting a report on Lamattina, DeStefano, and the Jacques Bless case. Leuci had not been doing his paperwork and he was being gently chided for it. Now Scoppetta's memo, crumpled up under the tapes, was on its way to Jacques Bless.

That Sunday, sitting at home on Staten Island, the thirty-eight-year-old Lamattina decided to listen to the tapes, and he spilled them out of the envelope onto a table. Scoppetta's memo fell out with them. Lamattina read it. It was a single sheet of unlined paper bearing no letterhead. It had been tapped out by Scoppetta himself, with many strikeovers. It was unsigned.

Lamattina telephoned DeStefano, and they hurriedly met. Both instinctively believed that the memo was exactly what it seemed to be. TPF-1 must be Leuci. They had been involved with Leuci now for well over four months.

They began to make telephone calls that became increasingly frantic. Was Leuci an informant? What were people's feelings about Leuci at this time?

One call went to Detective Nunziata. Nunziata would know about Leuci. Whatever he said could be both believed and acted upon. From Leuci's point of view, DeStefano and Lamattina could not have shown Scoppetta's memo to a more fortuitous choice. For Nunziata, above all else, was loyal to his friends.

When he had read the memo, Nunziata began to laugh. "If Leuci is a rat, my mother is a rat," he said. "Don't you know Leuci? He's flaky. He's trying to drive you crazy, and that's what he's done. You've been leaning on him, and now he wants to get even. He gives you the tapes, but he puts the letter in there. It's a joke. You probably owe him money."

Nunziata patted both of them on the back and left. DeStefano and Lamattina were not entirely certain, but they doubted this joke. The memo looked authentic to them.

On Monday morning Lamattina phoned Leuci and set up a meeting for dinner that night. Leuci sensed that something was wrong, and he brooded about it all day.

That night, when the three conspirators sat down to dinner in the restaurant, Leuci saw at once that the other two men were grim. Lamattina was about Leuci's height and weight. DeStefano was taller, and at least 100 pounds heavier. He sat there, stared at Leuci a moment, and then threw the memo across the table, saying, "Read this, and tell me what it is."

Leuci, looking down at Scoppetta's memo, blanched. He had only a few seconds to think up an acceptable explanation, but none came to mind. Nunziata had already provided him with one, but he did not know it. He had one reaction, and one only: I'm caught.

Could he lie his way clear yet again? An idea came to him.

"This is apparently Glazer's work," he said. "I knew that fucking Jew was a rat the moment I saw him."

Lamattina's face brightened at once, but DeStefano turned to him and said with disgust, "Are you a fucking moron, or what? Do you see the dates on that goddamn thing? Some of them are long before Glazer was even working with this guy. Some of these meetings Glazer was never at." He turned back to Leuci. "I want an explanation, and I want it fast."

Leuci pushed the memo back across the tablecloth. "I don't know what the hell it could be," he answered. "It's not mine."

"We're going to search you," said DeStefano.

"Go ahead," said Leuci. What was one more pat-down? And he stood up, holding his arms away from his body.

"Not out here, in there," snarled the fat man, jerking his thumb toward the rest room behind him.

"I'm not wearing a wire," said Leuci.

"We'll see," said DeStefano grimly.

In the toilet Leuci stood docilely while they stripped off his jacket, his tie, his shirt.

"See, what did I tell you," said Leuci. "You guys are crazy."

But it made the other two men, if possible, more frantic than ever. Nothing made sense to them, nothing. What is all this about, Bobby? they demanded. Who are you cooperating with? What are you trying to do to us?

DeStefano read the memo aloud, date by date, begging for explanation. Leuci chose not to respond. He ceased to say anything at all. When DeStefano came to the end of the memo, he looked up and said in an anguished voice, "This is not funny."

"You're right," Leuci said, "it's not funny. You guys are in a lot of trouble."

DeStefano turned to Lamattina and said, "Whack him. Kill him." But neither moved.

"What do you mean, kill him?" cried Leuci angrily. "I have seventy-five agents outside with machine guns. They'll blow both of you away."

All of a sudden, the fat bondsman, the crooked cop did not seem dangerous. For months they had seemed very vicious men. Often they had spoken about killing people or having them killed, about breaking informants' legs. But that was over. They were both, now, terrified.

"Relax, I can get you a deal," Leuci told them. But he wanted to get them outside where his backup agents were. "I can help both of you get out from under this thing. Let's get out onto the street and talk about it."

They followed him out of the restaurant, where they began to whine. "Oh, Bobby," DeStefano said. "We're in a lot of trouble."

Standing on the sidewalk, Leuci searched for his backup team. He saw no one. He began scratching his head—the agreed-upon danger signal. He scratched and scratched. But no backup agents ran up.

"What is that?" said DeStefano suddenly. "A signal of some kind?" the fat bail bondsman had begun to calculate. His mood had become dangerous again. Leuci's incriminating tapes would be worthless in court without the detective's testimony. There was no sign of seventy-five agents with machine guns. There was no sign of any agents at all. If Leuci was alone, then perhaps they still had a chance. Dispose of Leuci and they were clear.

Leuci's backup agents tonight were two IRS men and one cop, the cop he had been begging for, Patrolman Vinny Murano, who lived across the street. They had been driving round and round the block, and now, cruising past the restaurant again, they saw Leuci's signal.

"He's in trouble," said Murano.

But the IRS agent at the wheel was not sure. Perhaps Leuci was only scratching an itch, he said. They couldn't risk blowing his cover. Though Murano told him to stop, the agent drove by.

"He's in trouble," said Murano, lunging across the seat and turning off the ignition. As the car jerked to a stop, he sprang to the street.

Leuci was still scratching his head as Murano strolled up out of the darkness, stopped, and asked cautiously, "Hey, don't I know you?"

"Yeah, you know me," said Leuci. "Now arrest these two guys."

DeStefano and Lamattina were taken to the U.S. Attorney's office on Foley Square, where Scoppetta and Shaw offered them a chance to cooperate with the investigation. They wanted to cooperate, both said. They were frightened and bewildered. They wanted to think about it. Both promised not to blow Leuci's cover.

The Leuci investigation had lasted now almost a year. Scoppetta and Shaw felt it should be closed down that night. It was far too risky to let Leuci continue. They could not take the chance of sending him back onto the street.

Leuci, however, wanted to keep going, and he argued that Lamattina and DeStefano were in no position to blow his cover. How could they claim they had caught him out, when they were still out on the street themselves? It would be clear that they must be cooperating also. They could not afford to blow Leuci's cover.

Many conferences followed. At last the prosecutors agreed to accede to Detective Leuci's wishes. The investigation would continue.

From then on, Leuci became progressively more hot. Bit by bit Lamattina and DeStefano began to talk, to drop hints, and those to whom they talked, including some targets Leuci was still working on, began to put the pieces together, and to see the picture clearly.

Leuci believed he would be surfaced soon. He was treading a fine line, and it was getting finer every day.

17

THE RUMORS reached Mikey Coco.

Of all the mobsters Leuci had met, the one he cared about most and respected most was Mikey Coco. Coco had always been totally honest with him, and had never backed off from his word. If asked for a favor he would go to the ends of the earth to perform it. He seemed to trust Leuci absolutely, and if Leuci had gathered evidence against him, this was to a large extent his own fault. Leuci had been unable to avoid him. If he had been able to avoid Coco, he told himself, he would have done so. But Coco was a nosy, curious kind of guy, and he liked cops, particularly Leuci.

But now Coco had heard the rumors everyone else was hearing, and he kept phoning Leuci.

"Bobby, this is Sidney."

Coco wanted Leuci to meet him at once. Leuci, making one excuse after another, kept postponing this meeting.

At last, feeling that he had no choice if he was not to blow his cover completely, the detective agreed to meet Coco, and he arrived at the Baychester Diner, their usual meeting place, wearing his wire transmitter, and tailed by backup agents. He got into Coco's car.

Without even turning on his headlights, Coco sped out of the parking lot with a squeal of tires, made a U-turn, and was gone. He had again shaken the backup agents.

The headlights came on. Coco reduced speed. Leuci was alone with him.

"You have avoided me a couple of times," Coco said carefully. "You are nervous when you talk to me. You were never nervous before. I hear rumors you are wired all the time. I'm going to drive you somewhere, and I'm going to search you. And if you're wired—"

It was possible that the backup agents were still close enough to pick up Leuci's transmission. If he screamed for help, a great many patrol cars might be mobilized to search for him. But he did not do this. Instead he decided to brazen it out.

"You don't have to search me, Mike. I'm wearing a wire."

Leuci began lying fast. He was involved in an investigation. His home phone was tapped. The prosecutors he worked for knew about tonight's meeting with Coco, and had ordered Leuci to come wired. He disconnected one of the wires and showed it. "It's off, Mike. You can say what you want to say. Mike, trust me that I wouldn't hurt you."

Coco muttered, "I trust you. But people force people to do things they don't want to do."

Coco stopped in front of a restaurant on City Island, and they got out of the car. As they walked in past the bar, Leuci studied Coco's body, trying to see if the mobster had a gun. Coco was famous for not carrying a gun, but if he did have one, then whoever was with him was in trouble.

As they waited to be served dinner, Leuci continued to lie. His investigation had to do with cops and lawyers. "You people are separate," he said earnestly. "You have your own law. I'm not involved with you."

Leuci looked across into the hard, pockmarked face.

"You're lying to me," said the gruff-voiced mobster. "I've been in jail half my life. Do you think I'm fucking worried about going to jail? What did I do? I bribed you. They'll give me a year. Don't lie to me. Tell me the truth."

"Look, Mike, don't get angry."

"They caught you doing something, didn't they? If they caught you doing something, and you didn't come to us for help, then you deserve to get killed. Because you trust them more than you trust us."

Leuci said in a low voice, "No one caught me doing anything." This to Leuci was always the bottom line. No one had caught him. A man who squealed because he was caught was a rat. But Leuci, who had not been caught, was not.

He was a cop, Leuci told Coco. He had always been a cop. He didn't know how he had ever become involved with men like Mikey Coco. But to move freely within organized crime circles, to go to dinner with men like Coco had, at the beginning, excited him. He had felt a certain need to be wanted and needed by men who he knew were bad guys. "Do you understand all this, Mike?"

"No."

The waiter put plates down in front of them. When he was gone, Leuci began trying to explain about meeting Scoppetta, and talking with Scoppetta. "He got to me at a time when I felt that my world, all that I ever knew and believed in, had all gone down the tubes. I wanted to do something to show that I was a good guy, not a bad guy."

"Bobby, I never had any doubt that you were a good guy. Who were you being a good guy to?"

Leuci spoke about his father, who had always been so proud of him, and about his brother who had become a heroin addict.

Coco was surprised, "I didn't know that."

"Mike, I talked to you about my brother before. Your recommendation was that I break both his legs, and tie him to a chair. That wasn't the answer, Mike."

Neither was eating.

After a moment Coco pushed his plate away. "How bad am I going to be hurt?" he asked. "Don't tell me there's no case against me. There's got to be. I met that fucking Geik. Did you have a wire on that night? How long am I going to jail for?"

What was Leuci to answer to this? "I don't know, Mike. You're not going to get hurt that bad."

Coco called for the check.

"What's not bad by you? Five years? Ten years?"

Coco laid money in the dish on top of the check.

Leuci said, "I think the worst thing that could happen is that you get a year." The detective watched carefully, waiting for Coco's reaction. He didn't expect to get into a fight with him here in the middle of a crowded restaurant, but it was possible that, once back in the car, Coco would drive him off to where people were waiting. Coco could have set that up in advance.

But all Coco said was, "I could do a year standing on one hand. A year is nothing. Are you sure I'll get no more than a year?"

"I'm not sure," Leuci admitted. "I'm not a judge. As far as I'm concerned, you got extorted by Bernie Geik. You were the victim."

Abruptly, Coco laughed. "I've been a victim of you fucking cops since I started talking to you." Then studying Leuci, he asked in a softer voice, "And what's going to happen to you when this is over?"

"Perhaps they'll turn on me, and lock me up too. If they want to prosecute, there are things there."

"They are going to make you a hero," said Coco flatly. "But what they've really done is to make you a rat. Your father is going to be embarrasssed. Your cousin I don't want to even think about. Your cousin is going to have to explain to a lot of people how you got involved in this thing. Is anyone going to get hurt because of me? Bobby, that's very important. I introduced you to a few people. I vouched for you."

"I give you my word, Mike," Leuci said. "No one is going to get hurt because you vouched for me, or introduced me to someone."

They had been talking more than two hours, and this latest subject seemed the most dangerous so far. Leuci pushed back from the table and stood up. He did not want to give Coco time to consider who might be prosecuted because Coco had vouched for Leuci.

Coco said, "Sit down, Bobby. These people have turned you into a rat. You're not going to be able to live with yourself." He thought about it for a minute, then said, "I'm going to save your life. You meet me tomorrow morning at Kennedy Airport. I'll give you $75,000. You go anywhere in the world you want, and you get word back to me through your cousin or someone we can trust, and I'll send you another $75,000. You can start a new life. You won't be a rat." \

There was no one in law enforcement willing to give Leuci $150,000 to start a new life.

"Mike, where in the world could I go?"

They left the restaurant and started back to where

Leuci's car was parked. As he drove, Coco was silent. Finally he said, "I'll drop you off a couple of blocks away. I'll find a nice dark street." He looked across at Leuci.

Leuci said, "Mike, you kill me, and you're fucking dead."

Coco grinned, "Bobby, why do you talk like that? You worry too much. That's why you are in all this trouble. Ever since I knew you, you were a fucking worrier."

Leuci got out of the car and walked away without looking back.

18

TARTAGLINO'S TARGET was still corruption within the court system. The conduit was still to be Sergeant Perrazzo. Tartaglino's idea was to equip still another agent with plenty of money and a dazzling cover story, and to arrange for this man to be arrested by Sergeant Perrazzo. Perrazzo would process the agent in state court. Once inside the court system, the agent would begin bribing. He would bribe his way as close to the top as he could get.

To Scoppetta, to Shaw, to Leuci, this latest plan by Tartaglino seemed a bit complicated, perhaps unworkable, but as soon as Tartaglino, speaking in his quiet, immaculate way, had sketched in the details, all their skepticism disappeared, and they were once again filled with awe.

To begin with, the agent would be Carlo Dandolo. Dandolo was an Italian—this much seemed certain—but the rest of his life and past was murky. He had lived in France, spoke French, and had owned a café in Marseilles. He had lived in Turkey and in Syria, and at present lived in Lebanon and kept a café in Beirut. He was not a federal narcotics agent. Rather he was a frequent freelance employee of the bureau. If he had a criminal past, Tartaglino did not know about it. The man had worked for him on many major narcotics cases in Europe, and when Dandolo worked on a target, that target went to jail. Dandolo, Tartaglino said, was the consummate undercover agent, the consummate actor. He was the best the bureau had access to. He was very likely the best in the world, and he would be able to bribe any corrupt official he tried to bribe.

Tartaglino began now carefully to outline his plan.

Agent Dandolo would fly into New York and take a room at the Americana Hotel, and Sergeant Perrazzo would be informed both that he was there and that he worked for a rival Mafia family. Agent Dandolo, who would have money, would be ripped off by Sergeant Perrazzo, and then arrested.

It was better to keep Detective Leuci to the side this time, Tartaglino explained. A lot of people were suspicious of Leuci now. Perrazzo might be one of them.

Agent Dandolo would have to be arrested for something serious, but not too serious. A small amount of narcotics, perhaps. The kind of trouble that a habitual offender could reasonably expect to buy his way out of. He should seem to be a major narcotics dealer with connections all over the world. Tartaglino was hoping to catch one or several assistant district attorneys and judges who were willing to let such a man go for money.

So Agent Dandolo flew into Kennedy Airport, and checked into the Americana Hotel. Sergeant Perrazzo was notified. Perrazzo, as expected, selected two detectives he could trust, and explained what they would do.

But one of these detectives immediately refused to take part. "We're assigned to Queens robbery," he said. "How do we show up at a hotel in Manhattan and lock up a junk dealer? We can't do it."

This argument seemed sound to Sergeant Perrazzo, who said, "Okay, I got a guy I can call who has citywide jurisdiction."

He began to dial Leuci's number, but the other detective stopped him, "Don't call Leuci. I hear stories about Leuci. Call anybody but Leuci."

Still needing a detective with citywide jurisdiction, Perrazzo thought of Joe Nunziata, and phoned him. About midnight, the former mounted cop, the former SIU superstar, went with his partner to the Americana and knocked on Dandolo's door.

Within minutes Detective Nunziata was in a state of intense excitement. He had found Dandolo's passport. It was stamped with cities like Marseilles, Rome, Beirut. He had found Dandolo's little black book. In it were listed major Mafia drug traffickers from New York to California. It even had the home phone numbers of certain political figures with Italian names.

He had found an ounce of heroin sewed into the lining of Dandolo's suit. The markings on the envelope were in Turkish. He had found, he believed, one of the biggest dope dealers ever to have fallen into the hands of any cop.

But Detective Nunziata worked now not for the Police Department but for the Joint Task Force, and so he took Dandolo not to state court but to federal court.

Tartaglino's scenario was already in ruins—wrong arresting officer, wrong courthouse—but he decided not to abandon it yet. Instead, he summoned the two cops and their prisoner to Washington.

Leaving Nunziata and his partner outside, Tartaglino spoke to Dandolo alone.

"I can make these two cops," Dandolo told him. "These two cops are corrupt cops," Dandolo said. "I sense it."

Though the target was supposed to be district attorneys and judges, Tartaglino nodded. "Go ahead and do it if you can." His decision was made. The case would continue.

A moment later Detective Nunziata stood in front of Tartaglino's desk. "This Dandolo is a major drug guy," Tartaglino told him. "When he makes bail, I want you to stick close to him. Maybe he'll lead you to whoever he does business with."

Dandolo did make bail, using money Tartaglino gave him. As a condition of his release he was confined to the jurisdiction of the Southern District of New York State, and his passport was confiscated.

About two weeks then passed. In New York there were constant meetings between Dandolo, Scoppetta, Leuci, Shaw, and Tartaglino. Nunziata is a straight guy, Leuci kept telling the others, for he was terrified for his friend. To Leuci, Dandolo was a time bomb. Nunziata is an honest detective, Leuci insisted. Let's cut Dandolo into somebody important. Get him off Nunziata. Working on Nunziata is a waste of time.

Nunziata, as instructed by Tartaglino, did stick close to

Dandolo, and they had a number of meetings. Dandolo would return from each one and report. They were exploring the idea, he said, that Nunziata would allow him to bring in large amounts of narcotics. In his heavily accented English, Dandolo would quote lines and phrases he said Nunziata had spoken.

"That's not the way Joe talks," Leuci kept protesting. "Joe is a straight guy. Let's cut Dandolo into someone else."

Dandolo was meeting the detective regularly in a midtown restaurant called Friar Tuck, and then hurrying up to the investigation's cover apartment on the East Side to report to Tartaglino. It was a luxuriously furnished apartment in a luxurious building. Briefings, debriefings, and conferences were held there. It was the place Leuci went to put his wire on, or take it off afterwards. The phones were in use constantly on official business, and the assigned federal agents often slept there. Leuci kept urging Dandolo to be careful when he came to this apartment, because Nunziata was doubtless trying to tail him.

Dandolo was insulted. He had been worked on by the best, he boasted. Even the Gestapo had been unable to tail him. No one could tail him.

Leuci said, "Well, let me tell you something, my friend. If you keep coming here, Joe is going to follow you here."

Again Leuci turned to Scoppetta. "I want to see this guy record Nunziata. Let me hear those conversations he says he's having with Nunziata."

Scoppetta saw Leuci's anguish, but turned away from it. "If your friend is an honest cop, Bob, you have nothing to worry about."

Detective Nunziata, meanwhile, had attempted to follow Dandolo away from every one of their meetings at the Friar Tuck restaurant. Dandolo had never once led him back to the Americana Hotel. Instead Dandolo had each time shaken the tail. This led Nunziata to the conclusion that the Americana was a cover, and that Dandolo kept another apartment somewhere. He became convinced that if he could locate this other apartment, he might be able to drop Dandolo's entire drug operation, and seize an important quantity of heroin.

But where was this cover apartment? How to find it? Nunziata studied Dandolo, searching for a weakness. At last he found one—a waitress at the Friar Tuck who had caught Dandolo's eye. Nunziata went to the girl and gave her money to go with Dandolo. "You can go anywhere he wants to take you," he told her, "except to the Americana Hotel. All I want to know is where he takes you."

Dandolo took her straight to the investigation's cover apartment and bedded her.

Minutes after he learned this address, Nunziata was on the phone to Detective Carl Aguiluz, the best wireman in SIU, and shortly after that the two of them were in the basement attaching devices to the telephone box.

Upstairs, Leuci and the federal agents continued using the phone. Nunziata's tape recorder recorded every conversation.

Dandolo now offered Tartaglino a plan. It was urgent that he return to France, he would tell Nunziata. He would promise Nunziata to set up big arrests and an important seizure of drugs as soon as he got back. All this in exchange for his passport for two weeks—that's all he needed—two weeks in France. In addition, he would offer Nunziata $4000.

Dandolo looked around the room as if expecting applause. Tartaglino nodded thoughtfully. Basically the plan pleased him.

"Nunziata is not going to take that money," Leuci said. But there was a pleading note in his voice. "To Nunziata you are the biggest dope dealer he has ever dreamed of having. If he is just interested in money, it's better to wait. You can give him the biggest arrests he's ever had, and once he makes the arrests, he can sell the case for really big money, if money is what he wants. Why should he take $4000 from you now?"

"He'll take the money," said Dandolo smugly.

Dandolo would have to wear a wire, Tartaglino insisted in his soft, careful voice.

"Okay," said Dandolo, and he stripped to the waist and they taped it on him.

Tartaglino handed his agent the bribe money, $4000 in marked bills.

Dandolo buttoned his shirt back up, tied his tie, flashed his smug smile around the room, and went out the door.

Leuci had driven straight home, and there he blurted out the whole story to Gina. There was no doubt in Leuci's mind that if Dandolo came across to Nunziata the way he had said he would, if he ran the Sons of Italy routine—we're both Italians, trust me because I'm Italian—then Nunziata was going to fall for that, and probably he would take the money. Dandolo would find a way to get him to take the money.

Gina listened aghast.

Leuci wanted to phone Nunziata, warn him he was walking into a trap. But suppose Nunziata panicked, and did something crazy?

Leuci himself would be blown, together with many of the cases he had so carefully built up. That was the first certainty. A second certainty was that Tartaglino would have him prosecuted.

Leuci picked up his telephone, determined to phone Nunziata anyway, but he put it down again. Several times more he went to the phone, but he did not call his friend. Finally he left the house, went down to the beach, and sat on a bench facing out at the dark sea.

He remembered the day, looking nervous and very young, he reported to an office to be interviewed for possible transfer into the Narcotics Division. Several others also waited, including Nunziata. He was the only one not nervous. He was conservatively, expensively dressed. It was only the second time Leuci had ever met him.

Nunziata, waiting, began to tell horse stories—how once, when a suspect he was chasing tried to escape down into the subway, he had ridden his horse down the staircase after the guy, and had made the arrest.

Soon the waiting cops were laughing so hard their

nervousness was forgotten. A number of the clerks there had crowded around to listen to Nunziata. People always crowded around Nunziata.

The horse, he continued, was the dumbest creature living. The only way to teach a horse anything was with a left hook between the eyes. That was the way to make a horse respect you.

Leuci, watching the dark waves crash in, remembered all this and more.

In the Williamsburg section of Brooklyn where he had grown up, Nunziata had been a kind of mayor of his block. Little kids would cluster around him, would walk down the street beside him calling: Joey, Joey, Joey. Sometimes he played stickball with the kids. He could hit a stickball a mile. If teenage gangs of nonwhites came through knocking over garbage cans or beating up neighborhood boys, Nunziata would take them all on at once. He would thrash them, and they would not come back.

In the macho police society, cops often went out together at the end of a tour, and often enough they picked up women and did not go home. Not Nunziata, who was always in a hurry to get home to his wife Ann.

He was from a large family of working-class people, and this entire family looked to him as its leader. It had always been his ambition to save enough money to move out of the old neighborhood, and to live among educated people. He was very impressed by people who were educated. Recently he had bought a house in Great Neck.

A few years earlier the stars of SIU, and even of the Police Department as a whole, had been Sonny Grosso, and Eddie Egan, who had made the French Connection case. Egan and Grosso had since been transferred to other assignments—even as the film about it was playing in New York—just as Nunziata had since been transferred to the Joint Task Force, but when famous SIU detectives were spoken of, the three names were often mentioned interchangeably.

The three names had been inseparable also in the mind of Andrew Tartaglino. When first informed that Dandolo had been arrested not by Perrazzo but by Nunziata, Tartaglino had recognized the name instantly, and had dipped back into old files to refresh his memory. Tartaglino had then moved steadily, implacably forward.

And so on this particular night, with Leuci staring in despair at the sea, with Dandolo hurrying confidently through the streets toward Friar Tuck's restaurant, it was Gina Leuci who still had to act. The others—Tartaglino, Dandolo, Nunziata, her husband—all were acting out their roles with a kind of Calvinistic predetermination. Free will, it appeared, began and ended with herself.

After hesitating in an agony of indecision, she went to the telephone and dialed Nunziata's house, for she saw no other way out. It had become her job by default to save not only Nunziata, who was a friend, but also her husband. If Nunziata fell into Tartaglino's trap, it was her husband who would not survive.

He had betrayed already the Police Department code of silence, and also that code of silence that had its origins in the mountains of Sicily, and that had been brought to America by Leuci's own forebears, among others, remaining to this day a deeply rooted instinct in the breast of every young man of Italian origin. Silence and honor were the same. Now, in addition to betraying this ideal, he would also be betraying the cop whom he respected above all others.

As Gina waited for Nunziata's phone to be picked up, she had thought out, insofar as she was able, all possible consequences of her actions. She would explain to Nunziata's wife, or to Joe himself if he chanced to answer, that he must on no account meet with Dandolo tonight. Then she would hang up. Whatever happened, her husband would be clear. Tartaglino could give him a lie detector test tomorrow and he would pass it. She would never, never tell him what she had done, not tonight, not ever.

But there was no answer. She waited ten minutes, pacing, then dialed again. During the next hour she tried several times more, but there was still no answer.

Gina was a strong young woman, an Italian young

woman. She did not begin to weep. Though suffering intensively over what must now happen to both Nunziata and her husband, she accepted the decree of God, or fate, or whatever it was. She could do no more. What would happen now would happen, and it would be her job to glue the pieces of her husband back together again afterward, if she could.

19

IN THE NOISE AND BUSTLE of the Friar Tuck
restaurant, Dandolo, speaking in low, urgent Italian,
begged Nunziata for his passport. He needed just a few
days in Marseilles, he pleaded. When he came back he
would hand Nunziata an important case. He would
inform on a Frenchman, or a Syrian, or on some black
bastard. He would betray any of these rivals to his friend
Nunziata, but he was not an informant, he was an Italian,
and would never betray any fellow Italian. Nunziata knew
that. Italians could trust each other.

The deal, on whatever level he may have considered it,
sounded very good to Nunziata. Inevitably, this is how
one did business when enforcing the drug laws. One made
deals with scum like Dandolo. A detective learned to give
up one case in exchange for another that was bigger.

"And now I want you to take this four thousand
dollars," said Dandolo.

Nunziata, Dandolo's tape later proved, had at first
protested. He did not want the money. They were both
Italians. They trusted each other.

Afterward, certain members of the prosecution team
scoffed at Nunziata's protestations. To them it was
obvious from the tone of his voice, from its very
unctuousness, that his initial refusal was a formality only,
that he always intended to take the money. Others
maintained that he took it only because Dandolo kept
forcing it on him.

Nunziata handed $2000 to his partner, Detective Louis
D'Ambrosia, and pocketed the rest. "The money is an
expression of how I feel about you," said Dandolo, and he
jumped up and embraced Nunziata, kissing him on both
cheeks.

Nunziata then decided to check out his wiretap. It was

about one o'clock in the morning when he went down into the basement of the luxurious building on East Forty-ninth Street. He had not yet been back there, for it was Aguiluz who was supposed to monitor the tape from time to time.

In fact, Aguiluz had attempted to do so only once. He had gone downstairs into the basement and through the laundry room, walking right past a federal agent who was doing his wash there. This man watched, stupefied, as Aguiluz entered the storeroom where his tape recorder was hidden and began to move things around. The agent confronted Aguiluz and demanded to know who he was.

Aguiluz ran.

He ran upstairs and out of the building, with the agent in hot pursuit. The agent didn't know who Aguiluz was, and Aguiluz didn't know who the agent was. But both were cops, both knew something was not the way it should be. Both were not thinking, only reacting. Aguiluz sprinted down the street, into a crowded building, and out the other side. He dodged through hundreds of people, and at last when he looked back the agent was no longer chasing him.

This kind of thing had happened before to cops who installed illegal wiretaps. Usually the person in pursuit was the building superintendent or some busybody of a tenant. Nonetheless, the rule was never to go back to such a wiretap. It was too risky. Leave the gear in place forever. Abandon it.

Aguiluz was faithful to this rule. It was his gear he was abandoning. It was his job to check out the wiretap. It never occurred to him that Nunziata would go back there without him.

Nunziata, having descended to the basement, glanced around, listening carefully. The place seemed empty. He moved confidently toward the concealed tape recorder.

But the basement was not empty.

Upon losing Aguiluz in the crowd, the agent had called telephone company security, and what happened next was standard procedure. Telephone Security informed the Manhattan District Attorney's office that an illegal tap existed, and detectives from the D.A.'s squad were sent up to stake out the basement around the clock.

These detectives, as Nunziata reached for the tape recorder, were still staked out, and they grabbed Nunziata. He showed his shield and tried to laugh it off, one cop to another. It was a tap on a dope dealer. He expected them to let him go.

But too many superiors were involved, and they couldn't let him go. They made the proper notifications, and the superiors rushed in from all over, one of them Scoppetta.

Scoppetta and Nunziata had never met before. Scoppetta was grim. "You're in serious trouble," he told the detective.

Again Nunziata tried to laugh it off. "For what?" he demanded. "For an illegal wiretap? You must be kidding. This is the biggest case any of us have ever had."

"Not for an illegal wiretap, Joe," Scoppetta told him. "But for taking four thousand dollars."

In an instant, Nunziata's whole world crashed down around him.

Nunziata was allowed to go home. He was allowed several days in which to contemplate arrest, prison. He was the leader of his family. He was the hero of all the kids on the block. It was not possible for him to be arrested. So he had to seriously consider cooperating, consider denouncing cops he had worked with. The idea nauseated him. It made him crazy.

He called up various SIU detectives, though never Detective Robert Leuci, ranting unintelligibly into the telephone. A number of detectives, Aguiluz principal among them, went to his house, but he refused to let them in or to respond to the offers of money or the expressions of solidarity that they tried to shout to him through the door. At the end of two days, Nunziata was scarcely rational.

Strictly speaking, this was Scoppetta's show, but Tartaglino happened to be in town that week, so Scoppetta invited him to attend what was expected to be a showdown meeting with Nunziata in a motel room near LaGuardia Airport.

Detective D'Ambrosia was called in first. He was a young cop who had never been in trouble before. He was terrified, and willing to do almost anything to stay out of jail and perhaps save his Police Department career. Unfortunately, he was too new, he knew too little, there was no partner or superior he could give up in exchange for a break from the prosecutors, and they told him so. They told him that his only chance was to convince Nunziata to talk, for Nunziata knew plenty. Nunziata, if he agreed to cooperate, could perhaps save them both.

Then it was Nunziata's turn. He came into the motel room. His face was gray. The former SIU superstar was not visible, nor the hero of the Williamsburg section of Brooklyn, nor the tough, tough cop. He began to protest that he had never been in trouble before, that this was the only compromising situation in which he had ever been involved. Appearances were misleading here, he said, trying in a choked voice to convince these grim-faced prosecutors.

He had accepted the money only in order to make a solid bribery case against Dandolo. The money was still intact. He could turn it over to the prosecutors right this minute, and in fact wished to. He had believed Dandolo to be a major drug trafficker, and as soon as the Italian returned to New York Nunziata had planned to arrest him for bribery. With a solid bribery case against Dandolo, Nunziata had hoped to turn Dandolo, to force him to cooperate, to learn the names of his connections and the locations of his heroin drops.

Nunziata was pleading for his life.

Tartaglino had listened without emotion. He looked cool, immaculate. When he spoke, his voice was so low and soft that it was difficult to hear him. "Let's assume you're telling the truth, Joe," he said. "I think you might be telling the truth. You say you are."

Tartaglino paused. He spoke, as always, with meticulous care. "I'm going to give you a test," he said.

"Anything," said the anguished Nunziata. "What do I have to do?"

"Do you really want to cooperate?" said Tartaglino.

"Let's see whether you do. This first test I'm going to give you is a tough one. You get the tough ones first, and everything after that will be easy."

Tartaglino studied him.

"You have to do a good job, Joe. If you don't do a good job, then you're not helping us. You are an experienced cop, like I am. There are three things you have to do. I'll tell you what they are. The first thing is this. You go into a public phone booth, and you call Detective Sonny Grosso. You tell him to go out, get on a public phone, and call you right back."

Tartaglino studied the slack-jawed, ashen-faced detective.

"We're going to give you something written on a piece of paper," Tartaglino said. "When he calls you back, you are going to read it to him. It will say something like this: 'Sonny, I just found something out. The feds are on to us.' Then you are going to read him a statement of two or three lines."

Tartaglino paused. "I want to hear what Sonny's reaction is, Joe. If his reaction is 'But Joe, we haven't done anything wrong,' then we'll believe you. But if his reaction is 'Joe, you and me and Eddie Egan better get together and talk about it,' then I think some of us are going to decide you are lying to us."

For a moment the two men only looked at each other. Then Nunziata sprang to his feet. "I won't do it," he croaked. His voice fell amost to a whisper. "I can't take the test."

In the same quiet emotionless voice Tartaglino said, "You wanted a chance, Joe. You don't want to go to jail. Well, we've given you a chance. Sit down, Joe. Let me tell you something about yourself. You're a whore, Joe. You've been a whore since you put that uniform on, and all this business of you being a big hero is nonsense. You're a whore, and a thief.

"As far as I'm concerned," Tartaglino continued, "you have very few choices left. You can cooperate with us, or you can go to jail, or you can go out of here and shoot yourself."

The last alternative Tartaglino added almost as an afterthought. He was an expert at trying to turn a witness. Today, as always, he was using every argument that came to hand. As far as he was concerned, he had given Nunziata a better chance than Nunziata had sometimes given others.

"You decide what you are going to do," Tartaglino concluded quietly, "and you let us know tomorrow."

Nunziata went home, where he prepared a long rambling letter that proclaimed his own innocence, and especially D'Ambrosia's. D'Ambrosia was totally honest and had done nothing wrong, Nunziata wrote.

He spoke to his wife. He told her about the letter. In the morning he left the house.

He had an appointment to meet with Scoppetta to give his decision. He picked up D'Ambrosia, and the two detectives drove through the streets of Brooklyn with D'Ambrosia trying to convince Nunziata to cooperate, to save them both. Nunziata promised that he would not let his partner get hurt. "I'll see to it," he said.

They were already late for Scoppetta, but Nunziata had turned into the Williamsburg section of Brooklyn where he had grown up, and had begun driving up and down streets he had played in as a boy. D'Ambrosia supposed he was merely postponing as long as possible the inevitable meeting with Scoppetta. He was relieved when Nunziata at last pulled to the curb and instructed D'Ambrosia to telephone Scoppetta from that candy store there, to tell him they were on their way in to the federal building.

As soon as D'Ambrosia had entered the candy store, Nunziata withdrew his service revolver from his belt, pressed the muzzle to his chest, and shot himself in the heart.

Leuci was told on the steps of the courthouse. His stomach went into convulsions. Turning away, he began to vomit. When this ended, he entered a room where Scoppetta and other officials had been waiting for Nunziata to appear. Scoppetta asked the other men to leave, then said, "How did we get into this, Bob?"

They faced each other across the rug.

Leuci said, "I don't know. You did it."

Turning away, Scoppetta started to cry. Leuci started to cry. They stood apart, facing in opposite directions, weeping.

At last Leuci said, "Look, I'm just going to go away now. I'm going to go see Joe's wife."

It was SIU Detective Jack McClean who handled the wake for Ann Nunziata. McClean was everybody's Irish uncle. He had been a police kid—nearly every male in his family had been a cop, and he was an integral part of the Irish Mafia within the detective division. He was a first-grade detective who had lived through this kind of thing more than once. Now all that had to be done for Ann and for Nunziata's two kids Uncle Jack McClean took care of, and he also hosted the wake. It was Jack McClean who brought Leuci up to the coffin and stood with him there.

All the old SIU detectives were at the wake, Sonny Grosso, Eddie Egan, everyone. It was like an old family reunion, except that one of their number felt like a viper among them.

Much, much later it was discovered that the French Connection heroin, which had been kept as evidence in sacks in the police property clerk's office, was no longer heroin at all. The investigation showed that between 1968 and Nunziata's death in the spring of 1972, this heroin had been withdrawn from the property clerk's several times for presentation in court, and during one or more of these withdrawals someone had substituted pancake flour. On five of the withdrawal slips Nunziata's name appeared— apparently forged—and further investigation showed that the idea of such a ripoff had been Nunziata's also. Three years before his death he had gone to Robin Moore, author of *The French Connection,* and had suggested such a ripoff as the plot for a novel. He had hoped to share in the profits of this novel, but Moore declined to write it.

20

A YEAR and four months had gone by. Leuci had made more than a hundred clandestine tape recordings—not only with defense lawyers, but also with district attorneys, not only with Mafia drug dealers but also with bail bondsmen, not only with cops but also with federal narcotics agents. He had hurt only a handful of cops in all, none of them men he had cared about in the past. It was going to be possible to prepare more than thirty indictments.

But Nunziata was dead, and Leuci, it was clear, was close to the breaking point. At times he babbled. At other times, for no apparent reason, he wept.

He was also extremely hot. Rumors at SIU headquarters had grown ever more detailed and intense. Leuci was so hot as to be on fire.

Many times in the past the Harvard-educated Shaw had argued in private conferences with Scoppetta that the investigation should be cut short—it was too dangerous for Leuci. Always Scoppetta, the street fighter from the slums of New York, had argued otherwise—they were engaged in a dirty business, and such risks had to be taken—and always Scoppetta had prevailed. Now, in May 1972, both were in agreement. The danger was a factor, of course. But the main thing was that Leuci was played out. Emotionally he could go no further.

So the two prosecutors planned to pick up those few of Leuci's subjects who they imagined would agree to cooperate with the prosecution at once, the first being Sergeant Perrazzo. It was hoped that Perrazzo, once confronted with the evidence against him, would agree to wear a wire and to work undercover in his turn. The Leuci investigation would end, and the Sergeant Perrazzo investigation might begin.

The thing to do, they decided, was to come down on Perrazzo hard and quietly. Shock him. Bring him in immediately, lay the evidence out quickly, then show him the opening. Show him that he could save himself if he would agree to wear a wire and move against corrupt assistant district attorneys in Brooklyn and Queens.

All right, where should they pick him up? One possibility was to summon him to the offices of the U.S. attorney for the Southern District. Another was to arrest him at the detective squad where he worked. Instead, for maximum shock value, they decided to arrest him where he felt most secure, at home, and in the middle of the night. Two detectives from Internal Affairs went with Scoppetta to do the job. They had German names, and were not only considered professional hatchet men within the department, but were sometimes called The Gestapo.

While Scoppetta waited in the car, they knocked on Perrazzo's front door. He opened it.

"We want to talk to you."

Perrazzo, in pajamas, stared out at two men in topcoats. When they showed their shields, he said, "Come on in."

"I'm sure you don't want us to talk to you inside and wake up your family," they told him ominously.

Perrazzo got dressed and came outside. By then, terror already showed in his face. "Am I in trouble?"

"You have never been in more trouble, my friend. Did you ever hear of Bob Leuci? You're going to jail."

Perrazzo began to babble. "Why me? What did I do?" Standing in front of his own front door, he began screaming. "Why me? Why me? Why me? Why me? Why—"

By the time the two detectives and Scoppetta had got Perrazzo into the city, he had frozen up, and wouldn't—or couldn't—talk at all. After that, every time anyone tried to question him, he would begin to whimper, "Why me?" and then to scream in an anguished voice, "Why me? Why me?"

Later he was judged insane.

The secret investigation, it was clear, would not remain secret much longer. Shaw and Scoppetta were playing for time—time enough perhaps for one last case to be made, the biggest of all. The target was the office of the district attorney of Queens County.

But Leuci became obsessed with the notion that he would soon be blown, and that once this happened it would become impossible for him to explain his side of the story of Nunziata's death to those SIU detectives he cared about. It was Leuci himself who could keep the secret no longer. He decided to meet with several detectives, the most important being Carl Aguiluz. Nunziata had been Aguiluz's mentor too. In fact, Aguiluz had been closer to Nunziata than any other detective except for Leuci himself.

There was a restaurant on Twenty-third Street were SIU detectives often congregated. Leuci, knowing other detectives would also be present, arranged to meet Aguiluz there for dinner.

By this time, on explicit orders from Scoppetta, Leuci was accompanied everywhere by Vinny Murano, the cop who lived across the street. Murano had been ordered never to leave Leuci's side. To Scoppetta, Leuci was on the verge of a crackup. He was as fragile as a pane of glass. "Don't let him out of your sight," Scoppetta told Murano.

To meet Aguiluz, Leuci had first to get rid of Murano, or so he thought. Leuci begged his friend and bodyguard to let him meet with Aguiluz alone. But Murano refused. His orders were formal. How could he explain letting Leuci go to dinner with Aguiluz, he asked.

Leuci had a lie ready. He had lied so much he could hardly think straight any more. "Just tell them you dropped me off at the SIU office and then lost me," Leuci told him, adding, "I'm in great shape."

Murano said, "You tell me you're in great shape. You look awful. I don't know what goes on in your head."

Murano relented. He dropped Leuci off at the SIU office, then looked the other way.

Leuci went directly to the restaurant, where he sat

down at a table with Aguiluz and three other SIU detectives. Two he knew slightly. The third was new, and unknown to him.

The five detectives began to drink and talk and laugh. There was warmth and friendliness around that table, and Leuci talked of the old days when Nunziata used to be there with them.

The drinks worked on him. He began to relax, to feel really good. He was almost out from under this thing. In a few more days it would end, but before that he was going to tell his story to these men, his true friends. He was going to tell them tonight. He was going to tell them it wasn't his fault that Nunziata killed himself. He had had nothing to do with Joe's death.

Leuci went on drinking. Soon he was drunk enough that his vision of himself no longer hurt. Nothing hurt. He could talk to these men without being ashamed or afraid.

Finding himself alone with Aguiluz, Leuci said, "Carl, I'm going to tell you something. It will be a little hard for you to understand. But I want you to understand something." He paused. Even drunk it was proving harder to speak than Leuci had expected. "Some time in the near future you are going to hear all kinds of things."

Aguiluz said, "I know all that stuff."

"What do you know?" asked Leuci, shocked.

The story had been around forever, the Honduras-born detective told him. The story that Leuci was cooperating with prosecutors, that Leuci was supposed to be doing all sorts of strange things. Aguiluz watched him. "Everyone talks about you being a wreck," he said. "You must think we believe those rumors. Look, our friend Joe never believed them. Till the last day, he never believed anything bad about you. I don't believe it either. We know you. We know you would never do anything like that."

But Leuci was shaking his head into his drink. "Well," he said, "that's not entirely true."

Aguiluz turned white.

Leuci scarcely noticed this. He was closed in on his own pain. At last he was going to unburden himself to a man who cared about him, who would understand. He was going to unburden himself to SIU.

"I did some things—" He nodded drunkenly at Aguiluz, then added hurriedly, "I did nothing to hurt you. I did nothing to hurt Joe. Joe found himself in a situation that I had nothing to do with. I want you to understand what happened."

Now the words spilled out, a vast jumble of them: names, dates, cases. Most of this made no sense to Aguiluz. Leuci spoke of Dandolo, of Tartaglino coming up from Washington, of how he had once met Scoppetta, and had conceived the notion of trying to purify his own sins by moving against bigger sinners than himself, namely, the lawyers. He had wanted absolution, wanted to go back to the sacraments. But they had turned him against cops anyway.

The conversation had moved out of the restaurant. Aguiluz and Leuci were standing by Leuci's car in the street. Aguiluz was terrified. "I don't believe any of this," he said. "You are making this all up. Joe assured us you would never do anything like this."

The drunken Leuci had lied for months and months and been believed. Now he was telling the truth, but he could not, it seemed, make himself believed. Opening the trunk of his car, he ripped out the phony wall partition. Aguiluz stared at the tape recorder secured at the side of the car.

"I don't know what to say to you," said Aguiluz. After a moment he added, "You are telling me you had nothing to do with Joe. I believe you. How about us?"

"None of you guys are involved."

"I don't know how you are sleeping, but you better get home and get some sleep now. Do you want me to take you home?"

The other detectives had come out of the restaurant. They were clustered around.

"Can we help you in any way?" they asked. "Do you need any money? Do you need anything?"

Leuci said, "I'm not under arrest." Then he began screaming. "I didn't do this because they caught me! Don't you understand what happened here?" He was screaming, and in between phrases he was gulping for air. "I had nothing to do with Joe's death!" he screamed.

"You've got to believe that! I had nothing to do with Joe's death!"

"Take it easy," Aguiluz said. "You'll make yourself crazy."

The other detectives were trying to calm him down. "You'll do the same thing Joe did."

"I'm not going to do that!" Leuci screamed.

"How about giving us your gun," said Aguiluz.

"I'm not giving you my fucking gun!" Leuci screamed.

"We went through this with Joe," Aguiluz said. "He looked like you. He sounded like you. Are you going to do the same fucking thing? How bad is this thing?"

"Bad enough."

"How long has it been going on?"

"I don't know," Leuci whispered, close to tears. "A couple of years now."

"Let us take you home," Aguiluz said. "Give me your fucking gun."

"I'm all right," wept Leuci. "I can make it home."

He got into his car and drove away.

The next day Aguiluz called a meeting of SIU detectives and told what he knew. With so many men now in on the secret, inevitably the story reached the newspapers. There were headlines: a major investigation was about to break, and there was a Detective Leuci at the center of it.

The following day Bill Federici of the *New York Daily News* printed a story outlining each and every case. On Scoppetta's orders Leuci was immediately scooped up by detectives and put in protective custody in New York. He was not allowed to go home. Heavily armed agents from Tartaglino's office, together with detectives from Internal Affairs, surrounded Leuci's house in King's Park. But when they began to observe suspicious cars cruising by, it was decided to abandon the house and to keep Gina and the kids under guard in a hotel.

"A hotel?" Leuci asked, when he learned the decision. "What hotel? For how long?"

He would be testifying for the next two years or more, he pointed out, and perhaps he would not be safe even after that. Putting his family in a hotel was not the answer, he pleaded. He owned a cabin in the woods in the Catskill Mountains. He wanted permission for his wife and kids to go there to wait for him.

Scoppetta and Shaw mulled this over. Who knew about Leuci's cabin in the woods? they demanded.

"No one," Leuci lied. He had gone hunting there in the past with his former partners Mandato and Wolff, and other SIU detectives knew about the cabin also. But these men were his friends and would not hurt him, he believed.

Within hours Gina and the kids and all the belongings they could carry were convoyed upstate under guard to the rustic, half-finished cabin. Gina had loved her house on Long Island. She had lovingly polished many times every floor, every tile. She would never see it again. Even now federal agents were emptying it out. It was put on the market—to be bought, eventually, by another New York cop.

In a garage underneath the courthouse, federal marshals met Leuci. From now on they would be charged with his protection. Two unmarked government cars waited, together with six men carrying submachine guns. Leuci was exhausted and merely gazed at them. He wanted to know where his wife and kids were, he wanted to know if they were happy, if they were comfortable, and he wanted someone in law enforcement to understand what he had been through, how much he had suffered.

The chief marshal introduced himself: John Partington. He put his arm around Detective Leuci and led him to the government car. "I'm in charge of your security. You did your job for the past year and a half. From now on, until it's all over, it will be my job to take care of you and your family. I want you to forget about everything else."

A second marshal introduced himself: Ed Scheu. He was carrying a submachine gun. "Take my word for it," he said, "nobody is going to fuck with you when you're with us. They told us about you upstairs. We understand what you did. We think you have a hell of a lot of balls. From today on you have nothing to worry about except your wife and kids. We'll worry about everything else."

There were three marshals in the lead car, and Leuci

and three other marshals in the second car: the two cars as they started upstate were in radio contact at all times. Constantly they exchanged positions, and a short distance beyond the city limit two other cars were waiting, and a changeover was made. Marshal Partington kept up a steady stream of friendly conversation. Leuci should start thinking about where he wanted to live. "Pick a nice place where it's warm, because I'm going to come with you," said Partington. "Whatever you need, we are going to get for you." He knew the names of Leuci's kids. He knew Leuci's wife's name. "Anthony is fine," he said. "I spoke to Anthony. I spoke to Gina. She's fine. She's cooking you a spaghetti dinner.

When the two cars pulled up in front of the cabin in the woods, Gina came out, and they embraced. She said, "Did you see the people that are there?"

It was too dark to see anything.

Gina said, "Whatever direction you look, there's a man with a rifle. It makes me very nervous."

Partington assured her that none of the marshals would come into the house. They would stay outside.

Leuci said, "You are welcome to come into my house. There is not much room inside, but you are welcome."

The house was small. On the first floor were two bedrooms, and a living room-kitchen. There was a spiral staircase leading up to the second floor, which was an unfinished loft. Leuci had bought the property four years before, and had built the house himself, aided by his father-in-law and some friends who would come up for weekends. Now this cabin in the woods was home.

The next morning Partington phoned at 6 A.M. Apologizing for calling so early, he asked to come over. When he arrived, he explained that he had been up all night. He showed Leuci plans he had drawn up of the house, its access roads, and the points where marshals would stand guard. He also wanted a list of men Leuci felt might be threats. Leuci gave him the names of Mikey Coco, Sergeants Cohen and Perrazzo, John Lusterino, the lawyers Salko, Caiola and Rosner, and several others.

Later Partington came back with pictures of all these

men. "I know that this is going to upset your wife a bit," he said. "But we want her to carry these pictures. The marshal who will be with her at all times will have a set also. We're going to find out where these men are, and what they are doing, and we'll watch them."

Gina's house was gone, her life was constricted, but she never complained. She had been six years old when she became a refugee during World War II. She had owned nothing. Her parents owned nothing. Growing up, she had lived in a single room. She had come to the United States and had found work as a domestic. She had lived in a furnished room for a time, and for a time she had shared a two-room apartment with her aunt in Queens.

The house in Kings Park had meant a lot to her. Everything she had ever wanted in a house was in that house. It was hers. But now it was gone. Now this cabin in the woods was her home, and she was sharing it with a total of eighteen marshals. They had promised not to come into the house, but at night it was like Siberia up there, and she was not the woman to keep them outside.

There was only one bathroom in the cabin, and it was in the basement. She and her husband slept in the loft, and sometimes in the middle of the night she would have to come down the rickety spiral staircase that her husband had built. The staircase would shake and squeak. There would be marshals sitting downstairs watching television, and she would have to walk into the bathroom that was open on top and had no lock on the door, and she would die.

When morning came the marshals would take her son to school. They carried machine shotguns. This was an incredible weapon. The barrel was about eighteen inches long. The handle was short so that it could be fired from the waist like a pistol. These shotguns were loaded with double O buckshot, and it was said they were powerful enough to turn over a car. Each morning Gina would watch her young son go off to school with such men.

Leuci meanwhile was housed in a military barracks on Governors Island in New York harbor, commuting to the cabin only on weekends. Special grand juries had been impaneled, and he was testifying before them nearly every day. When it came time to testify in trials he was going to be cross-examined about his own previous misconduct, and he did not know what he was going to say. He was certain only that his old life was over, and that his future, in whatever direction he looked, was bleak.

Book Two

1

THE 100TH PRECINCT, Queens. On a hot summer day, two young cops patrol the Rockaway Beach boardwalk in a police jeep when their radio barks news of a cardiac arrest two blocks inland. They speed there. The house is a white bungalow with green shutters. They can hear a woman screaming. They dash into the house, and into the kitchen.

An old man. An old woman. The old woman, screaming, has her hands clasped to her head. The old man, half propped against the stove, gags and collapses.

One young cop rushes out to the radio to call for help. The second rookie straddles the old man, who has turned gray, and whose mouth is bubbling with spittle. He presses his lips—lips that have kissed girls—to the lips of this old man he has never seen before this minute, and who is dying.

The old woman is still screaming.

He has the old man's nose pinched closed. His other hand massages the bony old chest. He keeps breathing into the nearly toothless, spittle-soaked mouth. He is trying to breathe life into a corpse.

The kiss goes on and on, but resuscitates no one. The young cop's uniform becomes soaked with sweat. His fingers cramp on the ancient beak. His arm is numb but still massaging. His eyes burn. Sweat drips down his face and into his eyes.

Two blocks away, people frolic at the edge of the sea.

What seems like an hour passes. At last two older cops from Emergency Service Division burst into the kitchen. A hand falls gently on the young cop's back. The old man is dead, he is told.

But the young cop continues mouth-to-mouth resuscitation. "I can feel something moving inside his chest," he gasps.

The two emergency service cops pull him to his feet. "He's been dead at least ten minutes," one says. And then, "This is your first one, isn't it?"

The rookie patrolman, Robert Leuci, aged twenty-two, stares down on the old man whose last breath he has shared.

The emergency service cop has his arm around the rookie. "You done good, kid," he says, trying to comfort him. "You done all you could."

2

CERTAIN TAPES among the hundred Leuci had made
with more than forty individuals were more than four
hours in length. Voices were sometimes unidentified or
obliterated by background noises, but these tapes would
stand as the principal physical evidence in the trials to
come, and a task force of nine police stenographers was
brought in. Wearing earphones, they sat in banks day
after day, roughing out first drafts.

A second task force of assistant federal attorneys had
been assembled under Scoppetta and Shaw to sift
through the individual cases. These men were faced with
an embarrassment of riches—too many defendants, too
much evidence—and therefore with a bewildering assort-
ment of decisions. There were going to be, potentially,
thirty or forty trials. Where to start? Whom to indict? In
what order? Under which statutes?

Each morning, surrounded by bodyguards, the chief
government witness was brought in from Governors
Island to the Federal Courthouse, and each night he was
brought back again. He was more a prisoner than any
defendant. Though each now waited to learn his fate, at
least all were still free. Leuci was not free. He was not
allowed to leave the building.

Once inside the courthouse, the prisoner became king
and held court. He was crucial to every case, and every
day prosecutors and stenographers vied for his favors.

Leuci had never been busier. His ego swelled. The trials
could not take place without him. All these men needed
him. They were nice to him every day. No one else had
ever done what he had done, they told him. This was true,
and it was also what he wanted to hear. They worked
hard. He worked harder. He would work as late as anyone

wanted to work, or come in as early. Indictments began to come down.

He was almost happy. The future—when some or all of his new friends might turn on him—was still some months off. He had survived this far, he told himself. Whatever happened, he would be able to think of something. He was smarter than these prosecutors, smarter than any defense lawyer. He would find a way to save himself, no matter what.

In the meantime he was worried about Wolff, Mandato, and Cody, and about Vinny Russo, who was still another former partner. He was worried about Sheridan and Glazer too, knowing how they must be agonizing. Well, there was nothing he could do about Sheridan and Glazer, but he wanted to contact the others, who might be agonizing too—in their case, needlessly.

Unable to leave the courthouse, he telephoned Mandato. The conversation was very short.

"Do I have anything to worry about?" asked Mandato.

"No, you don't, Frank."

Silence.

Mandato had been a cop thirteen years. He had proven himself shrewd, calculating, and physically brave. He was also, like most detectives of his age and experience, worldly, cynical, fatalistic. If Leuci had truly gone over to the other side—far enough over to testify against him—then there was nothing he could do about it. He remembered meetings with Leuci during the past year and a half. Had Leuci taped them? He didn't know. Had anything incriminating been said? He didn't remember. What had Leuci told the prosecutors about their five years together before that? He didn't know this either.

Nor could he ask any of these questions. This was a telephone conversation, and one never knew who might be listening, either with Leuci's concurrence or without.

"Okay," said Mandato, "see you around." And he hung up.

This abortive conversation threw Leuci into black depression, and he began to beg the prosecutors to allow him to meet some friends in a restaurant from time to time. He was not a criminal, not a prisoner. They had to allow him to meet some old friends.

When this boon was not accorded him, he arranged to meet Wolff and Cody anyway, inducing his bodyguards to stop one evening at a steak house on the upper East Side. The bodyguards, two burly ex-motorcycle cops, were willing enough, for it meant a good meal paid for by Leuci, and they were sick of taking him to the movies every night. Inside the steak house, they took a table with their backs to the wall, from which they could, like Wild Bill Hickok in an earlier age, watch the entire saloon.

The three old friends ordered drinks. "I'm going to tell you right now," Leuci began, "neither of you have anything to worry about."

Wolff's reaction in person was the same as Mandato's by telephone. Perfect trust was gone. Question: Why had Leuci requested tonight's meeting? Question: Was Leuci wired even now? Question: Who else was listening to this conversation?

"I don't want you to start asking me anything," said Leuci. "None of this concerns you guys."

Wolff, studying him, said nothing.

But a big grin had come onto Cody's face. The older man socked Wolff in the arm. "I told you, Les. Bob wouldn't hurt us. Les, don't worry about it."

"Dave," said Wolff soberly, "you never worry about anything. You don't worry about whether you have your shoes on or not. I have to do the worrying for both of us."

The dinner was strained, and only Cody, who had had a few drinks, failed to notice it. Wolff's discomfort was so strong that presently, despite himself, he began to probe. How far was this investigation going to go, he asked, and in which directions?

But each question was interrupted by Cody, "Les, there's nothing to worry about, Bob would never hurt us."

"No further than it's gone already," said Leuci to Wolff.

Wolff, watching Leuci's face, nodded.

Partners spend eight hours a day in each other's presence for week after week, year after year. They interrogate subjects together, kick in doors together, go to court together, sit on endless surveillances together. They become, when the relationship is a good one, closer than brothers, closer than husband and wife. There are things one can't tell a wife. There is nothing one can't tell a partner, and the love of a cop for cop which exists everywhere, transcending all jurisdictional boundaries, is only an extension of the strongest love most cops have ever experienced, the love of partner for partner.

Similarly, to lose a partner can be a cop's strongest grief.

Outside on the sidewalk in the night the three detectives shook hands, and when Wolff and Cody had gone off together, Leuci stepped back into the custody of his bodyguards and went off alone.

3

LEUCI'S FIRST PARTNER is Jerry Schrempf. The two young cops who are straight out of the Police Academy patrol Rockaway Beach: sunstroke cases and rowdy teenagers in summer; in winter, nothing.

"You'll love it here," an older cop has told them. "You get the same check as the guy working Harlem. But there's nobody out here looking to take your head off, like in Harlem, and there's no money here, like in Harlem, either. Where there is money, there is bickering. One squad doesn't talk to another squad. One sergeant doesn't talk to another sergeant. But out here we have picnics. We have softball teams. You get sand in your shoes, and everybody loves each other."

But Leuci and Jerry want to feel themselves real cops. Both apply for transfers to the Tactical Patrol Force. TPF cops move about the city in squads, saturating high-crime zones.

However, as TPF cops the partners are split up. Schrempf is assigned to Brooklyn, Leuci to Manhattan. They meet often, though. "What am I doing wrong?" Schrempf complains. "I'm not making any more collars than a precinct cop. I'm looking for arrests, and I can't find them."

"Work the rooftops, Jerry," counsels Leuci. "You got all the junkies on the rooftops, and from up there you can watch the fire escapes for burglars." Imagination, cunning. These qualities come to other cops after years of experience. Somehow Leuci seems to have been born with them. "And Jerry, you stop cars. You ask for license and registration. You run plate checks. If it comes back bad, you can search the guy. You can search the car. Then you start coming up with guns, knives, drugs."

But Schrempf, who believes in civil liberties, is against stopping cars for no reason.

"It's legal, Jerry," Leuci points out. "And if you stop cars, you make collars."

One night Leuci's home phone rings at 3 A.M.

"Jerry Schrempf's been hurt. He stopped a car, and—"

"Is he okay?"

"We got the guy who did it."

"Is Jerry hurt bad?"

"He's dead, Bob."

Leuci goes back toward the bed. "Dead," he tells Gina. "I was with him yesterday, and he was fine. He's dead." He bursts into tears. "Jerry's dead."

Gina holds him in her arms in the dark. He sobs and sobs.

4

DESPITE THE FAILURE of his conversations with Mandato, Wolff, and Cody, there was one more former partner whom Leuci felt obliged to reassure, and this was Vinny Russo.

Good undercover detectives were rare, and were much in demand. One of the best, perhaps the best of all eight years before, had been Detective Vinny Russo. But Russo wanted to work only in Manhattan. Manhattan had the most dealers and biggest cases.

In addition, no skilled undercover liked to work with inexperienced detectives like Leuci. Undercovers were rated not according to how many buys they made, but how many arrests these buys resulted in, and inexperienced arresting officers often proved unable to find the sellers once the buy had been made. If this happened too often, the undercover began to lose ground in the monthly ratings.

Russo had agreed to work with Leuci in Brooklyn only after surviving a savage in Manhattan.

He had stepped into a hallway with three black men to buy drugs. Russo was an effective undercover because he did not look like a cop. He was small, almost frail. The three blacks led him up a narrow, malodorous staircase. There was no reason for this, so he realized he was about to be ripped off. Then the three men grabbed him. Russo had not gone for his gun soon enough.

The three men kicked and punched him. One took out a straight razor, and began slashing. The razor sliced through Russo's pants. They fell down. His gun fell out. Another grabbed up the gun, held it to Russo's head, and pulled the trigger. But the automatic was on safety. The man tried to cock the gun, but didn't know how.

All three men began kicking and beating Russo. They kicked in ribs. They slugged him with their fists, and with his own gun. They found his shield and tried to break his arm off at the shoulder. Russo was screaming for them to kill him.

A black woman, opening her door onto the hallway grabbed Russo and dragged him into her apartment, slamming the door on the three assailants.

"It's over for me," Russo had said, when Leuci visited him in the hospital. "I can't go in the street any more. I'm afraid, Bob. I'm too afraid. I've been beaten up too many times."

"Come back to Brooklyn with me," urged Leuci. "I'll take care of you."

"I don't want to be an undercover cop any more," said Russo through puffed lips. "I want to be able to tell people I'm a cop. I want to be able to walk up to somebody and say: you fuck, you, you're under arrest."

But Leuci talked to him persuasively for a long time. In Brooklyn he would be safe. No matter what happened, Leuci would be there to protect him.

And so for a number of years Russo had worked as Leuci's undercover, had communicated to the younger man not only his own techniques, but also his personal vision of the street and of street people. Eventually both men—Mandato too—had been promoted to SIU, where their success had continued.

Now Leuci wanted to see Russo. Although Russo was the more experienced detective, still Leuci had protected him from harm for so many years that he felt almost fatherly to him. He wanted to convince him that he had nothing to worry about from Leuci or from the prosecutors Leuci now worked for.

But Russo was an emotional, excitable kind of man, and Leuci found himself afraid to call him. Russo might imagine that his former partner was recording him, was trying to set him up.

So Leuci asked Gina to call Maria Russo, and from their cabin in the Catskills, Gina dialed the number. The conversation at first sounded fine. The two women asked about each other's children, about their husbands.

All of a sudden Gina began weeping. "Bob promises me he would never hurt Vinny under any circumstances," sobbed Gina.

"What are you doing?" cried Leuci, grabbing the phone out of her hand. "How do you know who could be listening?"

The constant police fear. Perhaps his own phone was tapped. Hurt Vinny? That single phrase might be enough to aim investigators at Russo.

"Why do you say such things?" demanded Leuci.

"Well, what do you want me to say?" sobbed Gina.

"Maria," said Leuci into the phone.

"Bob, don't be afraid," said Maria Russo. "Vinny wants to see you. You're welcome in my house any time."

Then Russo came on. "How are you? Are you okay? Will you come to my house? Do you have bodyguards out there? Bring them. We'll feed them all."

Leuci, hanging up, felt terrific. Russo was an SIU guy and still his friend. The perfect undercover agent was still his friend, and he looked forward to an Italian dinner at Russo's house next week.

Leuci's bodyguards escorted him there. But Russo stood in the doorway barring it. He stared at the two bodyguards.

"I don't want these IAD creeps in my house," he said.

The vast police brotherhood does not extend to cops who work for Internal Affairs Division, investigating other cops. Russo had his horn-rimmed glasses on. He seemed to have aged five years in the last few months.

"You're welcome in my house any time, Bob. But I don't know these guys."

"They're regular cops. They're my bodyguards."

"I don't want them in the house."

"Oh, Vinny."

"All right. Tell them to come in."

They came in. Once he started talking to them, Russo realized his mistake. Patrolman John Farley was a motorcycle cop. Patrolman Artie Monty was a childhood friend who had been in Leuci's wedding party. Russo poured out wine. In Russo's living room, the four cops talked about other cops, and about the department. But presently the bodyguards, realizing that this was a private meeting, went out to have dinner.

Once they had left, Russo said, "How did this all happen, Bob?"

"I couldn't begin to explain it to you. I don't want to talk about it. I want to enjoy my time here with you."

"Bob, from the day I met you, you were constantly giving out the deep sighs. I knew there was something wrong. What the hell was it?"

"It's too complicated. I don't want to talk about it."

Russo's son Jimmy came in. He was a big boy now, practically a man, Leuci told him. Russo bragging about his son's school work. "He's smart," said Russo. "He don't take after me, he takes after Maria." Then Russo bragged of his other son, who played football on the school team. He was proud of his two boys and his girl.

Dinner was served. Maria kept bringing out Sicilian dishes while Russo poured more wine. It got late. The kids were in bed. The three adults were all laughing and relaxed.

"Vinny, listen to Bob," said Maria. "Bob, Vinny is giving himself an ulcer. He's afraid something is going to happen."

"Nothing is going to happen," insisted Leuci. "Can't you believe nothing is going to happen? Do you think I would hurt you? Under any circumstances, do you think I would hurt you?"

"People make people do strange things," said Russo. "I don't know. What can you hurt me about? I'm a schmuck. Look, I've got cement on my hands." It was true. The foundation was cracking on the side of his house, and he had been trying to fix it himself because he couldn't afford to pay a mason to do it.

"Are you trying to convince me you're a hard-working guy? Not a money guy?"

"Bob, do you want to see my car? I've got an old, beat-up car. I can't pay for this goddamn house. I've got no money. Why would they be interested in me? I was never like you."

"What does that mean?"

"You were different."

"I was an arresting officer. You were an undercover officer. We worked together."

This remark caused a rather long silence.

"Those SIU guys treated me like I was a kid," said Russo after a moment. "They would send me out for coffee and things like that."

"You were a better detective than the whole bunch of them put together."

"Yeah, but I had no imagination. I couldn't put a case together. You guys were able to put those cases together. You and Nunziata and these other guys were incredible." He said, "Are any of the other guys in trouble?"

"Nobody's in trouble other than what you have read in the papers."

"Is anybody going to get—"

"Vinny, you're never going to get in trouble from me."

"I believe you. I really believe you."

"I want you to relax, enjoy your home. You have Maria, you're a second-grade detective. You're out of Narcotics now."

Russo, no longer undercover, had been transferred to a detective squad, where he investigated whatever crimes occurred each day.

"I love doing squad work," he said. "I can tell people finally: You are under arrest. All the years I was undercover and getting beat up, I wanted more than anything else to be able to tell people I was a cop. You're under arrest."

Monty and Farley were waiting downstairs by the car. Russo walked out to the car with his guest.

"Bob, I got three kids and a wife," Russo said. "I've got three years to do. I want to get out of this job in one piece."

"Vinny, you've got nothing to worry about."

They shook hands.

"My house is always open to you." Russo said. "At least you can relax here. I can see you laugh."

The car drove away. When it had covered a short distance Monty, whom Leuci had grown up with, turned and said to Leuci in the back seat, "You're never going to hurt that guy, are you?"

"Why should I have to hurt him? He has nothing to do with anything."

"He's worried. He's really worried, Bob."

"Those prosecutors," said Farley, "I don't trust those pricks. You are talking to them every day. You don't know when to keep your mouth shut. This guy seemed like a real nice guy."

Leuci stared out the window into the night. "If they ever come and take me, Bobby," Russo had said an hour ago, "they are never taking me to jail. I ain't going to jail. I got to whack myself out." After a moment he had added, "The only thing I want to do is see my kids grow up," and he had gazed searchingly into Leuci's eyes.

5

MIDNIGHT. A rooftop in a Bronx ghetto. Patrolman Leuci, aged twenty-three, watches two men lifting objects out of an apartment window onto the fire escape below. Burglars.

Patrolman Leuci's flashlight beam encapsulates them. One has a Vandyke beard. "Police officer. Stay where you are."

Leuci goes over the wall onto the ladder. But its steel moorings break loose from the mortar, and it swings out into space. Leuci rides it, trying to get back to the wall.

The two burglars sprint down the fire escape.

The terrified Leuci manages to drop onto the top fire escape. The burglars are already in the courtyard, running away. Leuci fires a shot down into the courtyard into pitch darkness.

"The fuck shot me," a voice screams. But the burglars keep running and escape.

When superior officers arrive, Leuci is standing beside a stack of loot, trembling. An investigation into the shooting begins at once. It is a legal shooting, but a bad one, and Leuci knows it. A shooting is morally justified in the presence of deadly physical force only. There was none here. The burglars were perhaps not even armed. In this precinct there is a cop known as "The Silver Bullet." He has killed three teenage kids in the last few months, each with one shot in the head. The precinct is bubbling.

The hospitals. He must check every hospital in the precinct until he finds his victim. In the first emergency room he comes to, doctors are taking a bullet out of the leg of a fifteen-year-old kid.

"Are you all right?" cries Leuci, grabbing the kid by the hand.

"You is some shot, man," says the kid, grinning. He is pleased to have been shot. His emotion is pride. Leuci's is overpowering relief.

The kid's mother rushes into the emergency room and begins to embrace the young patrolman. With tears in her eyes, she thanks him for not shooting to kill. She doesn't know about the dark courtyard. She imagines he shot her son in the leg on purpose.

The shaken Leuci leaves the hospital having resolved never to fire his gun again unless he is being shot at. Once he becomes a detective, he will carry this resolve one step further, and rarely even wear it.

6

THERE HAD BEEN, some months previously, a single meeting between Police Commissioner Patrick V. Murphy and Detective Second-Grade Robert Leuci. Leuci had insisted on it. He could go no further, he had said, without knowing that his boss approved of what he was doing. He wanted to hear this from the P.C.'s own lips.

Few cops had day-to-day contact with the Police Commissioner, and some never encountered one in person in their entire careers. The P.C. stood as a kind of god figure in their lives. He was the personification of all they stood for, and their attitude toward him was not far from the reverence and awe that other Americans accord to the President of the United States.

The meeting took place in a conference room in the Federal Building downtown. Scoppetta had told Leuci to wear a suit. This offended the detective.

"You don't have to tell me that. I know."

Murphy was late. Leuci sat with his back to the door. Scoppetta sat next to him, and U.S. Attorney Seymour next to Scoppetta. On the opposite side of the table sat Shaw, by himself. They waited for Murphy.

The door opened, and all stood up. Seymour was even taller than Shaw—about six feet six—and Murphy was a small man.

Leuci, in the presence of the Police Commissioner, feared that he would freeze up and be unable to speak, but Murphy, as he shook hands with them all, appeared scared too, like a father being called to the principal's office to defend a truant son.

Murphy sat in the chair opposite Leuci and would not look at him. He looked at Seymour or Scoppetta or Shaw when one or the other spoke. The rest of the time he looked at the table.

One by one, the prosecutors described the Leuci investigation. It was going terrifically well, they said. Terrifically well, to Murphy, meant that these men, this single second-grade detective, were knocking over his Police Department.

Murphy had been a New York cop more than twenty years, he said at last. He knew about corruption. Why, when he was a patrolman, the precinct cops used to get their police cars washed for nothing, rather than doing the job themselves. But he had put an end to that little practice. Police cars could now be driven directly to car wash garages and be washed professionally, and the city would pick up the tab.

Presently enough time had gone by, or so Murphy seemed to feel. Rising to his feet, he said, "I'm behind you one hundred percent," and he shook Leuci's hand. There was still no eye contact of any kind. During the final handshake Leuci, who had sat for twenty minutes unable to say a word, expected Murphy's gaze to meet his own. Perhaps some secret police message would flash across the void. But there was nothing. Murphy had walked out of the room.

Shortly afterward, however, Murphy appointed Three-Star Chief Sydney Cooper to head a new office monitoring the Leuci investigation and the cases that would arise out of it. The office was set up in a downtown office building, not only outside police headquarters, but even outside the normal police orbit.

Cooper at that time was fifty-two years old, and one of only four three-star chiefs in the department—there was a single four-star chief inspector—and he had commanded both the Inspections and Internal Affairs Divisions. He considered his new job, with its small staff and secret office, to be a demotion. Murphy didn't care about this. The Leuci investigation, to Murphy, was critical, and Cooper was the best and most reliable man he had.

Cooper was a big heavy man, with a bald head, a big nose, and a loud voice. He could be extremely funny, though most often his wit had a cutting edge to it. He seemed by far the smartest of the top cops around Murphy, and he had the most credentials, including a law degree. He had had management and computer training as well, and the previous year had begun the laborious job of computerizing Police Department personnel records. With no personal life to speak of, he regularly put in sixteen-hour days. He was known as a fierce corruption fighter—fiercer by far than Murphy himself.

Cooper had long ago terrorized the Police Department as a whole. No one, it seemed, had anything on Syd Cooper. He went where the evidence led him, and he was merciless. Cooper would not only lock up cops, he even seemed to enjoy it. Cops saw him as a shark swimming through their ranks. Although an amiable fellow to those who knew him well, Cooper was to cops in general the most hated and feared figure in headquarters.

But now he had been, to all outward appearances, banished, reduced in importance if not in rank. Murphy had even given out the cover story that Cooper was seriously ill and had been given this minor new office—its nature was kept vague—to tide him over while he waited out retirement.

His only job was what Murphy called "this Leuci business." However, there had been for many long months no Leuci business to occupy Cooper at all. He was not privy to the prosecutors' decisions, nor even to their knowledge. They would not let him close to the case. His vast energies were being wasted. Frustrated, deceived, he brooded constantly about headquarters. He longed to get back there, back inside the councils of power. He kept looking around for some means to do so, and at last he found what he was looking for. If he could not have "this Leuci business," then he would find a Leuci of his own. Arrests, headlines would all follow.

And he did exactly that.

Scoppetta telephoned Leuci with the news, "Cooper's got Frank Mandato."

7

TWO DAYS before his twenty-sixth birthday Leuci gets his gold shield—he is now a detective—and shortly after that he gets a new partner, Patrolman Frank Mandato, thirty-one, who has spent the last five years driving a radio car through the streets of the Seventy-seventh Precinct.

Mandato is six feet tall, weighs 185 pounds, and begins immediately to grow his sculptured black beard. Mandato is dark-complexioned, and his piercing black eyes seem to notice everything. His street sense, nurtured in the Bedford-Stuyvesant high-crime ghetto, is as acute as Leuci's, and by midsummer they are bringing ten felony narcotics arrests per month into the court system. By fall Mandato has his gold shield too.

One other fact about Mandato is not obvious at first: Mandato knows about money. The Seventy-seventh Precinct, like all ghetto precincts, teems with illegal bottle clubs, with street gamblers, with merchants willing to pay for additional police protection. The Seventy-seventh Precinct is a hotbed of payoffs to cops.

Although Mandato is five years older, Leuci was there first. It is Leuci who is team leader, and principally this is because the network of informants he has developed in Narcotics is his, personally. Most are addicts. The male addicts sometimes deal, and the female addicts are usually prostitutes. Their number fluctuates between six and ten, and their faces change. Some get arrested by other detective teams and go to prison. Some become terrified and no longer inform. Some disappear, and some die. Toward their informants, Leuci and Mandato obey the same rules all detectives obey. A junkie who gives up a street dealer is left alone. The street dealer who gives up a wholesaler is left alone. Any criminal is allowed to continue whatever his business may be provided he gives up someone worse than himself.

"Listen, these guys want to give me money," says Mandato one day. "They're junkies, but they are also selling dope themselves. Do you know how much money they make?"

"It all goes into their arms. They don't have any money."

One informant, a small-time street dealer and junkie, owns a candy store. His name is Nicky Conforte. He is standing in the back of his store when Leuci and Mandato enter. When they question him, he informs on his new wholesaler—name, address, location of the next drop. The wholesaler is a street-level guy, too. Still, it will make a nice arrest.

"Listen," says Mandato to the informant, "Bobby's short. Could you loan us a couple of dollars?"

The candy store owner hands $100 to Leuci and $50 to Mandato.

The amazed Leuci puts the money in his pocket.

The following week the two detectives call on the candy store owner again, and when they have finished questioning him he hands over another $100 without being asked.

There is a second informant who, to support his own habit, sometimes sells nickel bags out of his bodega. Leuci goes to question him, and afterward says, "I'm short. Can you lend me any money?" The words prove easier to speak than he had supposed.

"Why didn't you ask me? Any time you're short, Bobby." The informant rings up a "no sale" and hands across $100.

From then on, both informants pay regularly. Without being asked, too. This seems important. It is no shake-down. There is no extortion. It is not even a bribe, Leuci and Mandato tell themselves, for they give nothing in exchange. It is more like a loan they don't have to pay back.

The money is spent. Leuci is buying better clothes, eating in better places. The big thing is to be able to buy equipment—or so the two detectives tell themselves—to buy tape recorders, to buy eavesdropping gear. To buy a new car so that you can chase somebody in it.

Nunziata notices Leuci's new affluence. All the older detectives notice. Leuci realizes that he has crossed a threshold, that he is now one of them. He is accepted by other narcotics detectives for the first time.

Nunziata invites him to dinner, and when they have ordered, remarks, "You've earned a few dollars."

"Yes," says Leuci proudly. He is elated to have won Nunziata's approval. When he describes what happened, Nunziata laughs. "You're incredible. With your information and my brains, I'd be a millionaire."

This is a sixty-dollar dinner for two in an Italian restaurant on the lower East Side. It is Nunziata who picks up the check.

Leuci basks in his new acceptance by his fellow detectives. The important thing is to be able to make your cases, to make arrests, and to live a decent life, all the detectives seem to feel. Putting their heads on the line for everybody and going home with seventy-five cents in their pockets makes no sense. It's stupid guys who do that, or kids who don't know better. Now that Leuci has graduated, or suddenly gotten older, they see the change in him, and they like him much better because he is not only a good cop but also smart enough to earn money.

Nevertheless, Leuci continues, as is his way, to brood about all this. It has made a wound in his psyche that is trying to heal, but he won't let it. He keeps picking at the scab. In his heart he sometimes feels ashamed. He wonders if all the other detectives are secretly ashamed also.

He wishes he could talk to Nunziata about it, but knows he can't. It isn't done. He has never heard any detective talk about it. He imagines all the other detectives rationalize their conduct just as he does, telling themselves: As long as we all do it together, it isn't really so bad.

8

MANDATO WAS ALWAYS immaculately groomed, and his possessions were always immaculate also. It was because of this meticulousness that he fell into the hands of Chief Cooper.

He had left his car off at a body shop to have a dent knocked out and repainted—any car Mandato drove had to look sharp. The black man working on the car became conscious of the odor of marijuana. He searched the interior of the car but found nothing. Opening the trunk, he found what he was looking for. He was staring down at a bale of marijuana. It looked as though it weighed about ten pounds.

The black man went to the phone and called the police. A radio car team responded, contemplated the bale of marijuana, and matched the car to Detective Third-Grade Frank Mandato.

In any cop's lexicon of crimes, marijuana ranked at the very bottom, and in addition the rule said that you gave another cop a break. But this was a case the two radio car cops did not dare bury. For one thing, the black man's call had been logged in, marijuana had been mentioned, and the complainant was standing there, looking at them. For another, the Police Department, because of the Knapp Commission, was in the grip of a kind of corruption hysteria. No one knew who was investigating whom anymore, and the bale of marijuana perhaps had nothing to do with this Detective Mandato. Perhaps the target here was not Mandato but themselves.

And so they played it safe. They called IAD, and when Mandato came to pick up his car later, two IAD detectives were standing beside it.

Routinely Chief Cooper was notified. "Mandato is

mine," he said, and began rubbing his hands together with glee.

Mandato, who at this time worked out of Tenth District Burglary-Larceny, claimed under interrogation that the bale of marijuana was evidence he had seized in an earlier case. He had "forgotten" to turn it in to the property clerk's office.

This was perhaps true. By regulation, evidence had to be vouchered with the property clerk on the day seized, and returned there immediately after each court appearance, but the property clerk was in distant Manhattan, and Brooklyn detectives were constantly getting in trouble for letting their evidence stockpile.

Chief Cooper ordered all of Mandato's cases examined; this inquiry showed that certain packages of seized heroin had not been turned in to the property clerk either. Mandato promptly produced what he said were these packages. He had always intended to turn them back in, he said. They had lain "forgotten" in a locked trunk in his basement for months.

Cooper ordered the packages analyzed by the police lab. One contained more heroin now than when analyzed the first time. To Cooper, it was obviously not the same heroin.

Cooper had been a cop since 1941—thirty-one years—and believed he knew cops. It seemed clear to him that Mandato had intended to hold this evidence back indefinitely—until he retired, perhaps longer. If ever anyone called for it, then he would of course produce it. If no one called for it, then many years from now he would—do what? Sell it, perhaps, thought Chief Cooper.

And Mandato had been Leuci's partner, brooded Cooper. Mandato was an insider too. He would know the same crooked cops, the same Mafia hoodlums that Leuci knew. Mandato, if Cooper could only apply sufficient pressure, could become Cooper's Leuci.

Cooper had all the leverage needed, or at least he thought he did. Although criminal charges against Mandato probably would not stick—no jury, Cooper supposed, would send him to jail for what could be made to sound like administrative oversights—still he was clearly guilty of serious breaches of Police Department regulations, and for these Cooper could have him dismissed. Mandato had thirteen years in; two more and the first stage of his pension would be secured, three-quarters of half pay for life. How much money, Cooper asked himself, were we talking about here? If you accorded Mandato a generous life span, then the answer came back at around a quarter of a million dollars. Mandato need only to hang on another two years, and all that money would be his.

Mandato would cooperate, Cooper decided grimly, or throw away $250,000. Mandato, cooperating, would give up corrupt cops, detectives, and bosses. He would perhaps give up Leuci, too. The prosecutors were still insisting that Leuci was guilty of only three corrupt acts. Mandato would know better, and perhaps could be made to confirm Cooper's own suspicions.

Any success at all would sweep Syd Cooper back into Headquarters, perhaps at an even higher level than before.

Cooper had dealt with hundreds of corrupt and suspect cops, and he planned to crack Mandato with the same classic techniques that had always worked in the past.

Technique number one was to order cops to his office, and then leave them sitting in chairs in an anteroom for eight hours straight, without taking any notice of them whatever. At the end of the day Cooper would allow them to sign out and go home. On the second day the same scenario would be repeated, and on the third, the fourth, the fifth—for however many weeks or months it took until the cop cracked, and babbled forth whatever information Cooper sought. Cooper had never known this technique to fail.

But Mandato, summoned to Cooper's office, arrived with coffee and a bagel in a paper bag, and with books to read. He sat down in the anteroom, took out a book, and calmly read all day long. At the end of eight hours he signed out and went home.

The following day he returned with another paper bag

containing coffee and a bagel plus the same book, or perhaps another. And he quietly turned pages for eight hours. Cooper took no notice of Mandato, and Mandato—apparently—took no notice of Cooper.

Every day Cooper walked past Mandato several times. Normally Mandato did not even look up. Weeks went by. Cooper waited for Mandato to pace the floor, to ask anxious questions of the clerks and secretaries, to show fear. But he never did.

Finally it was Cooper who cracked. Becoming increasingly aggravated, Cooper began, when passing Mandato's chair, to attempt to bait him. Mandato, as always, was smartly dressed; his sharply creased slacks must have cost forty dollars, perhaps more. His shoes were hand-stitched.

"How can a piece of shit like you afford to wear such expensive clothes?" demanded Cooper.

Mandato only smiled. "My wife is very frugal. I'm sure, if you wanted to, you could afford to buy some decent clothes."

Cooper, fuming, went into his office and slammed the door. Though used to cops who trembled—literally trembled—in his presence, he was finding it impossible to intimidate Mandato, and he could not understand why.

But Mandato, however cool he may have seemed to Cooper, was badly frightened, and when Leuci one night rang his bell, he was glad to see his former partner.

"You can save your job, Frank," Leuci said.

"How?" asked Mandato. "Just tell me how."

"You can talk to these people."

"What should I talk to them about? Should I tell them what you and I did? Should I tell them what Les Wolff and I did? Should I tell them what Nunziata did with other people?" He shook his head. "I've got nothing to tell them."

The two ex-partners gazed at each other.

"Do I have anything to worry about?" asked Mandato. "Tell me. Is there something I should be concerned about? What have you told them?"

"I told Scoppetta I had done three things, and that's all

I ever intend to tell anybody, and those three things concerned only me. That's it. That's all they'll ever get from me."

"Then I have nothing to tell them," said Mandato.

"Maybe I can work something out. Let me think about it."

It was Leuci, via Scoppetta, who brought Deputy Commissioner McCarthy into the case. Mandato found Cooper crude, Leuci told Scoppetta. McCarthy seemed a sensitive man. If he would interview Mandato, then perhaps communication would be easier.

"I'll talk to McCarthy," said Scoppetta, and he did.

Deputy Commissioner William McCarthy was a former chief of traffic cops whom Murphy had brought back from retirement. During his police career, McCarthy had assiduously avoided not only corrupt cops, but also corrupt situations. He had rarely ever been tempted. Now, recalled as a deputy commissioner, he had proven to be a man of advanced management ideas, but underneath this veneer his personality was as rigid and unbending as ever.

In the presence of Cooper and two of Cooper's aides, McCarthy did meet with Mandato, but the conversation went nowhere, and very soon McCarthy became exasperated. "Tell me every bit of corruption you have ever seen," he demanded of Mandato.

"I've heard about a lot of corruption," said Mandato, "but I've never seen any."

"You have thirty seconds," said McCarthy.

"I don't know what you want to know," said Mandato. "I have never seen any corruption."

McCarthy rose from his desk and strode to the door, where he turned to Chief Cooper and said, "Suspend him. Take his shield and gun." And McCarthy walked out of the room.

Cooper in turn strode toward the door. "Suspend him," said Cooper to his subordinate, Lieutenant George Ahrens. "Take his shield and gun."

Cooper walked out of the room.

Lieutenant Ahrens turned to Dave Powers, a sergeant.

"Suspend him, take his shield and gun," ordered Ahrens, and he too walked from the room.

Mandato stood holding his gun and shield in his hands. "Is there anyone left, sarge?" said Mandato. "There's only you and me now. I think you got to do it." And he handed his gun and shield to the sergeant.

A short time later, forced to resign from the Police Department or be dismissed for cause, Mandato moved to Florida. There he experienced every cop's withdrawal symptoms—he felt for his shield a dozen times a day, and it wasn't there. This meant he was now alone in the world. Walking in the street, he kept hitting himself in the back pocket. All the time. He would get in his car, and realize he was not sitting on it. His shield was gone, and he could not get it back.

One day a police car pulled him over for speeding. He jumped out of his car imagining that he had nothing to worry about. His hand went to his back pocket. He would show the cop his shield and—

Oh.

The trooper came over. "License and registration."

He had been a cop himself, Mandato told him. Thirteen years. But he had just retired.

"They give you a card when you retire," said the cop.

So Mandato told him the truth.

The cop nodded. "License and registration," he said, and wrote out a ticket.

Mandato phoned Leuci in New York and recounted this story. "It's awful, awful," he said. "You got to beat them, Bobby. It's worth whatever it costs. You got to beat them. You got to hang in there."

9

TO MAKE ten felony arrests a month—sometimes
fourteen or fifteen—takes all of the young detective's
time. Leuci, now twenty-six, is in the streets of south
Brooklyn day and night, or else in court with prisoners.

One night while cruising, looking for someone to
arrest, he spies a beautiful Hispanic face. She looks
fourteen or fifteen years old. A child. She wears a
raincoat. Her long black hair is tied into a ponytail. Great
round alabaster face, enormous black eyes, full lips. A
beautiful face. He is sure she doesn't realize how beautiful
she is. She walks the same block prostitutes walk.

Leuci pulls over. "You shouldn't be here. It's
dangerous here."

She smiles. "I can take care of myself. You're a cop,
right?"

He doesn't like the way she says: You're a cop. But it
does not necessarily make her a bad girl.

"You're Babyface, aren't you?" She calls his name in a
kind of shout, alerting the neighborhood to his presence.

"You fool around?" asks Leuci, after a moment.

"No, I don't fool around."

"What are you doing out here then?"

She smiles. "I'm just waiting for somebody."

So Leuci drives off, but he comes back via a side street
and parks where he can look onto the avenue. She is
tricking. Men come up and she talks to them. Here comes
some crewcut kid. Leuci becomes terribly depressed. She
puts her arm in the kid's and off they go. Twenty minutes
later she is back.

Leuci gets out of his car, grabs her, and drags her into a
hallway.

"Open your purse."

She becomes nasty. "Who the hell do you think you are?"

He empties her purse out on the floor. He is angry at her, and doesn't know why.

"Take off your coat," he orders. When she resists, he yanks it off her.

And he sees the needle marks.

But it makes him more depressed than ever, because he finds her gorgeous. Black hair and eyes. White teeth. One rarely sees addicts with good teeth.

"How long have you been fooling around?"

"If it's any business of yours, since I was twelve."

"How old are you now, fifteen?"

"I'm nineteen."

"Have you ever been busted before?"

"Twice."

She puts her stuff back in her bag. She is looking up at him. "I'm warning you, Babyface. You leave me alone."

"I'll see you around. I catch you and you're going."

"You got to catch me first, smart guy."

A few days later, early in the morning, Leuci drives down Pacific Street toward court. There she is in the same raincoat on the same corner. Pulling the car to the curb, Leuci watches her from some distance away. When a black man walks up to her, Leuci pulls out into traffic and approaches very slowly. He sees him hand something to her, after which he starts to walk away.

Leuci pulls to the curb, gets out, and starts running. As he closes in on the girl, she smiles and shouts her greeting, "Hello, Babyface." Again she has alerted the neighborhood.

She has her hand closed. He grabs her hand and forces it open. Two bags of heroin.

The black man has run into a brownstone. Leuci takes her junk, cries, "You wait right here," and runs into the building after him. She may run, but he thinks she will probably wait, hoping he might give her back her junk.

In the brownstone, Leuci pauses to get his bearings. It's a rooming house. He runs up the stairs. When he gets almost to the second landing, he spies the black man.

Then a dresser drawer comes down the stairs at him. It goes over him, knocking him down. The black man runs up onto the roof. By the time Leuci gets up there, he is gone, either onto another roof or down a fire escape.

Scared and angry, Leuci goes back downstairs and outside. The girl is sitting on the stoop with her head in her hands.

"You're under arrest. Get in the car."

He processes her in the 78th Precinct, then takes her to court. All morning she screams and curses him. But wherever they go, he notices, people stare at her because she is so beautiful. This only depresses Detective Leuci. She could be anything, this girl, he thinks. With any brains at all she could go someplace.

She has a foul, filthy mouth. Her name is Maria. She is a nasty little bitch, but he cannot take his eyes off her.

Once in court, her fear becomes apparent. Her yellow sheet has come back. Leuci sees she has never been arrested before. Never gone to jail before.

"Do you know what it's going to be like for me in the Women's House of Detention?" she asks. "You are going to send me there. They are going to hurt me. There are bull daggers in there. The guards are bull daggers."

She is petrified and he is petrified for her.

"Get me out of here. I'm scared."

Leuci approaches the assistant D.A. "Listen, this girl wants to cooperate with me. Can I get her out?"

But the judge has left the courtroom. Leuci hurries to his chambers.

"Judge, I want a recall on my case."

But the judge, wanting to get home, refuses. Leuci goes back to the girl. She is sitting there, and is in tears.

"How bad is your habit?" he asks.

She starts screaming at him. "Fuck you and your medication. I don't need any medication. I'll get through this night without you. I'll get through this night."

Leuci goes home. All night long he thinks about her. He can't get her beautiful little face out of his mind. What is it like for her tonight in that prison full of lesbians?

The next morning he gets to Brooklyn early, and looks

to make sure her case is on the calendar. Eventually the truck comes. The prisoners file out of it.

She glares at him.

"Do you want to get out of here? Would you work with me? We'll make some cases."

"I'm not a rat."

"Do you want to go back in there tonight?"

"Just get me out."

At Detective Leuci's request, the assistant D.A. makes the standard approach to the judge. "The police officer has apprised me that the defendant will cooperate with the police Narcotics division. She has information about dealers."

As the judge listens, the girl reaches over and grabs Leuci's leg. She gives him a squeeze, and a warm childish smile.

Quickly Leuci straightens out her papers. When he comes out of the courthouse she is waiting by his car.

"Get in, I'll drive you home." After a moment, he asks, "What kind of habit do you have?"

"I don't mainline or skin pop. I haven't got a habit."

"All right. How about if I see you tonight? Get dressed up and I'll see you tonight."

"You would take me out?"

"Of course I'd take you out."

"You're terrific."

He goes to his office and talks it over with Frank Mandato. "She's a gorgeous girl, Frank."

"What are you going to do with her?" asks Mandato.

"I'm going to take her out."

"Why don't you just take her to a hotel and screw her? She's a fucking pross. Are you crazy? Do you want to take her to the movies? Buy her an ice cream soda? This is a Puerto Rican prostitute. So she's nineteen and pretty. In two years she'll have no teeth and seventeen needle scars in her arms."

"Frank, you've got to see her. She's like a saint. She is a beautiful thing. Where will you be tonight?"

Mandato plans to have dinner with several other detectives at an Italian restaurant near the courthouse.

"I'll see you there," says Leuci.

"Are you losing your mind? There are cops—all the guys in the office—"

That night he goes to pick her up. She is dressed all in black in a lace dress. A lace shawl comes up over her hair.

But when he tells her where they will go for dinner, she says, "That's where all the cops hang out."

"Yeah, there will be some cops there."

"You're not ashamed of me?"

"Of course I'm not ashamed of you."

All heads turn as they enter the restaurant. Leuci beams with pride. Mandato, who stands at the bar with four other detectives, comes over and introduces himself. "I heard about you," she tells him.

He looks at her, smiles at Leuci, and walks back to the bar shaking his head.

Joe Nunziata walks over and introduces himself, and after him, one by one, all the other detectives. From the bar they stare over. They can't stop looking at her. They are also giggling and drinking, making cracks no doubt, amusing themselves with their wit. Leuci doesn't care.

"What are we going to have?" he asks. "Some wine?"

"I'm very nervous in here. I don't like these guys. They are making fun of us."

"They are not making fun of us. Nobody would make fun of you."

"I have to go to the ladies' room."

When she has left the table, Nunziata walks over and says to Leuci, "Is your name Angel?"

"Joe, what's so funny?"

"Apparently this girl is in love with a guy named Angel. When she comes back, take a good look at her."

She comes back and sits down. "Do you know somebody by the name of Angel?" asks Leuci.

"Yes, my old man. How do you know that's his name? Oh, you saw my thing."

"What?"

As she turns he sees the word Angel tattooed across the muscle of her upper arm. But it is a tattoo done in the street. It is not a professional tattoo.

"Who did that to you?"

"Angel did it to me."

He almost starts laughing. By the time he has paid the check he has convinced her—or thinks he has convinced her—that she should work with him. He will bring in a female detective to walk with her in the street. They will make all sorts of buys, providing himself and Mandato with many arrests. Although afraid, she has said, "If you are with me, I will do it."

But when he calls for her the next day at her mother's house, she isn't there. Her mother has no idea where she is. He looks for her in the streets but can't find her. At length he gives up looking.

A week passes. At two o'clock in the morning Leuci and Mandato finish processing a prisoner, and leave the station house. As they walk toward their cars, a taxi cab stops nearby. Out step three passengers: Maria, another girl whom Leuci recognizes as a prostitute, and the black man who pushed the bureau drawer down the stairs on him two weeks earlier.

To Mandato, Leuci says quietly, "That's the son of a bitch who got away from me the day I locked up Maria."

The detectives start walking fast toward the three street people. Maria, spotting Leuci, again attempts to alert the neighborhood: "Hey B—"

Leuci slaps her, cutting off her voice, and Mandato grabs the black man, hustling him into a hallway.

In the hallway, Leuci has the suspect by the throat. "You're the guy that got away from me," he shouts. "You're under arrest."

Maria, next to him, is shouting that this is not the same man. The suspect is struggling, the two girls are shouting, and Mandato gives a sudden gasp. "Bobby, he has a gun."

The prostitute screams, "Hey, man, no guns," and gives a kind of strangled scream as the gun appears. Close to his head Leuci hears the trigger pulled twice, two loud clicks, no explosion.

Mandato pushes Leuci out of the way. He is on top of the suspect on the floor, gripping the gun hand. Leuci tears the gun loose. Mandato picks the guy up. Leuci is shaking so much he can only stand there, holding the gun. Mandato, gripping the suspect, is shaking also.

"He pulled the fucking trigger on me," Leuci says.

He gets his handcuffs out, but is shaking so much that, handcuffing the suspect, he cuts himself with the cuffs.

They walk the suspect into the station house. It's nearly three o'clock in the morning and the place is empty. The girls have gone, faded into the night. Upstairs they empty the gun out. Leuci stares at the bullets. "Regular fucking bullets," Mandato mutters.

Attempted murder of a detective is a heavy crime. The paperwork will take hours. After locking the suspect in the cage, Leuci and Mandato go out for coffee and pastry to sustain them through what is left of the night.

When they return, the desk officer stops them. "I don't see walking a guy in here that tried to kill a cop. You carry the fuck in, or you send him to the hospital, or you send him away in a box."

On the staircase they meet the squad detectives coming down. One says, "Let me tell you something, Leuci. If you don't teach that prick a lesson, the next cop he runs into he's going to blow him away."

Leuci apologizes. It was over so fast.

"Well, he's upstairs," the detective says.

Upstairs, the suspect lies in a heap in the corner of the cage. Froth and blood bubble from his mouth.

"Oh, shit, Frank, the guy is dead."

Rushing into the cage, they lift the prisoner up, wash him off, plead with him not to die. A lieutenant arrives, and looks down at him.

"I understand beating a guy up on the street," he says. "But in the station houses it don't make any sense."

By morning the suspect is well enough to appear in court. Later he is sentenced to one to three years for attempted felonious assault. His gun goes to ballistics that same afternoon. The ballistics detective identifies it by name. "He pulled the trigger on me twice," says Leuci.

The ballistics detective nods. "These cheap guns never go off."

But when he aims it into a test-fire box and pulls the

trigger, it fires perfectly. The room fills up with the noise and smoke of the explosion. Leuci and the ballistics detective stare at each other.

From time to time after that, Leuci parks his car down the block and sits there watching Maria patrol her street corner, tricking. He does not again try to use her as an informant.

10

THE FIRST TRIAL approached—*The United States
of America* v. *Edmund Rosner, Nicholas DeStefano,
and Nicholas Lamattina*—and with it would come
the moment Leuci dreaded, the moment when he would
be asked under oath to describe his own previous misconduct.

It was not this particular trial that caused now his sleep-
less nights, or the perpetual tightness around the region of
his heart. Rather it was the realization that from now on,
in his role as chief government witness, he himself would
be on trial too. The defendants would not take the stand.
Only the witness would take the stand, and once he was
there his credibility would become the issue, not their guilt.
Prosecutor and defense lawyer both would hammer. What
was he going to say?

To lie on the stand was perjury. But the truth would
impeach his credibility to such an extent that this trial—and
future trials too—would be compromised, probably lost.
If the truth were once spoken, then the Police Department
would have no choice but to dismiss him, the government
no choice but to prosecute him, a jury no choice but to send
him to jail—and with him would go all the detectives he
would have implicated: Mandato, Wolff, Cody, Vinny
Russo, and many, many others. Or so he believed.

The whole world would despise him, his new friends
as much as his old. If he answered truthfully, he would
bring down on himself and those he loved calamities
without number. The truth would condemn him to death.
It was lies, and lies only, that could set him free. And so
he resolved in advance that he would lie. He would say
nothing.

He worked every day with the assistant U.S. attorneys who would prosecute the case.

Weekends, in the Catskills, he would go out of the house, walk into the woods, and brood. He would try to think it all through. But he was never alone. Always at least two heavily armed marshals trailed him and sometimes, not understanding his need to be alone, his absolute need to think this thing through, they would stride along at his side chatting about the weather, or about football. Then the weekend would end, and Leuci would go back to New York, to his bare barracks room by night, to the corridors and offices of the Southern District Courthouse on Foley Square by day.

An all-out effort to convict Lawyer Rosner, Bail-bondsman DeStefano, and Detective Lamattina had been ordered. As many as three assistant U.S. attorneys were assigned to help prepare the case at one time. Leuci worked at their sides, and this work went on literally night and day.

Leuci had made twelve recordings with one or another of the defendants. The transcripts had to be absolutely accurate, for the defense could be expected to challenge every line, and the various background noises made this difficult. The transcripts went through draft after draft until each line, each incriminating statement, was as accurate as they could make it.

After that, the prosecution's case had to be virtually memorized both by the lawyers and by the chief witness. Day after day, week after week, all these men studied, tightened, honed their case.

Scoppetta and Shaw, busy on other cases, were not involved in trial preparations, and so Leuci, ostensibly to keep them informed, took to dropping into their offices several times each day. They were his sole emotional support, although they didn't know this. They perceived neither the nature of his dilemma nor the extent of his suffering. What was he going to admit on the stand?

He had never asked for nor been promised immunity from criminal prosecution, much less immunity from Police Department charges. He had not needed immunity, because he had not been charged with anything. There was no evidence against him. To get immunity now he would first have to admit to the prosecutors that he needed it. He would first have to confess to actions they did not suspect. Nor was there hope under any circumstances of acquiring immunity for his former partners.

From Scoppetta and Shaw, who cared about him, he needed answers to questions he could not pose, legal advice that he dared not ask for. Scoppetta and Shaw were prosecutors. The law was inflexible. Leuci's questions alone would reveal the guilt he was concealing. They would be obliged by law to take action against him or be guilty of crimes themselves.

No, he would have to lie.

Leuci's only comfort was that they were there. They had strength, and to stand near them gave him the illusion of strength—enough, at least, to get through each day.

"I think I'm going to be leaving soon," said Scoppetta one morning. "I think I'm going to be given an important appointment." He was elated, and trying to keep from grinning.

Leuci did not grin.

Scoppetta was about to be appointed New York City's Commissioner of Investigations—the man charged with investigating corruption in any and all New York City agencies. This was a cabinet level post, equal in rank and salary to the Police Commissioner.

"I'm very happy for you, Nick," said the stricken Leuci.

A few days later, when Scoppetta's appointment was confirmed, the prosecutor came out from behind his desk and embraced Leuci, saying, "I've got it."

Scoppetta beamed with happiness, and held the detective by both shoulders.

Leuci went back to work.

The chief prosecutor in the Rosner case was a young lawyer named Elliot Sagor, and as the trial date neared he had begun working fourteen to fifteen hours a day, and weekends as well.

Around eleven o'clock one night, while editing tapes with Sagor, Leuci wanted to go to Vinnie's Clam Bar in Little Italy. Sagor told him this was crazy. It was too dangerous, and besides, they had to go on working. Probably they would have to work all weekend.

Frustrated from hours and hours of listening to the same tapes over and over, Leuci lost his temper.

For a moment they glared at each other. Then Leuci grabbed up Sagor's tape recorder and threw it down on the desk. Yanking Sagor's jacket off the coat tree, he tried to tear it in two. He upended Sagor's desk. "And furthermore, I'm going home this weekend."

Leuci's bodyguards had burst into the room, which was a shambles. Leuci was trying to get at Sagor. The two cops grabbed Leuci, and pulled him off.

"If you can find a way to get home and get back here by Sunday," said Sagor, "I'll let you do it."

From the next room Leuci phoned Marshal Partington, who arranged to put a customs helicopter at his disposal. On Friday evening Leuci was driven to the Wall Street heliport, and the machine took off into a clear night, flying up the East River over the bridges. He was going home to the north woods, and there he would try to store up in two days enough strength to get through next week. From the helicopter the view of his city at night was breathtakingly beautiful. He saw this beauty, but was too much involved with his own problems to enjoy it. Scoppetta was gone, but at least he still had Shaw.

And then Shaw too received an important new appointment. He was named head of the New York office of the Justice Department's Joint Stike Force Against Organized Crime. He cleaned out his desk and moved across the plaza to new offices—and new concerns.

Every day the strain on Leuci built higher. Every day the time when he would testify—and be cross-examined—came closer. Every day Shaw telephoned: "Are you all right?"

From time to time Leuci was still invited to dine with Shaw and Margaret in the couple's Brooklyn Heights apartment, and it was there one night that Shaw said suddenly, "I need a good Jewish undercover detective. Do you know anyone?"

Shaw in his new job had begun to put together a

scheme designed, if it worked, to break organized crime's stranglehold on New York's heavily Jewish garment industry. The Jewish detective would be furnished with money with which he would buy a garment business in partnership with a garment executive who had come to Shaw for help. Once installed in the garment business, the detective would become subject to and take part in shakedowns, shylock operations, truck hijacks. The investigation would last at least two years. And the detective would be in grave danger most of that time.

"I can't tell you about the case," said Shaw, "except to say that if I can find the right Jewish detective, it can be a great case."

"I think," said Leuci after a moment, "that the guy you're looking for is Les Wolff."

Shaw nodded. "Does he have any skeletons I should be warned about?"

Again the pull in two directions at once. But Wolff was a great detective. More important than that, with Shaw behind him, he would be safe from such people as Chief Cooper.

"No, none," answered Leuci. "Les Wolff is your man."

The Rosner-DeStefano-Lamattina case was almost ready for trial. "The only thing left to prepare is your cross-examination," said Sagor. "Get a good night's sleep tonight. Tomorrow come in early, and we'll start on that."

Now it comes, thought Leuci. He had only hours left in which to decide. How much was he going to tell?

He communicated his decision to Sagor the following morning. He would admit nothing. "What are you telling me?" The prosecutor responded. "That you now admit no misconduct of any kind? What about what you told Scoppetta?"

Leuci attempted a confident laugh. "I was bullshitting."

Sagor stared at him.

"It wasn't me," said Leuci. "I was talking about somebody else."

Sagor nodded his head up and down. "You'll have to

excuse me," he said, and strode toward the door. "Have your lunch brought in here. Order it sent up."

He went out.

Leuci's bodyguards came in from the outer office. "What are you going to do?" asked one. "Are you going to tell him you did something? You have to be out of your fucking mind. You'll lose your job. You can't tell him anything."

This was the conclusion Leuci had come to also.

"Don't tell them anything," advised the other cop.

Into the office walked Mike Shaw. He was wearing jeans and a sweater. He said to the two cops, "Will you excuse us?"

The two cops, looking surprised, left the room.

"Bob, I want to tell you something," began Shaw earnestly. "I couldn't care less if you sold junk. I couldn't care less what you've done in the past. I know you for what you are now. What you were three years ago, two years ago, even one year ago—that's not what you are now. You're a different man now. You've changed your life. But if you allow yourself to take the stand, and then perjure yourself—I understand why you might want to do that, but if you do it, you would lose me as a friend. I would know that you had lied. You would force me into a position where I would have to take the stand and testify against you, because I know that you've done things. You've told Nick that you did things."

Shaw paused. A pleading note came into his voice. "You're not going to put me in that position, are you, Bob?"

"Mike, why do I have to pay that price? Why do I have to get on the stand and tell what I've done. Tell me, why?"

"Because it's the truth. It's as simple as that. That's the difference between us and Rosner, because we're going to get on the stand and tell the truth."

The phone rang. Shaw picked it up, spoke for a moment, then handed the receiver to Leuci. "Talk to him. It's Nick."

"Bob, you've gone too far to turn back now," said

Scoppetta. "You've told me what it is. It's not so terrible. People will understand."

"I'm embarrassed, Nick. I'm ashamed."

When Leuci had hung up, Shaw called in Sagor and his boss, Robert Morvillo, head of the Criminal Division. "This guy is going to be the best witness you ever had," Shaw said.

"If he tells the truth he'll be the best witness I ever had," said Morvillo.

Shaw turned back to Leuci. "Margaret is waiting for me. I've got to go home." He turned to the two prosecutors. "Prepare him well. Let him know what he can expect." Shaw turned back to Leuci. "See you soon."

"See you soon, Mike."

Morvillo sat down at the desk, smiled at Leuci, and said, "Okay, detective, tell us about your misconduct."

"It's so hard."

"Let's make it easy for you. What did you tell Scoppetta? Start from the top."

"What was the first time?" said Sagor.

"The first time?"

"Tell us about it."

And so Leuci told the following story to the two prosecutors—the same story he would later tell in open court.

"It coincided with my cousin getting out of jail," he began haltingly.

11

IT IS four years ago, 1968. A lieutenant, Aaron Mazen, arranges to meet Leuci secretly in a restaurant. There he tosses a case folder onto the table. "Something's wrong with this case," he says.

Leuci begins to go through the folder. It is a narcotics investigation involving wiretaps. Leuci recognizes the names of the targets: Mikey Coco, Stanley Simons, Louie Legs, and the Indelicata brothers, Joseph and Sonny Red. Mazen wants Leuci to find out why the detective in charge made no arrests, and to decide whether the case is worth pursuing by a new team of detectives.

A day or two later Leuci is sent by his parents to his Aunt Rosa's house, because John Lusterino has just got out of jail. Perhaps they need help over there.

Leuci has not seen his cousin in thirteen years. Lusterino is now thirty-nine, but his blond hair is gray and he looks forty-nine. He is solidly built. In jail he spent half his time in the library studying law, and the other half in the gym lifting weights. He has been out two weeks but already sports a beautiful tan.

Lusterino's conversation is predictable. He is shocked to learn that Detective Leuci sometimes operates against Italians. "There's a million niggers out there selling junk," he says. "There ain't enough niggers for you? You have to work your own people?"

They go for a ride in Lusterino's new car. "Putting people in jail ain't going to put bread on your table, Bobby," Lusterino says. "It's better you sit down with them. See what you can work out. You help people out with a problem, they won't forget you."

For some minutes Leuci broods over the import of

these words. At last he decides to risk an exchange of information with his cousin. After exacting a promise that Lusterino will not burn him, Leuci shows his cousin photos of the targets of the investigation that has somehow gone bad.

"Johnny," he says hesitantly, "if you know any of these people, I just want to know three things about them. Are they in junk? Are they in it now? Can I make a case against them? All I want to do is avoid wasting time."

Lusterino laughs. "You're with me a day, and you're trying to make a rat out of me."

But later Leuci's home phone rings. It is Lusterino.

"Be at the corner of Elizabeth and Kenmare at six o'clock sharp on the button. Legs will be there and Joseph Indelicata. They want to talk to you."

"Wait a minute, wait a minute," cries Leuci. His head pounds. "You're making a big problem for me, Johnny. If the feds have a tail on these people, and I meet them—"

But at six o'clock Leuci is at the corner of Elizabeth and Kenmare. Louie Legs leads him into Charlie's Oyster Bar. They are joined by Joey Indelicata, who begins to curse.

"This fucking spic. What does this whore motherfucker want from us? What has he got?"

This is the first Leuci realizes that he is on a shakedown. The detective who has the case is threatening to arrest these hoodlums unless they pay.

"I don't want to be in the middle," Leuci says. "You want to talk to the guy, I'll try to get him down here."

"We're going to kill him. He don't know it yet, but this whore is going to get three in the head."

Leuci gets up from the table, finds a phone, and calls the detective at home.

"For these two pricks you're going to pull me out of my house?" he answers grumpily. "All right. All right. Give me half an hour."

Leuci is worried about safety. "These are bad people," he says when the detective arrives.

"They're scumbags. They're all scumbags. You don't

have to worry about them or nobody like them. Where are they?"

Although the detective is thirty-four, his deeply tanned face is as smooth as a boy's. His wavy hair is prematurely gray. He wears a double-vented blue blazer with gold buttons. There is a knife-edge crease in his tapered tan gabardine slacks.

The two detectives enter the bar. Leuci expects Legs and Indelicata to curse the detective to his face. Instead their manner is conciliatory.

"A beautiful guy like you," says Legs. "Ain't you got anything better to do than go around making up stories? I think it's time you cut the shit. You gave us a figure and it's a big figure. It's a fucking outrageous figure. What have you got to give us a figure like that?"

"Louie, we aint' got you good, we got you beautiful. All you fucking clowns talk too much. We've been sitting on your telephone for a month. We got a warrant. It's all legal. All nice stuff for the D.A. We've got an earful of you, we've got Sonny Red and—"

Indelicata jumps up, enraged. "You spic bastard. You motherfucker. My brother Sonny has got nothing to do with nothing. Don't you dare. Don't you dare bring his name into this. He's not in this. He's not in nothing."

The detective laughs. "Your brother's in this real good. He's in it up to his guinea ass. What's more, as a man on life parole for murder, he's not supposed to associate with you criminals. If we can't work something out, I go to the parole board with my notes off the wiretap, and that will be it for your brother. Back in the can for good. Seventy-five grand or you can say bye-bye to Sonny."

Legs and Indelicata are furious. "Who you think you're dealing with here?" cries Indelicata. "You think you got women here who you lay a lot of bullshit on?"

"Your brother is on life parole," says the detective. "Life parole."

Indelicata looks drained. "I'd sooner kill you tonight than have my brother go back into the can for nothing."

The detective, annoyed, gets up from his chair.

"You fuck," cries Legs. "That fucking shield you've got

ain't no bulletproof vest, and don't you forget it."

The detective gives a disgusted wave of his hand, and walks out.

Leuci jumps up. This is a fellow cop they are threatening. "Watch your mouth. You hear me?"

The two detectives leave the restaurant.

"These guys are killers," says a worried Leuci.

"They talk a lot of shit," snaps the other man. "They're tough. We're tougher. We've got the biggest fucking gang in the world. There are thirty-two thousand of us." Leuci looks at him in awe.

A few minutes later Leuci reenters the bar and sits down with Indelicata and Legs.

Indelicata says, "I don't want that spic bastard making moves against Sonny Red. My brother ain't got nothing to do with this. Nothing. And that spic knows it."

"Let's talk numbers," Leuci says. "He says he wants seventy-five grand. What's the best you guys want to do?"

"If he promises on the heads of his kids that he'll stay away from my brother, if we never hear from him again—" The two Mafiosi look at each other. "You tell that motherfucker we'll give him seventy-five hundred not to see his face again."

Leuci goes across the street to the bar where the detective waits. "Seventy-five hundred," he reports.

The other smiles. "We'll take it. What do you want, half?"

Leuci is bewildered. Is it that simple? Can an SIU detective simply walk in on big people like this and score $7500?

After a moment Leuci replies, "I'll take two thousand and the name of your stool." The detective is said to have the best informant in the city.

"You pick up the money and bring it to me," he agrees, "and I'll give you the stool."

The money is paid in two installments. "You took care of a real headache for us, kid," Leuci is told. "Sonny Red knows what you done for him. If you ever need a favor from Sonny Red, you got it."

Three years later the favor comes back. On a street

corner in Little Italy, Sonny Red tells DeStefano, "If you kill him, you better be sure he's a rat, because he's a friend of ours."

This was Leuci's story to the prosecutors. It was unsupported, and the other detective was one of the most decorated cops in Police Department history. His commendations, among them the Medal of Honor, covered two full pages, and they attested not only to his shrewdness, but also to his bravery. No criminal prosecution against him was ever initiated on Leuci's charges, for the alleged crime was already five and a half years in the past, and no corroborating evidence or witnesses could be found.

He was, however, brought up on charges in the Police Department trial room in 1975, eight years after the alleged crime, and Leuci's testimony was taken. Although trial commissioner Philip Michael wrote in his opinion that he did not disbelieve Leuci, nonetheless he noted that he could not convict an officer with such a record on the unsupported testimony of a fellow officer. The detective was permitted to retire from the Police Department with full pension rights.

12

"THAT WAS the first time?" asked Morvillo.

"The first big score, yes." It was his first meeting with his cousin after thirteen years, and his first meeting with the legion of Mafia hoodlums who became his contacts within organized crime and, in some cases, his friends.

"What else?" demanded Morvillo.

Leuci described selling, for $10,000, a botched case that Bernie Geik, who was an SIU detective at the time, had been trying to put together against Mafia drug dealer Stanley Simons.

There was a cynical half-smile on Morvillo's face, and his head nodded up and down. "How much did you get for that?"

"Twenty-five hundred dollars," said Leuci.

"That makes forty-five hundred so far. What else?"

Leuci described accepting $1000 for putting Mikey Coco together with Detective Dick Bell.

Morvillo nodded. "What did you do with all this money?"

Well, he had bought three cars in two years, he had bought fancy clothes, he had gone into expensive Italian restaurants with other SIU detectives. His eyes were on the floor, and his voice had dropped so low it was almost a whisper.

Nodding, Morvillo strode to the door, but when he had grasped the handle he turned abruptly. "You want to know something?" he said. "You're a fucking crook."

"I know that."

"You should be in jail."

"I know that."

Morvillo's voice rose. "Why aren't you in jail? You tell me why you aren't in jail."

"Because no one caught me," Leuci said. "What I just told you, you weren't good enough to catch me at."

"Oh?" said Morvillo, and a big smile came onto his face. "Is that what you are going to say on the witness stand? Because when you testify, you're going to be asked that question. The reason you are not being prosecuted is not because no one caught you. Because, in fact, once you told us, we caught you. The reason you are not being prosecuted is because we see fit not to prosecute you." Warmth came into his voice. "Because what you did is something special." He paused. "It's not going to be easy, Bob."

"I know it's not going to be easy."

"When you're on the stand, there will be a lot of name-calling. You're going to have to try to explain these three situations. That's all there were? Three?"

Leuci was not under oath, and he could go no further today.

All the following week, Sagor and Morvillo, who had now decided to try the case himself, worked late into the night preparing Detective Leuci for cross-examination. Over and over again they hammered at him, trying to trick him or trap him exactly as the defense lawyer was sure to do.

"What else have you done, detective?"

But Leuci remained firm.

With the trial now less than a week away, the defense lawyer, Albert Krieger, asked to interview Leuci.

"You have to give your permission," Morvillo advised him. "If you don't want to do it, you don't have to."

Leuci thought about it.

"He wants to size you up, I suppose," said Morvillo. "But it's also a chance for you to size him up."

The meeting took place in Morvillo's office. Leuci, as was his way, examined the man sartorially first, and after that examined his manicure, his scent, the hair in his ears. Krieger had a totally shaved head. He was beautifully, expensively dressed. His fingernails were lacquered, his after-shave lotion pungent.

Krieger's questioning was low-keyed, almost gentle. It

focused immediately on Leuci's past misconduct. Each question seemed carefully thought out in advance. Each was delivered in a soft, calm voice. Leuci answered the same way.

Morvillo, seated behind his desk, said nothing. When the questioning had gone on for some time, Krieger glanced toward Morvillo. "This Detective Leuci is a very charming guy," he said. "I believe we are in a lot of trouble."

"I know you are," answered Morvillo with a smile.

Krieger stood up, closed his briefcase, and prepared to leave.

"You're very disarming, Mr. Krieger," said Leuci. "I hope you are going to be this kind to me in court."

"You can bet that I won't be," answered the lawyer. "We're dealing here with a man's career, and with his life. Eddie Rosner is not such a terrible man."

"That's open to conjecture," said Morvillo.

Krieger peered at Leuci. "Three acts of misconduct, eh, detective? Three acts in eight years? I want you to know that I've done a great deal of work in the narcotics area. I've defended narcotics users, narotics dealers. I defended Detective Kelly a few years ago. Did you know Detective Kelly?"

Kelly had been an SIU detective. "I know Kelly," said Leuci.

"I know you know Kelly. And Kelly knows you. I've spoken to a number of addicts who have come forward and who will testify during this trial. They say they know you too. They say that maybe you are guilty of more acts of misconduct than you admit to."

"Well, they're lying."

"They very possibly could be. It's not unusual for someone to come in and lie about someone else. But when we get into court, I want you to understand that I'll be asking you questions about specific people."

Morvillo had jumped to his feet. "Hey, Al, let's not get carried away here. Okay, Al?"

"I just want Bob to know what to expect."

As Krieger walked out of the office, Leuci's eyes were

fixed on the back of the lawyer's bald head. Morvillo's eyes were fixed on Leuci.

"Bob, look at me," the prosecutor said. "I want to ask you one last time. I promise you I won't ask you again. Is there anything else in your past besides these three acts of misconduct?"

Morvillo and Leuci looked intently at each other. Elliot Sagor glanced from one to the other.

"What are you asking me, Bob?" asked Leuci.

"I'm asking you if there is anything else besides these three situations?"

After a moment Leuci said, "There is nothing else."

Morvillo nodded several times. "There fucking better not be, because if that man comes into court and proves that there is, then you're going to get locked up for perjury."

A perceptible choke had come into Leuci's voice. "Suppose he brings in a witness to testify that I've done something else?"

"He can walk in a hundred junkies, a hundred dope dealers. That's not what I mean."

There was a moment of heavy silence. "I understand what you are saying," mumbled Leuci.

"Okay, I'll see you at the trial."

Leuci went out of the office. Addicts. His mind was churning. Which ones had Krieger got his hands on?

13

A FREEZING COLD NIGHT in February. Leuci has just driven home to Kings Park, fifty miles from the city, when his phone rings. It is his informant, Johnny, and he is sobbing. "Bobby, I'm sick, I can't sleep."

They have worked all day together, making buys, setting up arrests, and in the morning will work together again. When Leuci left him two hours ago, he had had one bag of heroin to get him through the night.

"Whatever it was, Bobby, it wasn't heroin. It made me sick, Bobby."

Gina is sitting up in bed.

Johnny starts crying. "Bobby, I can't sleep."

"Johnny, can't you go out in the street and see anybody around? What about your girl?"

"She's gone. Oh, Bobby, please come back and get something for me."

In the middle of the night Leuci gets in his car and drives back into Brooklyn. Johnny lives in Red Hook, not far from the piers. Leuci rings his bell, and he comes out. His nose is running, his eyes are tearing, and he's retching.

"Get in the car, John. We'll ride down to the Union Street station house. I may know a detective in the squad."

Leuci parks outside the station house. Upstairs in the squad room he finds a detective he knows slightly.

"Listen, do you have any stuff around?" Leuci asks. "I need it for a stool of mine."

"I'm not in Narcotics," says the detective. "I don't know if I have anything in my locker or not." But in a moment he returns with a crumpled glassine envelope. Leuci looks at it. Thanking the detective, he goes down to Johnny. Right away Johnny grabs the envelope. A big grin comes into his face. He holds the envelope to the light, flicks it with his finger, taps it. "Yeah," he says, "there is stuff here. Come on, Bobby, take me down by the water."

As he drives, Leuci glances into the back seat. On the seat, Johnny has his works already laid out. His hypodermic is an eye dropper with a needle attached. His bottle cap and string are ready. He's rubbing his arm.

Leuci has parked. In the back seat of the car Johnny is heating his bottle cap. Suddenly he screams. Leuci, who is trying not to watch, turns sharply in his place. The "heroin" is fizzing up like Alka-Seltzer.

"I don't know what this is," sobs Johnny. He throws it down. "What am I going to do, Bobby?"

Near the piers lives a man named Pollock who sells nickel bags out of his house. Leuci drives there and parks out front.

"You gotta buy me something, Bobby."

But Leuci has no money.

So he studies Pollock's house. It sits by itself amongst the piers. Up the street Leuci spies someone coming—by his walk, obviously a junkie. Hands in his coat against the freezing wind, the junkie goes into Pollock's building.

In the back seat, Johnny is sobbing. "Oh Bobby, you gotta buy me something."

Leuci says, "Johnny, when that guy comes out I'm going to take him. I'll take whatever he just bought off Pollock and give it to you."

"Good, man," says Johnny. His tears stop. He is bouncing up and down with glee.

"Get down out of sight," snaps Leuci.

The junkie comes out of Pollock's house, and as he passes the car Leuci, who has slumped down, sits bolt upright. Immediately the junkie starts to run. Leuci springs from his car and runs after him. Behind him Johnny is running too. They run through the piers. Leuci, furious, catches up to the junkie and dives at him, a flying tackle that knocks him down. As he buckles, Leuci punches him as hard as he can in the face. He can feel the junkie's nose crunch. The junkie screams, but the scream becomes a whimper. "Don't hurt me, Babyface. Don't hurt me."

Leuci is sitting on his chest. Behind him Johnny is screaming, "Kill him, kill him."

"Johnny, go back to the car."

This junkie's name is Vinny. Leuci knows him—a kid from the neighborhood. Now his nose is shattered, he's bleeding, and he's shaking like an infant.

"Where is your junk?" snarls Leuci.

"Don't take my junk. Please don't take my thing. I've been out all day stealing, man. I made twenty-five dollars, enough to buy a spoon."

A spoon is five bags.

"I've got to take it, or lock you up. One or the other."

"Take half of it, don't take all. Please let me go home. Don't lock me up."

"Wait right here," orders Detective Leuci. Clutching the spoon bag, he goes back to the car. The night is freezing cold, and Johnny cowers now in the back seat.

"Do you have it, Bobby? Give it to me."

Leuci is consumed by an almost overpowering hatred. He hates both of these addicts. Opening the spoon bag, Leuci pours half of it into the envelope the detective gave him.

"Here. Now take your fucking works and go home." Johnny lives three blocks away. "Run the fuck home. If you get locked up, you're on your own. I'll see you in the morning."

"Thanks, Bob. Thanks a lot, man. You did good, man. You have some left hook, man."

Leuci returns to Vinny, who is sitting on the curb crying and bleeding. Blood from his nose is all over his face, his clothes.

"My nose is broken," he sobs. "I'm sick."

Leuci hands him the bag of heroin that contains now only two shots. "Get in the car. I'll take you home."

A young woman opens Vinny's front door. She looks from him to Leuci and back again.

"Don't worry," says Vinny proudly. "I have something."

At once she has forgotten Leuci. "Oh, thank God, thank God, where is it?"

He gives her the bag containing two shots, and at the

sink washes his face. "I'm sick," he says. "I'll be all right, though. As long as she's okay."

She comes out of the bedroom. "Did you save me anything?" asks Vinny anxiously.

She wears a kind of half-smile. "I blew my first shot," she says.

"You fucking liar," screams Vinny.

"I had to take two," she whines. "I blew the first one."

"Oh, you liar. Didn't you even leave me enough so I can get through the night?"

Leuci almost bolts for the door. But Vinny runs after him. "Bobby, do you have anything in the car? Can't you give me something, Bobby. Bobby, please. Bobby—"

On his way home, Leuci reaches Exit 40 and starts seeing trees again, starts seeing a whole other world.

14

MORVILLO RARELY TRIED cases himself, but this one had turned very big. Media interest in Leuci was high—*Life* magazine had devoted a full-scale profile to him—and there was equally intense interest in the fate of the clean-cut lawyer, Rosner, partly because of the two characters, DeStefano and Lamattina, with whom he seemed to have associated himself. In the days preceding the trial, Morvillo was obliged to devote considerable time to dealing with the press.

Ten times a day other prosecutors, stopping by his office, volunteered to help him with any unfinished tasks. Morvillo himself began to feel anxiety. He began to talk frequently about how good a lawyer Al Krieger was, and about how much Krieger must be costing Rosner.

His one nagging worry was Leuci. He didn't know how Leuci would behave on the stand, under pressure. He didn't know if the jury would believe Leuci. Several times he considered giving his star witness a lie detector test, but when he talked it over with his assistant prosecutors, all advised him not to risk it—not because they doubted Leuci, but because he had lived a double life for so long and because he seemed to them now so emotionally fragile that the apparatus would not be able to test him fairly. Hook his blood pressure, his pulse rate, and his sweat glands to the machine, and very likely he would register a lie the moment you asked him his name. The polygraph instrument, under certain conditions, was virtually infallible, Morvillo believed. However, in no way did Detective Leuci match these conditions, or so it seemed to him.

In addition, he and his aides understood and sympathized with the ever-tightening strain under which

Leuci lived. He was now, in a certain sense, a man without a country. He would never be able to go back to his past. He had become a man without a past. He had no future anyone could discern—certainly not as a cop in New York—and his present was bleak as well, inasmuch as he had no real home and could draw little sustenance from his wife and children, whom he saw only on weekends. No wonder he sometimes seemed to them close to a breakdown. To question his credibility now, Morvillo decided, might throw him over the edge. If that happened, not only would Detective Leuci be destroyed, but so would the case against Rosner, DeStefano, and Lamattina.

As jury selection began, Lamattina abruptly pleaded guilty to two of the seven counts against him. Two days later DeStefano also capitulated, and Morvillo found himself rushing to restructure his case against Rosner as sole remaining defendant. Before testifying, Leuci would be obliged to confess in open court to past misconduct of his own. Morvillo had wanted Rosner on trial with the other two men. Leuci would have seemed like a choirboy by comparison. Also, Rosner would surely have seemed tainted when standing in the same dock with two such men.

So now what?

Morvillo could perhaps use Lamattina and DeStefano as corroborating witnesses for the prosecution, but if he did so, they would taint only Leuci. The jury, with three admittedly corrupt law enforcement officers arrayed against him, might sympathize entirely with Rosner.

Morvillo decided he would call Leuci only.

With this decision made, Morvillo's nervousness left him. And on the appointed day he strode into a courtroom that was as packed and as tense as a football stadium. Sagor, in his opening statement to the jury, described Detective Leuci as a thirty-two-year-old police officer who almost two years ago had come forward of his own volition, had confessed to several past acts of mild misconduct, and then had conducted a sixteen-month undercover investigation at great risk and peril to himself.

Krieger then made his own opening statement, asking the jury to understand what had happened to this young lawyer—Rosner was then thirty-six—who had been under indictment by the federal government, and who had been very worried about that indictment. And then who should come forth, continued Krieger, but this super-slick detective with his offer to save Rosner's life. This super-slick detective offered to provide Rosner with information outlining how the government had framed him in that pending case. Would any human being not buy such information? Throughout the trial Krieger would continue to ask the jury to compare the life and the lifestyle of Eddie Rosner, whose pregnant wife could be seen in the front row of the courtroom, to the life and lifestyle of the main witness against him, corrupt Detective Robert Leuci.

Calling Leuci to the stand, Morvillo began by asking the same questions that the detective had already answered hundreds of times when testifying against defendants he had arrested. Will you tell us by whom you are employed? And in what capacity? And for how long? Then Morvillo said, "Now, Detective Leuci, while you were employed by the New York City Police Department, did you engage in any acts of misconduct? Will you tell the jury generally what those acts were and when they took place?"

Leuci on the witness stand was terrified, but so far he appeared only very nervous. Morvillo calmed him down, and suddenly Leuci felt comfortable. He was a cop on the witness stand, and this was nothing new to him. He was a member of the New York Police Department. Morvillo kept calling him "Detective Leuci," soothing words to him, until at last Leuci was able to convince himself of the one central fact: I'm not on trial here, Rosner is.

With that, a great calm came over Leuci, and he began to explain the three situations already described to Morvillo in private, in which he had taken money. As he spoke he tried to judge the reaction of the jurors. He thought he could see them nodding with sympathy, as if they understood how he had been put in a compromising spot—how he had been offered money, how in a moment of weakness he had taken it.

Leuci looked out over the crowded courtroom. Every seat was taken. There were standees in the aisles. Except for arraignment court at night, he had never before testified in a full courtroom. He had never before looked out on rows of reporters taking notes.

"In addition to these situations," asked Morvillo, "did you ever engage in any other misconduct of any kind?"

The courtroom had gone silent. The jurors leaned forward expectantly, and when Leuci had answered several sat back nodding their heads in agreement.

"No, sir," said Leuci in a clear voice.

And so the focus of the trial moved to the defendant, who sat with his head down, while Leuci described the wearing of transmitters into restaurants, and the passing of documents to DeStefano in exchange for money.

Sometimes Leuci studied notes before replying. Often he coughed nervously, or sipped from a glass of water. Then the jurors donned earphones, were handed transcripts, and the incriminating tapes were played— four hours of them.

DeStefano: "Are you going to get me those grand jury papers?"

Leuci: "If there's any way possible, I'll get them."

DeStefano: "Here you go." And he had handed Leuci an empty pack of cigarettes containing $1150.

Leuci: "What's here?"

DeStefano: "Eleven and a half."

In the tense courtroom another tape was threaded onto the machine.

Leuci: "All right, all right, all right, so listen. I'll put that—I'll put that to him. Fifteen hundred dollars for the grand jury minutes, and aside from that, more important, a thousand I'm getting, you know."

Rosner: "How long will it take to get them?"

Leuci: "Well, let's find out. Like I said to him, you know—"

DeStefano: "We don't get it pronto, then we don't need them."

Rosner: "Doesn't do us any good to get it at the last minute."

The jury also listened to a conversation in which Rosner took part, about a missing narcotics informant Leuci was asked to find; Leuci expressed reluctance for fear the informant would be killed.

Now Defense Attorney Albert Krieger, shaven head shining, advanced toward Leuci in the witness box and cross-examination began. Krieger started slowly, calmly, underplaying his role, taking Leuci step by step back to the three admitted acts of misconduct, probing for details, asking the same questions over and over again, seeking through repetition to discredit the witness.

Krieger: "At this point, did you believe yourself to be committing a crime?"

Krieger: "So from the time you went to contact Mr. Simons, you knew that you were committing a crime?"

Krieger: "Did these detectives know at that time that you would be receptive to the proposition of selling evidence?"

The witness became increasingly nervous.

Krieger: "What did you do with the money?"

Krieger: "Where did you count the money?"

At the end of the first day of cross-examination, Leuci was standing glumly in a little room beside the courtroom, when Shaw came in.

"You were fantastic," said Shaw. "You were calm, quiet. The jurors were looking at you and we sensed that they feel sorry for you."

Well, maybe.

The trial continued. Turning to the tapes, Krieger read certain conversations from the transcripts, for he wanted the jury to hear again the vicious, sometimes obscene language employed by the chief government witness. He wanted the jury to hear again how Leuci had described Rosner on tape as "that cheap Jew," and again as "that goddamn cheap Jew."

The presiding judge, Arnold Bauman, was Jewish. There were Jews on the jury. Later Krieger made a short speech to the effect that we don't need Buchenwald or

Auschwitz—we have Leuci.

Some defense attorneys not only scream, but also call witnesses vile names. Krieger's technique was far more subtle. Leuci was now on the stand for the third straight day, and Krieger's approach was still low-keyed, almost intellectual.

In predictable sequence came his next series of questions. Apart from these three corrupt situations to which Leuci had just admitted in open court, had Leuci committed any other corrupt acts? Nothing? In eleven years as a cop? In eight years as a narcotics detective? Come now, detective. Had he never perjured himself in court? Never made an illegal wiretap? Never taken money from informants? Never given drugs to informants? Never sold drugs himself? Never?

Leuci had convinced himself of his own righteousness. He was telling the absolute truth about Edmund Rosner.

And so to each of Krieger's direct questions, Leuci answered: No.

Krieger focused in on informants.

"You never gave heroin to informants?"

"No, never."

"You're telling me now that in all your years in narcotics, you never gave a piece of narcotics to anyone?"

"I never did."

"Do you know a man named Richie Carti?"

"He's an informant of mine."

"Did you ever give Carti heroin?"

"I never gave Carti heroin."

"Did you ever give Carti heroin to sell?"

"I never gave Carti heroin, period."

"Do you know a man named Frank Reggio? Did you ever give Reggio heroin?"

15

INFORMANTS LIKE REGGIO can be used for a month, three months if they are lucky. Despite instructions to the contrary, they stay in their own neighborhoods most times. They take the undercover detective to dealers they know—who, when arrested, know right away who the informant was. The dealer or his lawyer reads the affidavit and they figure it out: I sold to only three guys that day, to my brother, to my brother-in-law, and to this fucking Reggio and that guy that was with him that looked like a fucking cop, and that I've never seen since or before.

Informants become exhausted from getting beaten up. They become petrified of the street, but they have the sickness. They have habits that they have to take care of every day, and now the only people who will give them drugs are cops.

This adds up in Brooklyn alone to twenty-five or thirty addicts at a time who can no longer go in the street, can no longer buy narcotics, and who now count on policemen. They will work with any cop, cops from Safe and Loft, cops from local precinct squads. They become informants. That's the only thing they do, and they aren't even good informants.

They go down to the courthouse every day. They know which detectives are there, and they wait outside by their cars. Most detectives will give heroin even to another detective's informant. If he has anything, he will give it to them. This is no longer in exchange for work. These guys are finished as informants. The heroin is given away out of pity.

Narcotics detectives are paid every two weeks at the First Precinct. On payday hundreds congregate from all over the city. From a junkie's standpoint these are hundreds and hundreds of bags going into the station house to be paid, and they line up and stand there begging.

Some detectives laugh and walk by. Some mock them. Most, like Leuci, give. This is illegal, but not hard to justify. The junkie is probably twenty years older than I am, the detective thinks, and how does a man deal with another man who cries and begs? Impossible. I just can't deal with it. I do whatever he wants me to do. I give him something that costs me nothing, that he needs.

There is no fear to walking around with junk in their pockets. Nor in asking another detective for some bags. Yet some detectives are very careful. One has an old diary; he keeps bags in the cut-out pages of this diary in his pocket. Others have magnetic key boxes that they stick under the dashboard or hood of their cars.

Some are less careful. Once Leuci gets a call from the cleaner, who has found three bags of heroin in his pocket.

"What the hell is this? Is it heroin? I know you are a cop, but there has to be something wrong."

"Yeah, it's heroin." Leuci takes the bags and goes home. He is not afraid of arrest. Who is going to arrest him, IAD? The IAD guys are focused on gambling corruption, and so far have left narcotics alone.

Inevitably, addict-informants become almost part of Leuci's family. They are as dependent on him as his own children. He becomes convinced it is his responsibility to take care of them. After a day's work, each addict crawls back into some hovel. It seems heartless to leave him without anything, to be sick, when he has been with you for weeks.

Often in the middle of the night his home phone rings. The informant may be sitting in the Waldorf Cafeteria, or some such all-night place, alone or in a group, and he is high, stoned out. He wants to talk to a relative, or to somebody who cares about him, to say that he is feeling good. It is a different kind of talk, quiet, relaxed. Addicts' lives seem to have some kind of normalcy when they are high.

"You know, I used to have a house," one tells Leuci one night.

16

"DID YOU EVER give Reggio heroin?"

At times Reggio would shine and wax Leuci's car for hours, and when Leuci finally came out of the station house, or out of court, Reggio would greet him with a big grin, hoping to be rewarded with a bag of heroin.

The names kept spilling out of Krieger's mouth, even the street names, names like Pale Face, Blood, Young Blood.

"No. Never."

"All right," said Krieger.

Later, he began calling each of the named addicts to the stand. One by one they were walked into the courtroom, sworn in, and interrogated. Some were high, and stoned, and sick. Each testified to heroin deals with Leuci.

At last Judge Bauman asked Krieger how many more such witnesses he intended to call. A good number, Krieger replied, for Leuci—Babyface—was infamous, and such witnesses as these were available in a line that would stretch out around the block.

"They have smelled up my courtroom for the last day and a half," Judge Bauman said. He remarked that he had sat in judgment or otherwise dealt with narcotics addicts and dealers for years, and found them to be totally venal, totally unbelievable. Any jury, he believed, would feel the same.

Leuci had convinced himself still again that he had told the jury the truth. Whether, as a corrupt detective, he was involved in three situations, or three thousand, didn't matter. He had been able to face Rosner and say: I was a corrupt cop. Therefore he was being totally honest with Rosner and with the jury, and the jury now should judge the facts of the case, based on the recordings that he had made, and on the fact that he had been honest in admitting his own wrongdoing.

And so the jury retired to deliberate.

"Are you angry with me?" asked Leuci. He and Morvillo were waiting it out in Morvillo's office.

"No, I'm not angry with you. You did a great job. I just hope I didn't forget anything. I hope my summation was okay."

The verdict, after twelve hours of deliberation, was guilty on five of the seven counts.

In Morvillo's office, a kind of euphoria broke out. Every attorney in the building seemed to want to shake Morvillo's hand, to pat him on the back.

"You did it!" they cried. "You did it!"

But Morvillo said softly, "Not me, him," and he pointed to his chief witness. "He did it."

"I'd just like to get home now," said Leuci.

Shaw was there. "You were a great witness," he said.

Scoppetta telephoned. "Congratulations, Bob. Keep going. This is only the beginning."

Only the beginning. Leuci had already realized this for himself.

"It's not over for Rosner," said Morvillo, who stood with his arm around the government's chief witness. "There are going to be appeals and motions."

"What do you mean?" asked Leuci, alarmed. "He was convicted by a jury."

"He has money to spend. He's not going to sit still for this. He's going to ask for a new trial."

"Based on what?"

"New evidence. Don't forget, you admitted to only three acts of misconduct."

"That's right."

"Rosner apparently doesn't believe that, and neither does Krieger. They'll try for a new trial. You can expect a lot of motion papers."

"It's not important to me what Rosner believes," said Leuci. "What's important to me is what you and Sagor believe."

Leuci and his bodyguards went downstairs and out of the building.

Another trial came with a rush—the two detectives who had accompanied Sergeant Perrazzo to the hotel room to rip off the supposed drug courier, Federal Agent Sandy Bario. Leuci took the stand and was sworn in. Same questions, same answers. Better, rougher lawyer, who hammered the witness until his mind numbed, and he began to fear that in a moment he would crack, and begin to babble.

On to the next cases. More tapes to study and restudy, commuting to the Catskills weekends. More facts and details to dredge up out of memory. Shoveling snow away from the door of the cabin. More testimony to prepare. More prosecutors to fend off, to win over.

In an unstable world, prosecutors' offices were and are unstable at ten times the national average, a hundred times. The criminal justice system moves with the speed of a glacier, an inch at a time, but prosecutors move on like lightning. Most come in as assistant D.A.'s assistant U.S. attorneys at the age of twenty-four or so, fresh out of law school, at ridiculously low salaries. A year later they are trying major cases against defense lawyers of thirty years' experience, who earn sometimes hundreds of thousands of dollars a year. Some young prosecutors are naturally gifted, and win cases right away. Most are not and don't. Either way they learn their trade, and in less than five years resign to become rich lawyers in their turn. To say this is not a condemnation, merely a description, and five years of public service is more than most men give.

Scoppetta and Shaw had moved on. Morvillo was about to go into private practice, with Whitney North Seymour close behind him, and Detective Robert Leuci at the start of the new year, 1973, was handed over to a new young prosecutor, Richard Ben Veniste, twenty-nine. Ben Veniste would not last long. Within a few months he would move to Washington to direct the investigation into the Watergate coverup, passing Leuci on to still another assistant U.S. attorney.

Each of these shifts was, to the detective, as painful as a

divorce, but there was never time to grieve. Instead, with
each change he set out immediately to court the
replacement. He wanted each of these men, in effect, to
fall in love with him. Only then would they want to
protect him when—when what?—when whatever was
going to happen finally happened. Leuci didn't know
what this would be, or how soon. But he sensed perfectly
well that it would be dreadful.

In fact, each of these men in turn did fall in love with
him. They found him intelligent, observant, extremely
perceptive too, and these are admirable qualities in any
man. Furthermore, they believed that what he had done
and continued to do required uncommon courage.

But more than all this, his entire being seemed turned
toward them. He was tremendously open and vulnerable.

On the fourth floor of the Southern District Courthouse Leuci's telephone rang. One of his bodyguards
picked it up. With his hand over the mouthpiece, he said
to Leuci, "Hey, there's a guy on the phone. It sounds like
he's not a cop. He says he's The Baron."

"That's my stool," said Leuci. "I'll talk to him." The
Baron, he knew, had been working as an informant for
the Bureau of Narcotics at a salary that may have reached
at times $1000 a week. He was an outstanding informant.

Leuci put the phone to his ear. "They cut me off the
program about three weeks ago," said The Baron. "I'm
going to blow my house, I'll probably blow my boat. My
car is in hock. I'm in all kinds of problems."

"Larry, what are you trying to tell me?" Leuci had gone
weak with the sudden onrush of terror.

"You understand, Bobby. I'm flat broke. I've got kids,
I've got a wife. I've got the same kinds of problems you've
got."

"Larry, I don't know what you're trying to tell me,"
said Leuci. "Do whatever you've got to do. Just don't lie."
The terror was making him babble. "I'll be seeing you
around, Larry."

"Yeah, I guess so," said The Baron, and he hung up.

Someone's paying him to testify against me, Leuci told
himself. Who's paying him? What will he say? Will it be

believed? Leuci was trying to think, trying to consider his options.

An hour later he reported the conversation to Ben Veniste. The lawyer, apparently unimpressed, told him to make a memorandum about it and put it in the files.

"He'll come in and say I did all sorts of things, maybe," said Leuci.

"Let him come in and prove it to me," said Ben Veniste. "Fucking creep."

Leuci, smoking incessantly, waited and worried. It was too late to do anything else.

Allegations charging Leuci with perjury, and other crimes as well, were even now being prepared. In a few hours they would reach Morvillo's desk.

17

LEUCI, aged twenty-eight, is brand-new in SIU, and The Baron is the first SIU informant he has ever seen. Until now he has known only street informants, most of them addicts.

The Baron, whose name is Richard Lawrence, has come to him as part payment for the shakedown of the Indelicatas. Having been given The Baron's phone number, Leuci calls and introduces himself, and they arrange to meet on Houston Street and Avenue D. Though the other detective has promised him to Leuci, the decision will be made by The Baron himself, who is probably auditioning a number of new narcotics teams.

It is said that The Baron can work with any narcotics team he chooses. He is a fantastic informant who works off and on for the Bureau of Narcotics, for the Treasury Department, and for the Police Safe and Loft Squad, as well as for Police Narcotics. Leuci will have to sell himself to this man.

At last The Baron's car pulls up—an oil-green Eldorado with a black vinyl top and a telephone on the back shelf—and The Baron steps out. A tall, forty-two-year-old black man, he wears a full-length fur coat, though it is summer, plus a green fedora that matches the color of his car. His shoes and socks are green also. He is a strange-looking dude, Leuci thinks. He has a scar that runs from behind his ear across his cheek and over to his chin. Another scar runs from behind the other ear straight across his throat.

"Some scars," says Leuci.

"Combat marks, man. Combat marks."

Both men climb into The Baron's Cadillac. As he

drives, The Baron puts on his stereo. They ride up and down the streets of the East Village. "Can you get me some goods?" asks The Baron.

"What are you talking about? What kind of goods?"

"Can you get me some goods? You know what I'm talking about."

Leuci thinks about it.

"Larry," he says presently, "I don't know you, you don't know me. I know you worked this road for years. Let me tell you where it's at, as far as I'm concerned. I'll work day and night with you, and I'll make any kind of worthwhile case. You get in any kind of trouble, I don't care if it's homicide or what, and I guarantee you within an hour after you're locked up I'll get you out."

Leuci pauses. "There is only one difference between you and me. You are a connection. You are a dope dealer, and I'm a cop. We ain't going to switch them roles. You are not going to become the cop, and I'm not going to become the dope dealer. You want to do something in the street, you do it. I'll be there to protect you. But don't ask me to become a fucking dope dealer. Are you a junkie, Larry?"

"Am I a junkie? Do I look a fool to you?" The Baron's face has darkened. He pulls to the curb, leans across and pushes open Leuci's door. "What did you ask me here for? The kind of deal you offer I can get from anybody. I can work for any team, for any detective or federal agent in the city. What the fuck do I need you for? You're going to keep me out of jail. Big deal. I need somebody I can get stuff from all the time."

"Larry, here's my home phone number, I'll work with you. I want to work with you. But those are the conditions. You're not turning me into any fucking dope pusher."

"The kind of cases that I make, there is a lot of money around, man."

"You are talking about something different now. If there is money there, you are an equal partner."

"I'll think about it, and let you know," says The Baron.

A pensive Leuci watches the Eldorado drive away. He

is convinced he has blown the audition. He will never hear from The Baron again.

Back at SIU, Leuci recounts the story.

"This guy is not some jerk from Harlem," remarks another detective. "He's a connected guy. Promise him anything he wants. If you have to promise him a package to get him, then promise it."

"You promise it," retorts Leuci. "This guy works for the feds, he works for the D.A.'s office. He's a professional stool pigeon. If you think I'm going to put my life in his hands, you're crazy. I'm not looking to do twenty-five years."

"All right," said the other detective. "But if you could have got him, you would have been in fantastic shape."

Two weeks later, Leuci gets a call at home about eleven o'clock at night. He can hear music in the background. "Bobby? This is Larry. Same place, same time tomorrow, right?"

Leuci phones Mandato at once. "Hey, The Baron called me."

The next day The Baron gets out of his car wearing a big grin. It is as if the previous conversation never took place.

"I have a guy up in the Bronx," The Baron says. "An Italian kid. Thinks he's a big-time connection. I think I can buy a thousand-dollar package off him."

"How about you just talk to the guy?" suggests Leuci.

"I don't go around talking to people. I'm The Baron." Then he adds, "What is the reason for me to talk to some guinea in the Bronx? If I go talking, I'm talking about buying a package."

"What are you telling me, Larry?"

"Give me a thousand dollars."

"Go fuck yourself."

But Leuci seeks to persuade The Baron to meet this connection. "At least let us take a look at him," he pleads.

Finally The Baron agrees—and then he spends the next hour lecturing Leuci on how to put the case together. He knows where the Italian comes from, how he operates, and suspects who his Mafia contact must be.

Leuci listens with his mouth open, marveling at The Baron's knowledge and skill. No wonder all the teams want him as an informant!

After a couple of days Leuci receives another call. "I'm going to meet this guy tomorrow up in the Bronx near the Concourse Plaza Hotel."

Leuci and his team set up surveillance across the street in the park. From the park they watch this amazing actor who is The Baron take over. He sticks his finger in the guy's face—a tough Italian guy, supposedly—then turns his back on him, walks away, comes back, smiles, cajoles. The connection has his head down. He looks up, he shrugs. What do you want from me? The Baron steps back and yells at him. Finally The Baron gives a disgusted wave of his hand and strides away.

The detectives have a prearranged meeting place down by Yankee Stadium. When The Baron arrives, he beckons them to join him in his Eldorado, "I don't want to sit in your cramped piece of shit."

For the next several weeks they watch The Baron operate. He keeps bargaining for bigger and bigger loads, moving upward in rank from connection to connection. He requires very little direction. Evidence stockpiles.

Finally Leuci and Mandato make arrests. They grab two men and an eighth of a kilo of heroin. They are in the station house processing the arrests when The Baron calls. Leuci meets him outside.

"Do these guys have any money?" The Baron asks.

"They have no money."

After a moment The Baron says, "I have to see something out of this. This thing has taken eight or nine weeks of my time."

"We got a good case going," responds Leuci. "This thing can go higher. We are into some major Mafia junk dealers."

"So don't you think I ought to see something?"

"There's no money here. At the end of the case maybe there is going to be some money."

"Maybe."

They stare at each other.

"Let me go back and talk to my partners," says Leuci.

Back in the station house he huddles with Mandato and two other detectives assigned to the case. "We have an eighth of a kilo, maybe a little bit more, of evidence," he begins. "I'm petrified of giving him anything. Let's throw in some money together." But the others refuse. They vote unanimously to pay off The Baron by giving him a piece of the package.

Leuci gets an evelope and pours into it about an ounce of evidence, worth maybe $6000 on the street. Then he walks outside and gets into The Baron's car. They sit side by side.

"Man, you better find someone else to work with you," says The Baron. "I'm not going through all this bullshit for nothing. Working for the feds I can get a thousand a week, five hundred a week to do this shit."

"Larry, you did a great job, I want to thank you," says Leuci, and he steps out of the car, leaving the envelope behind him on the seat.

The Baron's electric window comes down. "Hey brother, nice day today, isn't it?" he says, He is grinning.

"It's going to be a good day," agrees Leuci. He is thinking: He's smart enough not to say anything about it. It's over now. I did it.

But back in the station house he begins to worry. He has heard of some sort of atomic test that can trace the route of a package. It can match a kilo of junk to other junk found elsewhere and can determine that both came from the same original package. This fuck could be working for the government, Leuci worries, and if they come up here and seize our evidence, they will prosecute me. Leuci is not worried about the heroin going into some black kid's arm, he is worried about twenty-five years in Attica. If The Baron turns on him—

As a young man The Baron was twice convicted of armed robbery; he spent eleven and a half years in jail. Today he owns a gypsy cab company, a laundromat, a beauty parlor. He has a wife and five kids and lives in the suburbs. He is also a street wholesaler. He has street dealers working for him, making him not quite a major narcotics mover. He operates with impunity because a legion of law enforcement agents, including Leuci now, have chosen not to arrest him in exchange for information.

As time goes on, The Baron constantly pressures Leuci for junk. Leuci becomes increasingly afraid of him, but at the same time more and more dependent on his information. The Baron is at the root of all his major cases. The Baron knows who's dealing and where the junk is coming from. He can cut into any operation. Leuci's instinctive fear increases in direct proportion to The Baron's demands for junk.

About twice a year The Baron gets arrested by other teams. Each time Leuci rushes to court, speaks to the district attorney and judge. The Baron gets out on parole, and they go back to work.

18

AND SO The Baron's allegations, purporting to describe his past dealings with Leuci, duly reached Morvillo. Morvillo and his aides were stunned. The allegations laid out names, places, and dates, and described crime after crime in detail. If true—and the details were so precise that they had the ring of truth—then Leuci was one of the most devious felons of all time, and they themselves had been gulled.

Morvillo's first reaction was personal: How is this going to look in the newspapers? How am I going to look? His second reaction was outrage. "I'll lock him up myself," he muttered to Sagor and the others. "I'll try the case myself."

Only after that did a certain calm obtain, and they began to study the charges. The Baron was alleging that illegal narcotics deals took place between himself and Leuci from 1968 up to and including the summer of last year. That is, Leuci had been buying and selling heroin during all of the time he was also working undercover for the government, according to The Baron.

The Baron, or whoever had written this script, had broken these deals down into four categories. He charged first that, several times a month, from 1968 through 1971, Leuci had supplied him with heroin which he diluted and sold; he had then paid Leuci for the cost of these packages. Second, on numerous other occasions Leuci had given him portions of the narcotics seized in cases in which he had assisted Leuci in setting up the arrests, in exchange for which he gave Leuci money and three automobiles. Third, he had been personally involved in transactions where Leuci had sold heroin to three other individuals known as "Slim," "Cornbread," and "The

Saint." Fourth, after Leuci and The Baron had profited financially for most of 1971 from supplying a Buffalo group with heroin, Leuci had arranged the buyer's arrest; the heroin seized at the arrest was the same heroin Leuci had supplied.

1971 was the undercover year. The prosecutors felt sick. They wished to read no further, but had to.

"Another 1971 case in which I received seized narcotics directly from Leuci," they read, "involved the arrest of three people at a Spanish grocery store on the southeast corner of 122nd Street and Lexington Avenue. I had given Leuci information concerning "Cadillac" Joe. When the narcotics arrived in a van, the arrests were made: seven ounces were seized from "Cadillac" Joe, and one ounce from each of two people in the store. Leuci and I later met at Houston Street and Leuci passed me an ounce in his car while we conversed.

"In another case I informed Leuci that I had seen seven kilos of heroin at a particular house on Atlantic Avenue in Brooklyn. Mr. Hershey from the Brooklyn district attorney's office called me to check the information in order to get a search warrant. Four persons were arrested that night, including a woman known as "Clementine" (who subsequently was sentenced to 15 years). A seizure was made at the house of heroin, narcotics paraphernalia, and guns. Leuci gave me three to four ounces of heroin from the seizure."

Now The Baron described meeting Leuci near Broome Street, which was the site of the police property clerk's office, where Leuci handed over heroin still contained in Police Department evidence pouches. The so-called French Connection ripoff of some 300 pounds of heroin evidence from the property clerk's office had come to light only a few weeks previously. Obviously The Baron, or The Baron's ghost writer, was suggesting that Leuci was involved in the ripoff.

"If this is true," muttered Morvillo, "then all our cases will be bad."

"Over the course of my dealings with Leuci," the allegations read, "I regularly gave him money. For a long period of time I gave Leuci approximately $100 a week. I also purchased and gave to Leuci three automobiles in 1969 and 1970: a 1966 yellow and red Oldsmobile (purchased at Fair Motors, Mount Vernon) for Leuci's brother; a 1966 or 1967 blue Plymouth (purchased also at Fair Motors, for about $500–$1000) for Leuci's wife; and a 1966 or 1967 blue Ford Country Squire station wagon (purchased at Manor Lincoln Mercury, Mall Street, White Plains, for approximately $1100) for Leuci's wife. Leuci did not reimburse me for these automobiles; nor did I ask him to.

"To my personal knowledge, Leuci supplied heroin to many other individuals. During the course of my relationship with Leuci I was personally involved in Leuci's transactions with three of these individuals: "Slim," "Cornbread," and "The Saint." I was involved in the "Slim" transactions in two ways: for a period of time Leuci supplied packages of heroin for Slim and me to divide; and sometimes I also helped Slim sell some of the heroin that Slim had received from Leuci. Slim had a barbecue store on Fulton Street, one block north of Washington Street, Brooklyn. Slim and Leuci, I was told, had been friends for years. Leuci introduced me to Slim and then Slim and I worked together making cases for Leuci in Brooklyn.

"During this period, Leuci moved around with New York City Detective Frank Mandato. On at least half a dozen occasions, Leuci and Mandato notified me along with Slim at Slim's store that they had a package of heroin for us. Slim then sent a woman named Jesse or her husband, whose name was also Jesse, to pick up the package. Slim and I then divided up the package on a table in a small room behind the kitchen, which we entered through a hole behind the stove. Slim took about a whole kilo each time for which he paid approximately $32,000. After dividing up the heroin, Slim and I would separate and then a day or so later we would meet with Leuci or Mandato to settle prices. When Slim gave me part of his portion of the heroin to sell I paid Slim the money for it. On several occasions Slim, myself, and

Leuci sat in Leuci's car and discussed these transactions. I was present on two occasions when Slim paid Leuci thousands of dollars for the cost of the heroin."

"This is sickening, sickening," said Morvillo, and he gave orders for The Baron to be brought in and interrogated.

This was done. Under severe questioning The Baron stuck to his story. He would be glad to get on the stand and testify against Leuci, he said, and would do this for nothing. He also wanted to work steadily as an informant for a fee of $5000. He was advised to go fuck himself.

But the prosecutors were worried, and they began trying to check the details of the allegations. When some of the cases and individuals mentioned proved not to exist, they became cheerful, but when the three cars had been traced, they became terrified. Because two proved to be registered in the name of Gina Leuci.

The Baron was advised that if he would take a lie detector test, and if he passed it, the government would be glad to pay him the $5000 he had requested. At this news, The Baron's scar-crossed face broke into a broad grin, and he agreed.

He was flown to Washington and driven to the offices of True Security in Alexandria, Virginia, where he was hooked up to the polygraph sensors. The results were sealed and sent back to Morvillo in New York by courier on the first shuttle the following morning.

Leuci had spent the night, as usual, on Governors Island, and his bodyguards, as usual, had telephoned the office after breakfast to say they were starting in. But a lieutenant got on the phone, demanded to speak to Leuci personally, and then ordered him to report to Morvillo's office forthwith. "Forthwith" was the most curt—and the most urgent—command in the police lexicon.

The detective had become a kind of human seismograph. He was able to measure at once any eruption that occurred in his life, no matter how small, no matter how distant.

Forthwith. Immediately came the terrible tightening in Leuci's stomach. He and his bodyguards got on the ferry and crossed to Manhattan. It could be any number of things, Leuci told himself. Inside the Federal Building he walked down the hall past people with whom he had exchanged smiles every day for months. Today there were no smiles. No one came out of his office to say hello. They all know, Leuci thought. Whatever it is. They all know something terrible is going to happen.

As he neared Morvillo's office on the fourth floor, fear came on strong, and he said to himself, "I'm not going to survive this fucking thing. There is just too much out there. I'm never going to be able to get through this. But I've got to get through this. Whatever it is, I've got to get through it."

He walked into Morvillo's waiting room. The prosecutor's secretary was an Italian girl who always claimed to be looking for an FBI Irish husband. Other mornings Leuci had kidded her. Today she gave him a queer expression, told him to take a seat, and after that wouldn't look up.

Leuci sat down on the couch. Presently Morvillo came out of his office, said nothing, not even good morning, and walked past Leuci into the hall.

"What the hell is going on?" said Leuci to the secretary.

"I don't know," she said vaguely, avoiding his eyes. "He is screaming in there all morning. It has something to do with a lie detector test."

Leuci's panic became total. He is going to make me take a lie detector test. How am I going to get through this thing? How am I going to get through this day?

Morvillo, crossing back into his office, glanced at Leuci, then at the envelope in his hands.

"I haven't opened this envelope yet," he said. "In it are the results of a lie detector test. I want to tell you something. If they are positive, I'm going to prosecute you myself."

"For what?"

"Did you ever hear of the crime of perjury?"

"Do you want to tell me what this is all about?"

"You'll know in a minute." He went inside and slammed the door.

Leuci waited.

The secretary's console buzzed. She said, "Go in. He wants to see you."

Morvillo was sitting at his desk.

"I want you to read this material," said Morvillo, and he tossed The Baron's allegations across the desk.

Reading, Leuci said automatically, "This is bullshit."

"All of it?" said Morvillo. "What if I told you we checked and found that the car part of it is true."

Leuci started to say, "Give me a break," but when he looked up Morvillo was grinning.

"They came to us, I want you to know, five days ago with this thing," said Morvillo. "We didn't know what to do. The Baron came in. We offered him money if he passed a lie detector test. We gave him a series of tests and he failed them all."

Leuci's heart was pounding, but he had started to sense that he was all right. "What did you ask him?"

Morvillo pushed across the questions. There were only about a dozen. The polygraph can measure only yes or no answers. All questions must be phrased with great specificity so as to demand a single yes or no response. Whoever had phrased these had confined himself exclusively to the most serious of The Baron's charges.

Did you and Leuci sell narcotics together?

Did you ever share money with Leuci from the sale of narcotics?

Did Leuci ever give you heroin in evidence vouchers near the property clerk's office?

Each time that The Baron answered yes to these questions, the graph needle had gone off the page.

Morvillo now was ecstatic. "I feel terrific, Bob," he said. "Bob, I felt sick for five days."

"Why didn't you tell me about it?"

"Tell you? Bob, we were deciding on how we were going to lock you up. How was I going to look in the paper?"

These are not my friends, Leuci was telling himself. Tomorrow they could prosecute me and never think twice about it. I have lost all my friends on the other side by now. I have nobody. Then he thought: Sooner or later these people are going to turn on me. There is no escaping this thing.

"By the way," said Morvillo," we want you to explain these cars. We find that both are registered in your wife's name."

"Those cars are mine," said Leuci, "but I never gave him narcotics for them. I paid for both of them. One was an old bomb, and the other was better. I probably paid in cash for them. I don't know."

"So you actually have those cars?" said Morvillo. "How the hell can you take cars from an informant?"

"This happened a long time ago," said Leuci. "The guy owned a taxi cab company. He owned a fleet of cars. I got cars from him for a couple of hundred dollars. I would have had to pay seven or eight hundred some place else."

"He's an informant," said Morvillo. "You don't take things from informants."

"Look, I paid for those cars," said Leuci, and he telephoned his wife, who soon called back to say she had found a canceled check endorsed by The Baron, paying for one of the cars.

Morvillo was jubilant. So was Leuci. They were patting each other on the back.

When Leuci came out of Morvillo's office, his bodyguards read the news on his face. "You did it again," one said. "You got out of it, whatever it was, didn't you?"

Nodding, Leuci thought: But for how much longer?

19

ENTERING the cocktail lounge, three men approached the table where the owner, John Lusterino, sat alone. One threw a newspaper down. It landed hard and split open in front of him.

The bar went instantly silent. In the world in which Lusterino moved this was already an insult. Lusterino was known to have a violent temper.

However, he only locked eyes with his visitors, proving to onlookers both that he knew them, and that they had weight.

Voices were raised. One of the men was thumping a particular article—it concerned Leuci's role in an upcoming trial—with his thumb. Lusterino shook his head several times.

All three visitors stomped out of the lounge.

Lusterino went to a phone and started a message via his mother through his aunt's household to his cousin. Leuci should phone him at once on a matter of great urgency.

Several days passed before the message reached its destination, and a telephone connection was made. Some men had been in his place, Lusterino told Leuci. "They're looking to hurt you, Bobby."

There was a short silence while Leuci digested this news.

"They think you should be hit," Lusterino continued. "I agreed with them. Do you expect me to defend you? I'm not your lawyer, Bobby."

Leuci began to ask quick, nervous questions. Who were the men, did he know them?

"They wanted me to do it," Lusterino interrupted bluntly. "I said, hey, the kid's my cousin. He's my uncle's son. I said I wouldn't do it." After a moment Lusterino added, "I also said I wouldn't interfere. I feel I owe you this much. I owe you a warning and that's all I owe you. Watch yourself, Bobby."

The conversation lasted some time longer. Leuci said he was sorry if he had embarrassed Lusterino, or put him in a position where he would be looked on with less respect than in the past. It was a way of saying: I hope you're not going to be killed because of me.

But Lusterino only laughed. "Listen, anyone I ever introduced you to, anyone that ever wanted to meet you, I always told them you were a cop. Fuck them." And he hung up.

Leuci's protection was already tight. With so many trials depending on him, his life was a valuable commodity to the government. Up to eighteen marshals working three eight-hour shifts guarded the cabin in the Catskills, and six cops guarded Leuci in New York. All these men had been screened for their integrity, for a wrong guard could have sold rights to his life for a lot of money.

Next a private investigator from Los Angeles came forward with information about a plot to assassinate Leuci by attaching a bomb to his car. The private investigator was a former New York police lieutenant. In a Las Vegas casino he had chanced to overhear the plot being discussed by three men. Even the name of the technician who would attach the bomb had been mentioned.

Leuci became paranoid. In the street the sound of a car starting could cause him to shudder, and he approached his own car each time with fear. I'm the guy that's supposed to start the car, he would tell himself, inserting the key. I'm the guy responsible. He always started the car himself. His bodyguards, meanwhile walked to the corner and stood with their fingers in their ears. This usually broke the tension, and everybody laughed.

In the Catskills the cabin stood at the end of a long dirt lane off an already isolated country road. The access lane, with heavily armed men posted along it, wound through the woods to a clearing where the house was. It was an expensive place to guard and an uncomfortable place to live—both for the marshals and for the Leucis. In winter the snow drifts piled to the windows, and in spring the mud rose up over the children's shoes. Because of the isolation, the marshals were rotated every three weeks or so. Gina and the kids were not rotated, nor was Leuci, who had to be driven up there every weekend by bodyguards, a minimum six-hour round trip.

Pressure to move the family became strong.

"I love being up in the mountains in our place," Gina told her husband one Friday night. "But I want our family in a home. This is a summer cottage. I look out the window and my kids are always by themselves. Or else they are playing with men with guns. I want them to be in a neighborhood where there are other children. I want to put a bedroom set together. I want to put a living room set together." Her voice got wistful. "I want a home."

She didn't know about the active investigations into threats against her husband's life, only that the government now decided to relocate the Leucis in northern Virginia. Leuci was flown down there one weekend. He saw and bought a house. The following weekend Gina was flown down and shown the house, and some time after that they moved in. There were no guards on the family in Virginia.

Nothing else changed. Leuci continued to live in the barracks on Governors Island, continued to commute home on weekends, although now it was via Eastern Airlines shuttle; his bodyguards now drove him to the airport every Friday night, and picked him up there every Monday morning. Usually the bodyguards arrived at the terminal an hour early to check out the waiting room first.

One Monday morning they spotted a man who, to their eyes, looked bad. They didn't like the hard-eyed stare with which he scrutinized every arriving passenger. And from the moment Leuci came out the gate, this individual's eyes never left him.

There were three bodyguards that morning: Bill Fritz, Artie Monty, and John Farley, all patrolmen in plain-clothes.

Leuci's bag came off the plane. He picked it up and walked toward the exit doors. When he glanced back the man was following. Monty and Farley were walking beside him. Fritz had gone to get the car.

"We'll walk to the parking lot," said Leuci. "When the car comes up we'll jump in and take off. Let's see what he does."

As Bill Fritz pulled up in the car, they saw the man running to his own car.

Leuci looked out the back window. He watched a late model green Chevy spin out of the parking lot and come up behind them. Everyone tensed up. They drove out of La Guardia onto the Grand Central Parkway. The green Chevy was still with them.

"This guy has got to be crazy," said Leuci. "He's all by himself. There are four of us here. He knows I'm a cop, so I've got a gun. He's got to believe you guys are cops. You all have guns. We got four guns facing one guy."

Monty tried a joke, "Maybe he's got a machine gun under the front seat."

Fritz was hitting eighty. They raced down the parkway. The other car, weaving in and out of traffic, stayed with them.

They sailed up an exit ramp, sped along the service road, and jumped the stop sign. The green Chevy did likewise.

"This fucking guy is chasing us," said Leuci.

They pulled into the next street, stopped the car, threw open the doors and sprang out, guns in their fists, seeking cover. Leuci was behind one car door, Monty behind the other. Farley and Fritz both left the car and ran to the sidewalks, where they crouched behind whatever protection was there.

The Chevy spun around the corner into a residential street blocked by their car. The driver hit his brakes and slid to a stop ten feet away. As he did so the four cops came at him from four different directions, their guns pointed at him.

He put his hands on his head and his head on his steering wheel. Farley pulled him out of the car. The guy sailed out on the fly, his feet never touching the ground.

They searched him. He was not armed. They searched the car but found nothing. He seemed terrified, and he began to claim that he was a horse player. He waited by the shuttle every Monday. Horse trainers would fly up from Virginia and Maryland, go into the city and place enormous bets at the offtrack betting. He would follow them, stand on line behind them, and dump down whatever money he could scratch together on whatever horses they bet.

The four cops threw him into their car. All the way to the Southern District courthouse he pleaded that he had nothing to do with any crime they thought he was doing.

Seeing Leuci come off the plane wearing a leather jacket and boots and a pair of brown slacks, the man insisted, he had taken him for a horse trainer. He kept mentioning a particular trainer's name. "You look just like this guy," he insisted, over and over again.

Leuci said, "You better be right. I better look just like this guy."

The man was thrown into the grand jury, where he swore that he didn't know Leuci, had never heard of Leuci.

Two members of the Police Commissioner's Special Force drove him to his home in Queens. They found an apartment that was empty except for a bed, a table, one or two chairs and a very sad woman who was the man's wife, and who told the story of her husband's sickness. He had long since gambled away all their savings. He was in debt to everyone in her family, in debt to everyone in the neighborhood. He had at one time owned his own taxicab. He had sold his taxicab, sold his medallion. The apartment was cluttered with thousands and thousands of scratch sheets everywhere. So maybe his story was true. Or maybe, in his desperation, he had accepted a hit contract he was incompetent to carry out. He had an Italian name and low-level Mafia connections.

The attitude of Leuci's bodyguards changed dramatically. From then on they treated their jobs as serious business. Whenever they moved they moved professionally.

In the end, the only hit contract carried out was on Lusterino.

Lusterino had grown up in the Brownsville section of Brooklyn in a neighborhood that now, in 1973, was almost entirely black. In his childhood it had been heavily Italian and most of the families had emigrated from the same few Sicilian villages.

Lusterino's father, Marino, was a mason trying to support six children. They lived in a railroad flat that always smelled strongly of cooking oil and tomato paste. All the Lusterinos were big and fair-skinned, and Johnny was a blond with strong arms and a barrel chest.

His first arrest occurred April 1, 1948—grand larceny, auto. The charge was dismissed. The car thief became a burglar. Three years and only two arrests later he was sent to Elmira, his first time inside. When he came out he graduated to membership in a ring hijacking truckloads of furs. Others were caught, not him, but someone informed and, after fighting the case for almost two years, and having been arrested twice more on gun charges in the interim, he was sentenced to ten to fifteen years for first degree robbery. In prison he played on the same football team as Mikey Coco and Sonny Red.

By then he was what the Mafia world knows as a "made guy." He had been taken into full-fledged membership. He was one of the fortunate few. He had proven himself early, and so when he came out of jail he would be given things outright. He would be given money, and the opportunity to make money. Of course he would have to keep paying the men who made him.

Lusterino had a clear perspective on life.

"A man who hasn't spent time in prison and is in street life is not a complete guy," he said once. "It's in prison that you get your real education."

To Johnny there was white and there was black. One might think that men who had stayed out of jail would be called bright, but in Lusterino's world it was the opposite. "So and so is okay," he would say, "but he's never done a day's time." There were no gray areas. A man who hadn't been to prison was probably an informant.

Lusterino believed in rules that were simple to follow. There was nothing he would not do to help a friend—or to hurt an enemy.

When he came out this last time after so long, he was like a man lost. He was amazed at the progress of the world in his absence. The year he left for jail the girls had worn skirts to their ankles. Now they were in miniskirts. He would sit in his lounge watching the young people dance. "It's hard to believe," he would say, shaking his head. He married a go-go dancer from his lounge, a sweet, beautiful young girl named Bea—she was nearly twenty years younger than himself—and very quickly he fathered two children.

He was constantly hustling to make money, and he was constantly on the verge of going to war. People who had been in prison with him came into his lounge, and he gave them money. He often handed his "kid cousin" hundred-dollar bills for no reason.

But one day a friend asked Johnny if he had access to counterfeit money; after making a few calls, Lusterino found a suitcase full of it, which he handed to his friend over the bar. The friend then went to meet his buyer, who was a federal informant accompanied to the meeting by a Secret Service agent. Not only was the friend arrested, but so was Lusterino who had tailed along behind to watch the sale go down.

Whenever Johnny was on the street, law enforcement watched him closely. In the various Mafia albums kept by the police, the FBI, and others, Lusterino had a page to himself marked "at large." It was not clear what he did in organized crime, and so, although most albums called him a captain in the Colombo family, at least one rated him no higher than soldier.

He had moved his mother out of the railroad flat and

set her up in a semidetached house in a quiet street in Queens. It was there that men came to get him one night in March 1973. He had just kissed his mother good night on the porch. There was a brief struggle. A gun appeared. Lusterino got into a car with them, and was never seen again.

Rosa Lusterino had witnessed this, but she told detectives investigating the case that she had recognized no one, knew nothing. They got nothing more out of her.

Though Johnny's body was never found, and though no one was ever brought to trial, the detectives had little difficulty amassing information. As was usual after Mafia hits, the underworld seethed with conversation, and they soon learned the names of two of the three men involved. They also concluded that Lusterino was unquestionably dead.

He was forty-four. He left his wife Bea, who was twenty-six, and two sons, aged three and one, and a shaken cousin.

"Was Johnny killed over me?" Leuci asked himself. When he lay in bed in the dark, he was already seeing faces: Nunziata, Sheridan, Perrazzo. Now, night after night, his cousin's face was there, too, head thrown back, laughing. When in a temper, Lusterino didn't scream or shout, he laughed. He had a crazy, scary laugh, and no one ever laughed back.

Night after night, lying in the dark, Leuci asked himself: Who took him? But any of those men who used to frequent his bar could have done it. What was more difficult to understand was how Lusterino had let it happen. Lusterino would have seen them coming—he bragged that he could always see an enemy coming. Always look for a guy with a smile on his face, Bobby, he used to say. Look for a guy who's smiling, who never smiled before.

Did they torture him before they put him to death? Whenever the police found bodies in the trunks of cars, the guy had usually been tortured first in some grotesque way. Leuci had met a number of the men who performed such tasks.

From then on, Leuci worried about being captured. If a car pulled up and men opened fire on him, or if a bomb went off when he turned the ignition key, it would all be over in an instant. But if they captured him, it would last a very long time.

Mike Shaw realized how much the Lusterino hit had upset Leuci. "You're not holding yourself responsible, are you?" inquired the prosecutor.

"No," Leuci insisted.

"You're blaming yourself," said Shaw. "You're not responsible for other people's actions."

But in the night Leuci continued to see Lusterino's face laughing. He continued to worry too. If they take you, he told himself, you can't talk your way out, or buy your way out. These people don't want an explanation.

For months Leuci continued to ask about Bea and the kids. He asked his mother—he found he couldn't call Bea directly. Rosa Lusterino, Leuci was told, had urged her daughter-in-law to begin dating again, but Bea so far had refused, saying, "Not until I'm positive." But the day came when she announced to the family that she had begun going out with men again. "I want to find a father for my children."

That night in the dark Leuci again saw Lusterino's face, head thrown back, laughing.

20

THAT SPRING still another young prosecutor, Assistant U.S. Attorney Rudy Giuliani, twenty-nine, took over the Leuci cases, and he began to prepare the witness for his next important trial: *The United States of America* v. *Benjamin Caiola*. It was a good strong case. The recordings were unequivocal. The Mafia lawyer had clearly attempted to bribe Detective Leuci.

But Giuliani was troubled nonetheless. Leuci's testimony might be a problem. Giuliani had studied all Leuci's previous testimony, particularly in the Rosner case, and now, every day, he was studying Leuci in person. He saw an emotional young man who wanted everyone to like him, even his natural enemies. If he met Caiola right now he would want Caiola to like him, even as his testimony sent the lawyer to jail.

Leuci was also, Giuliani saw, guilt-ridden, worried, easily upset. Why so guilty? What was he worried about? He displayed a tremendous need to explain why he did what he did, but the explanation never entirely satisfied the young prosecutor. Because Leuci, despite such limited previous misconduct of his own, had made a major commitment to do dangerous, dirty undercover work for the government over a long period of time. He had accepted an enormous burden that was—or so Giuliani perceived—inconsistent with his personality. Why? Now, afterward, he was still deeply troubled. Why?

To Giuliani there had to be a better explanation for Leuci's conduct than the one advanced—a crisis of conscience—and what other explanation could there be than fear of prosecution. Leuci had admitted three acts of misconduct, but he could not have feared prosecution on any one of them. The only witnesses were Mafia men who would never testify.

So what else had he done that he feared being arrested on?

Up close, Giuliani found Leuci an extremely complicated man. He was enormously sensitive to other people and to their problems. He was a sympathetic listener, a charming talker. He was, Giuliani sensed, a man of integrity.

Yet he was deeply troubled. None of it added up. His personality didn't match with the facts.

Studying the Caiola case, Giuliani came up with still more questions, but no answers. Caiola had operated with impunity for years. Law enforcement considered him as evil and as dangerous a man as Rosner, but had never been able to make a case against him.

Then along comes Leuci. He goes straight to Caiola and elicits a bribe. Why was the lawyer so off guard? So sure of Leuci?

Just how much did this cop, Leuci, know?

Giuliani's suspicions were strong only at night when he was alone. In Leuci's presence he succumbed to the warmth and openness of the detective's personality. He believed his assurances.

"I wouldn't commit perjury. Are you crazy?"

Face to face, Giuliani found Leuci one of the most credible persons with whom he had ever dealt. Nonetheless, as he began to prepare Leuci's cross-examination, Giuliani resolved to try to break him down. To make him admit anything he might be concealing. He believed he could do this where Morvillo and Sagor had failed. Morvillo had prepared the Rosner case at night while running the Criminal Division in the daytime. Sagor did not have the right background and personality to understand Leuci.

But Giuliani had himself been brought up in an Italian family, and had spent time on the streets. Later Giuliani had graduated magna cum laude from both Manhattan College and New York University Law School.

The prosecutor realized that if he broke Leuci down, if other acts of misconduct came out, this would prove perjury, which would upset the Rosner verdict and probably make a successful prosecution of Caiola impossible as well. Still, he would have to do it if he could. His oath of office demanded it.

All this time Giuliani had also been negotiating with Caiola's lawyer, and now the defendant suddenly decided to plead guilty to conspiracy to use interstate facilities to further the crime of bribery. He was sentenced to a maximum term of three years in jail.

This was a great relief to Giuliani, whose suspicions of Leuci became moot. He watched Leuci prepare, with other prosecutors, many additional cases. But none ever came to trial. The detective never took the stand, and this was a relief to Giuliani, too.

Bail bondsman Dominic Marcone, an associate of DeStefano, pleaded guilty without trial. He got two years.

Drug dealer Mikey Coco pleaded guilty also, and went to jail for three years. Case after case was disposed of similarly.

Queens Assistant District Attorney Norman Archer did go on trial. Marked bribe money had been found in his safe. Leuci was not needed as a witness, and was not called.

As for Leuci, the only cloud on his horizon, and it seemed a small one then, was the Rosner appeal. Rosner was on bail, his appeal pending. Meanwhile the ex-lawyer had submitted two post trial motions to trial judge Arnold Bauman, requesting formal hearings. The motions were granted, but Leuci was not required to testify either time. Now, as the year ended, the Court of Appeals handed down its ruling. Rosner's conviction stood. The defendant, it seemed, would go to jail at last.

After him would go many, many others, for these cases were so strong that nearly every defendant could be expected to plead guilty: the Mafia hoodlums Marchese, Tomasetti; the Tolentinos Senior and Junior; the lawyer Salko; and the many compromised cops.

For Leuci this was a time of almost total security, and

it lasted many serene months. He was the hero of the Southern District Courthouse—look how easily all these bad people were being put out of circulation—and for month after month his credibility was not questioned.

He was the hero, in fact, of the entire criminal justice system. Partly because of the official corruption he had revealed on all levels, Governor Rockefeller had appointed a Special Prosecution Force headed by Maurice Nadjari to watchdog the entire justice operation. For the first time in history an attempt was going to be made to clean up not just the station houses, but the courthouses as well.

Nadjari was a firebrand—unpredictable, capricious, and blindly tenacious once he fastened on a scent—and this Leuci realized, could one day be a problem for himself. But mostly Leuci exulted that he was there, a lawyer whose principal function was supposed to be to investigate his own kind. Because credit for this went directly to Detective Second-Grade Robert Leuci.

It was possible, some days, to imagine himself the hero he had always wanted to be.

Meanwhile, his home life was good. In northern Virginia, Gina was happy with her new house, their children played in playgrounds with other kids, and Leuci was there every weekend without fail.

His friends were doing well. He met Les Wolff for dinner several times. In the garment district, Undercover Detective Wolff had penetrated the Mafia at an extremely high level. Major indictments were coming. Wolff was pleased with Leuci for having got him the job, and no longer distrusted his former partner. Mike Shaw, still directing the Federal Strike Force, was thrilled with Wolff.

And Assistant U.S. Attorney Giuliani, whom Leuci considered now an extremely close friend, had been promoted to head the Special Prosecution Section, and then the Narcotics Section as well. Still only thirty, he was now the third most powerful prosecutor in the U.S. Attorney's office.

Leuci even had, for the first time since his conversations with Scoppetta, a viable long-term future, or so it seemed, for in Washington he now met regularly with Tartaglino. The Bureau of Narcotics had recently changed its name to the Drug Enforcement Administration, but Tartaglino was still Number Two man there, and he too seemed to have succumbed to Leuci's warmth, his charm, his obvious vulnerability, his desire to be liked. The federal official talked often now of the detective's future—something Leuci had scarcely dared think of himself—when all these cases would be over.

"We are going to work out something for you," Tartaglino promised.

Once he showed him a written agreement he had negotiated with Police Commissioner Murphy. As soon as Leuci's cases ended, he would be picked up by the Drug Enforcement Administration; his salary would continue to be paid by the New York Police Department, his pension would continue to build up, he would still be, a cop.

This sounded like a dream to Leuci.

Tartaglino talked about assigning Leuci to a task force he would form and send to Trieste. Or maybe Leuci should go to Syria and Turkey to make buys of opium. Maybe buy it all up for the government. "I have all sorts of ideas for you," he promised. "So don't be concerned about your future. You've done your job and you are going to be okay."

But he doesn't know the whole story, Leuci would think. Other times he would tell himself: He's so much smarter than the others that of course he knows. But he doesn't care as long as I never tell him.

One day Tartaglino spoke of still another task force. He was collecting agents from all over the country to go to the Mexican border. "It's not the nicest kind of assignment in the world, but it's not bad," he said. "You would work on the border with the Mexican police."

"Mr. Tartaglino," said Leuci, "I'll do whatever you ask me to do. My big fear is that I will embarrass you."

"You have said that to me before and I don't want to hear it anymore," answered Tartaglino. "You are going to get me thinking that you may embarrass me. Why do I have to think about that? There is no reason why you should embarrass me. You've told them everything. Are you going to tell them any more? No? Then that's it."

21

THERE WAS no keystone which, plucked out of the arch, caused the entire edifice to collapse. There was not even the steady undermining of any foundations. The collapse was sudden and total, and not even particularly dramatic.

It began with a series of events that apparently were not related.

First, the Baron's allegations reappeared as a formal affidavit. This time it was deposed in the proper form and place, and duly sworn. It was a legal masterpiece. the work of Rosner's new lawyer, the renowned constitutional scholar Alan Dershowitz of Harvard. This affidavit swayed Judge Bauman, who agreed to accord Rosner a hearing, and set a date for it. Detective Leuci would be obliged once again to take the stand. Once again he would be questioned under oath about himself.

Then, too, although Leuci had admitted during Rosner's trial to only three acts of misconduct, a memo out of the files of Tartaglino now came to light that outlined a fourth. At dinner at Shaw's apartment two or more years ago Tartaglino had badmouthed cops to such a point that Leuci had angrily described almost the first corruption he ever saw, because it was by federal agents. After executing a search warrant with the two agents, he and Mandato had met them in a bar, where $200, taken by one of the agents, was split four ways. The two cops had not even known until the split that money had been taken.

Tartaglino had made a memo of this conversation—fifty dollars' worth of corruption by Leuci—then had forgotten about it. So had Shaw. So had Leuci. But Assistant U.S. Attorney Elliot Sagor, obliged to answer so many questions by Rosner and others, had sent formal requests to every federal agency for any and all information on Leuci that their files might contain.

When the Tartaglino memo came back, Sagor was furious, and he summoned Tom Taylor and George Carros to his office. Taylor and Carros had both served in the Leuci investigation. Both had been promoted by Tartaglino as a result; they were now among the highest-ranking Drug Enforcement officials in New York. But they had gotten no publicity out of the investigation, had come to resent Leuci, who had made headlines.

Now in Sagor's office Carros and Taylor were scared. This oversight would seriously embarrass Tartaglino. It could subject the Justice Department to ridicule.

If Sagor reported them to Tartaglino, then their civil service futures might be in jeopardy. They would suffer while the crooked cop, Leuci, got off scot-free once again.

When they left Sagor's office, Leuci was waiting to go in. They cursed him. After that, knowing that success would remove all heat from themselves, they launched their own investigation into past misconduct by Leuci.

A third event in the series at this time was Special State Prosecutor Maurice Nadjari's announcement to the press that he had solved the ripoff of 300 pounds of heroin from the police property clerk's office. He hadn't, but it now became incumbent upon him to do so, and fast, and rumors began to circulate that Detective Second-Grade Robert Leuci was a solid suspect in the case. These rumors were fed by Leuci's appearance at Nadjari's offices day after day for interrogation.

And finally, SIU Detective Carl Aguiluz was indicted for perjury and offered a deal if he would cooperate.

Leuci had been informed of Aguiluz's arrest in advance. Assistant U.S. Attorney Wally Higgins called him in. "I sat through the Rosner trial, and I think you were great," Higgins began. "I'm going to ask you a favor. We are going to lock up a detective from SIU."

"Who?"

"Carl Aguiluz. Do you know him?"

Leuci's head began churning. So did his stomach. "Yeah, I know him."

"We're going to take him in the next couple of days. We

thought you might talk to him. He might do the kind of thing that you did."

It's coming to an end, Leuci thought. Aguiluz. Who else do they have? What other investigations do they have going on that I don't even know about?

"He testified in the grand jury," explained Higgins. He was pleased with himself, and totally unaware of the turmoil he had created inside Leuci. "We are sure he's committed perjury. So we got him. We can indict him and have him locked up. After that we're going to try to turn him. Maybe you can help us convince him to cooperate."

As Leuci left Higgins's office, the names of every SIU detective he had ever known flashed like file cards through his head. Who had Aguiluz worked with? Which of these detectives had Leuci also worked with? Who, if compromised, could finger whom? But he knew Aguiluz. Aguiluz was not going to cooperate. Then he thought about the Rosner hearing coming up, and about The Baron's affidavit, and about Nadjari's investigation, and about Carros and Taylor, who were interrogating The Baron and trying to move their investigation under the aegis of the U.S. Attorney's office in Brooklyn, because Leuci had no friends there who might protect him. Now Aguiluz.

It was all closing in on him at last.

"Things are getting really bad," he told Gina that weekend.

"What's so bad?" she asked. "We've gone through it. It's over now. I never thought we would survive it, but we did."

"What if I told you there was a chance I would be arrested?"

"What?"

"Because I never told them all the things I did."

"What does that mean? Who is going to arrest you? Scoppetta and those people? Bob? After all this, you could be arrested by the same people who got you to do it?"

From then on Leuci lived in a state of steadily mounting terror.

22

SPECIAL PROSECUTOR NADJARI was not the only man investigating the French Connection heroin ripoff. Eight other prosecutors also wanted to solve it: the elected district attorneys sitting in each of the five boroughs; the special narcotics prosecutor whose jurisdiction covered the entire city; the U.S. attorney for the Southern District whose jurisdiction covered Manhattan, the Bronx, and Staten Island; and the U.S. attorney for the Eastern District, whose jurisdiction covered Brooklyn, Queens, and Long Island.

The French Connection ripoff was the most celebrated crime any of these men might ever hope to solve, and all had active investigations going. So did the Police Department itself.

All these investigations proceeded along the same lines. At the start, investigators assigned to the job merely went around asking questions of persons active on the narcotics scene—the range extended from street junkies to detective commanders—and one of the first questions asked was always this one: who do you think did it?

The name Leuci was mentioned often. Again and again investigators were urged to take a close look at him. Surely he was involved in the ripoff in some way. Only a crime of this magnitude would explain why, when they had had nothing on him, he had volunteered to cooperate with the prosecutors in the first place. His sixteen months undercover was no doubt an attempt to save his neck in advance. All the prosecutors knew he had had the best organized-crime connections of any SIU detective. He could have used these connections to funnel the heroin back into the street.

Motive plus opportunity. To the cynical police mind, this equaled not logic but proof. The next step was to locate hard evidence against Leuci, and a great many investigators began digging. Apparently the heroin had been withdrawn over a period of months. Leuci's movements during these months were scrutinized. A search was begun for secret bank accounts. Samples of his handwriting were surreptitiously obtained and matched by handwriting experts against the withdrawal vouchers.

All this time the name Carl Aguiluz was mentioned frequently also. Detective Aguiluz was probably not involved himself, investigators were told. But he was a key guy in SIU. If anyone could unlock the French Connection case, Aguiluz could. Was there any way to make Aguiluz "cooperate"? Could he somehow be forced to talk?

In the offices of the U.S. attorney for the Southern District, Rudy Giuliani was not yet listening to the rumors about Leuci, for whom he still felt enormous sympathy. But the rumors about Aguiluz sounded good to him, and he pondered them. There had been for a long time a possible perjury case pending against Aguiluz. It was a weak case. There was enough to indict, not to convict, and the case had nothing whatever to do with the French Connection ripoff. But an indictment would be a hook into Aguiluz. It might be enough to make him talk.

Cops feared indictment far more than ordinary citizens, and they had good reason. Once indicted, they were immediately suspended from the Police Department. Emotionally, this meant moving about the city stripped of gun and shield. Financially, it meant their pay stopped. They were out of work during all the months and sometimes years that the indictment pended.

In addition, an indictment, even one that resulted eventually in acquittal, always resulted in a second trial by the Police Department. In the Police Department trial room, hearsay testimony, co-conspirator testimony, and other such evidence became fully admissible, and conviction became almost a foregone conclusion. Conviction meant, usually, dismissal without pension rights. It meant going out into the streets to find a job, and who would hire an ex-cop dismissed for corruption? Indictment to a cop meant his life was ruined.

At length the decision was made to indict Aguiluz and make him sweat. Scare him enough and he might crack. He might give up information on the French Connection ripoff.

The perjury case centered around an informant of Aguiluz's named Frank Ramos, who was maître d'hôtel at a midtown Spanish restaurant. Through Ramos, and through illegal wiretaps which Ramos had allowed him to install in the restaurant, the detective had learned of the imminent arrival of a major shipment of heroin. But when he went to stake out the site of the drop, he was recognized by federal agents, who protested that this was their case, and that Aguiluz must leave the scene at once. The dispute was carried to higher levels, and a political accommodation was made. Police Department brass ordered Aguiluz off the case.

Furious, anxious about his informant, Aguiluz went to a telephone and warned Ramos to stay away from the drop area. When the feds subsequently blew their arrests, they blamed Aguiluz, claiming he had warned the suspects they were there, and a grand jury investigation was opened into these charges. One of the first witnesses called was Frank Ramos.

Previously, a federal undercover agent had made two narcotics buys off Ramos, who was, therefore, in serious trouble. When told that he could lighten his sentence if he gave up Aguiluz, Ramos did not hesitate. Only a small part of his testimony proved critical. He put Aguiluz in his bar at a certain hour, and Aguiluz, testifying before the same grand jury, denied it.

Several other witnesses were found who corroborated Ramos's testimony—sort of. They put Aguiluz in the bar just before the time specified by Ramos and denied by Aguiluz. Thus the alleged perjury was a considerable distance removed from any crime Aguiluz may or may not have committed, and it was unlikely that any jury would ever vote to send the detective to jail for it.

Nonetheless the indictment came down, and late on a Friday night in January he was arrested and brought to an undercover office that federal prosecutors sometimes used. During the next several hours various prosecutors and agents attempted to question Aguiluz. Some spoke softly to him. Some railed at him. All attempted to persuade him that he should, and must, cooperate.

But Aguiluz continued to insist that he was an honorable cop and an innocent man. The perjury case against him was persecution, pure and simple, he said. It would never stick. Furthermore, there was nothing to cooperate about. He had committed no corrupt acts himself, and knew no detective who had. He knew nothing about the French Connection ripoff.

Leuci, who had been summoned to the cover office shortly after the interrogation of Aguiluz began, had since been cooling his heels in an anteroom. He was there, supposedly, to help persuade Aguiluz to cooperate, but three hours passed before the exhausted questioners, withdrawing, invited him to take his turn. "He's not going to turn," they asserted, "but see what you can do."

And so Leuci stepped into the office in which Aguiluz waited, closed the door, and sat down opposite him. Aguiluz, he saw, was terrified.

Leuci's own motivation at this time was not clear to him. If he could convince Aguiluz to talk, he would be in for another round of praise and handshakes. His friendships with the prosecutors would become firmer than ever. he would be the hero of the Southern District once again, and perhaps his friends—Giuliani and others—would urge the city's other prosecutor to leave him alone. Some of the heat would be off him.

On the other hand, if Aguiluz cracked and began to name names, it could be dangerous. Still, Leuci felt one step removed from whatever Aguiluz might reveal, for they had never worked a single case together.

He studied the man across the desk from him, and tried to decide how to start.

"You have to live with yourself and what you've done," burst out Aguiluz. "I'm not you. I'll never give up my partners and the guys I've worked with."

This was the start of a vitriolic outburst against "the feds" that lasted ten minutes. Leuci's first job was to separate himself in Aguiluz's mind from the men he so bitterly denounced.

"Carl, you're in bad trouble. You have to tell them whatever they want to know. It's the only way you can save yourself. We're cops. If I were in your position I'd have to do the same!"

Aguiluz continued to rant. There were federal agents as deeply involved as he was in this Ramos case. When they had rousted him from the drop site they had made him leave all his illegal gear in place, and had continued the wiretap themselves.

It made Leuci think that Aguiluz's problems could be limited to this one case, and he began urging him to name these specific federal agents. But Aguiluz only cursed the men outside this room. He would never cooperate, he said.

Leuci knew what a brilliant detective Aguiluz was. He knew that Aguiluz loved being a detective, and had no other life. And so he began to bring up some of the great cases Aguiluz had made hoping to appeal to the Hispanic detective's pride. Aguiluz, listening, fell silent, and stared at the floor.

Leuci said, "Is this the way it ends, Carl? Do you want to go to jail? To West Street, tonight? They're going to put you in jail, Carl, tonight."

"Why does everybody hate cops?" asked Aguiluz. "Why do they turn on us? Why do they persecute us?" It was a cry from the heart of every cop everywhere.

"I spoke with them," Leuci said. "They told me they would take it easy on you."

The desperate Aguiluz was thinking only of prison. "Can you come to West Street with me?" he begged. "Can you stay with me tonight? I'm not Nunziata. I can handle it. All I need is someone to help me get through tonight."

Leuci left the room to report. "He's going crazy in there. Let me leave with him now," Leuci told the prosecution team. "Give him his gun back and his shield. Let me take him out of here as a policeman. Don't take him out of here as a prisoner. Give him time to think about doing this as a policeman."

They agreed. An amazed Aguiluz took back his gun and shield.

Leuci took him to a restaurant on Long Island. Leuci's bodyguards sat apart while he and Aguiluz ordered drinks at the bar. They talked about Nunziata. Why had he done what he did? Look at the mess he had left Ann in, and the kids. Why had he let them beat him? Aguiluz mustn't let himself be beaten by them in his turn.

"Just tell them what they want to know," Leuci said. "When it's over, they'll relocate you in another part of the world. You can start a new life."

Aguiluz did not look up from his drink. "If I was to agree to cooperate," he said in a low voice, "I would tell them everything."

Oh God, Leuci thought. "Great," he said out loud. "Tell them everything." Just tell them a few things, he silently pleaded.

By the time Aguiluz got home he was calmer. Leuci had made some good points, and now Aguiluz pursued thoughts of his own. The feds were onto him, he reasoned, and they would never let him go. If he got out of this indictment, there would be another close behind it on something else. They would hound him till they got him.

Finally, having made his decision, he came in to the Southern District and began to tell his story. His debriefing lasted three days, and the prosecutors were amazed by it. None of them had ever before dealt with a cop who held nothing back. Aguiluz told the worst things first, and he solidly implicated his partners, Peter Daly and Joe Novoa; if they had been like brothers to him, it did not show. Aguiluz, Daly and Novoa had not seized 100 kilos of heroin and cocaine, it seemed, but 105 kilos. Aguiluz had held five back, and sold it. He and his partners had stolen tens of thousands of dollars from drug dealers. They had sold prisoners their freedom in exchange for tens of thousands of dollars more. Aguiluz's recital was so shocking that his "minor" crimes, by the time he got to them, seemed hardly worth noting down.

Yes, he had perjured himself in court—twenty or more times, in fact. He had given junk to informants hundreds of times, had planted dozens and dozens of illegal wiretaps.

Aguiluz seemed a cold man, at least this was the mask he had assumed: much of his tale was uttered in a monotone, without any emotion. But at other times he tried to justify his conduct. Every narcotics detective he had ever known gave junk to informants, he said. The informants were sick, and no man with any compassion could turn his back on them. As for perjury in court, this was mandated by the stupid search and seizure laws, and by the need to put drug dealers in jail. The wiretap laws were equally stupid, for without illegal wiretaps most cases could never be made.

Some of the prosecutors debriefing Aguiluz nodded in sympathy at such reasoning. It was true that the laws might be written better, and now was not the time to argue that each law, right or wrong, was sacred—to argue, that is, that the law was the law. Abstract concepts had never yet convinced a street detective, and the important thing was to keep Aguiluz talking.

Stealing money from junk dealers was, to Aguiluz, justifiable also. Most would be out on the street on bail before the arresting detective was, and right back dealing again. Most would have no difficulty whatever fixing their cases at some stage of the system. They would buy bondsmen, district attorneys, judges. They were so rich they could buy anybody. Most could be hurt, could be put out of business, in one way only, and that was by stealing all their cash at the moment of arrest. As for selling them freedom, for the most part this was done only when, because of a scarcity of evidence, a legal arrest could not be made anyway.

Aguiluz had an explanation for holding back five kilos out of his monumental seizure. He had been so euphoric to have made such a case, to stare down at so much junk, that he had scarcely known what he was doing, he said.

He had held the five kilos out. Afterward he could never explain why, even to himself.

Once he found himself stuck with the junk, he did not know what to do with it. He couldn't turn it in—he would go to jail for having held it back in the first place. He found he couldn't flush it down the toilet either, for it was worth too much money, and his partners knew he had it. Daly and Novoa wouldn't believe he had flushed it away. They would think he was holding out money.

For weeks he drove around with five kilos of narcotics stashed in the trunk of his car. Finally he, Daly, and Novoa got together, talked it all out, and decided to get rid of the junk. All three got into the car and drove down to the river. They had resolved to empty the sacks out, spill dust onto the current. The junk would float away. They would be rid of it.

But once they stood on the embankment they couldn't bring themselves to do it, and they talked the subject out once more. Together they had done what no one else they knew had ever done. They had been through The Door. It should have changed their lives, but on the other side was —nothing. A newspaper clipping.

Like most SIU detectives, they had become used to money at the end of a big case, and this one was much more than a big case. This one was "The Door." And there was no money there. There was no reward of any kind. All they were left with was these sacks of junk that they had unthinkingly, almost inadvertently, held back. At their feet the water rushed by fast enough to carry away all the drowsy misery in the city.

They turned away, put the sacks back into the trunk, and drove off. A day or so later Aguiluz had begun disposing of their merchandise. He sold it in installments for safety's sake, and shared the money with Daly and Novoa. What difference did five more kilos make going into the New York narcotics market—none. Or so he told himself. So all three told themselves.

It was a dirty story, but also a sad one, because Aguiluz had been not only a great detective, but even, at the start of his career, as idealistic as most other young cops.

One other quality came through Aguiluz's long recital—his extreme bitterness toward Leuci. Bob Leuci was lying to them, he advised the prosecutors again and again. They should not be so shocked at what Aguiluz was telling them, because their star witness had done the same or worse.

Clearly he blamed Leuci for plenty—for Nunziata's death, for provoking the entire investigation into SIU detectives, even for having persuaded Aguiluz himself now to cooperate. Aguiluz, having made his deal with the prosecutors, was going to be obliged to plead guilty to felony charges twice, once in the Eastern District, once in the Southern. Leuci, meanwhile, had not yet even been indicted. Why the hell was Leuci getting away with all this shit, while he, Aguiluz, was required to plead guilty? He would do it, he said, but he didn't like it, and he wanted them to know that this character Leuci wasn't the angel they thought he was.

The listening prosecutors kept demanding that he give specific facts of misconduct by Leuci, but Aguiluz said he didn't have any. Leuci had kept his deals to himself, he explained. Contrary to what people seemed to think, detectives did not sit around in a circle describing the scores they made. The only people who knew specifically what you were doing were your own partners, and he had never worked a case with Leuci. Leuci had worked on Italian organized crime, while Aguiluz concentrated on Hispanics. Still, it had been clear to everyone in SIU that Leuci was making money.

In the absence of specific information, Giuliani and the other Southern District prosecutors decided that they were not really interested in Leuci at this point. They were interested in corroborating Aguiluz's other revelations. So they picked up his brother-in-law, Sal Buteria, who was not a cop; and his sergeant, Jim Sottile; and a young Spanish-speaking detective named Luis Martinez. All three cracked quickly; they corroborated Aguiluz's stories, and they agreed to cooperate themselves.

Using the dates Aguiluz had provided, the prosecutors subpoenaed the bank records of his supervisor, Lieutenant John Egan. These records showed that Egan, on the day following virtually every score, had made substantial deposits to one or another of his many savings accounts.

It remained now to nail Aguiluz's partners, Daly and Novoa. One score, according to Aguiluz, had been divided up in a room in the Taft Hotel. So the Taft's records were subpoenaed. These showed that the room in question had been registered in the name of Detective Peter Daly. On the day following another score, Detective Novoa had bought a new car for cash.

Giuliani and his assistants were too busy to think about Leuci. In a single day some two dozen SIU detectives were indicted and arrested, so many that the prosecutors had to meet with them almost in groups. All were offered deals if they would cooperate. Many of them, at that point, brought Leuci's name into the conversation: "Give me the same deal you gave Leuci, and sure I'll cooperate. Just give me the same free ride he's getting."

Aguiluz, meanwhile, was sent across into Brooklyn to be interrogated by Eastern District prosecutors under Tom Puccio. His revelations were equally juicy there, and Puccio ordered other SIU detectives brought in and questioned.

At once Puccio in Brooklyn began listening to the same anguished voices as Giuliani was hearing in Manhattan.

"I'm not admitting that I did anything," said each detective he talked to. "But if I did do something it wasn't any worse than what Leuci did."

Puccio decided to meet with Giuliani. As they talked there seemed to be an echo in the room, and both heard it. "Leuci is as bad as we are. Leuci is lying to you. You are closing your eyes to it, because he's your pal."

But Leuci was no pal of Puccio's. They had never dealt with each other. Remarking that he had a few ideas he might try, Puccio left the meeting and went back to his own office. From then on the belt began to tighten around Leuci.

Giuliani summoned him. All the detectives were saying that Leuci was guilty of more than three things, the prosecutors began. Giuliani was troubled and it showed.

He cared about what happened to the detective opposite him. "Are you sure there's nothing you want to tell me?" Giuliani's tone was kindly. When Leuci, wearing his most sincere smile, insisted that there was nothing to tell, Giuliani showed him out.

Puccio summoned Leuci to Brooklyn. Leuci, who arrived nervous, was soon at ease, for this new prosecutor seemed at first as casual and friendly as all the others.

But there was method to Puccio's casualness. He began by praising Leuci and Aguiluz almost interchangeably. Both were brave, both were admirable. As for Aguiluz, the prosecutors were going to do for him whatever they could.

Leuci did not like to be equated to Aguiluz. Aguiluz had been caught, and he had given up his partners. Leuci himself had done neither. However, Leuci kept silent while Puccio prattled on.

Suddenly the prosecutor's smile vanished, and his voice went hard. "You're Babyface," said Puccio, "aren't you? We've come upon an old allegation against you, and the witness is sitting outside."

Puccio, watching Leuci carefully, noted a sudden tightening of the brows, and he wondered if this indicated guilt, or only surprise at the abrupt change in mood.

Leuci said he didn't know what case Puccio might be talking about.

So Puccio described it. Some years before, Leuci and his team had executed a fugitive warrant. They had kicked in a door and arrested the narcotics dealer inside. While they were processing the dealer in the station house, his partner and the partner's wife had arrived with a $5000 bribe. So all three were charged with attempted bribery as well.

"Oh, I do remember the case," said Leuci. He was smiling. He remembered the case with pride.

Suddenly Puccio said, "There was four hundred dollars taken at the scene of the arrest, according to this allegation."

Puccio was under heavy pressure from Taylor and Carros. It was they who had dug up this old case. They wanted Leuci indicted on it. They had the dealer himself outside willing to testify.

It would be a pretty flimsy indictment.

Puccio was trying to decide what to do. He was trying to read guilt or innocence in Leuci's face. The job of a prosecutor was no exact science, and bluffs sometimes broke cases wide open. The Aguiluz perjury indictment had been largely a bluff, and look at the result. But he didn't want to bluff a guiltless man.

"Who took the four hundred dollars?" Puccio demanded.

Leuci at first did not comprehend. "The guy offered us five thousand, and we locked up all three people for it."

Puccio said coldly, "Sometimes it's hard to tell who is lying, and who isn't. But it's my feeling that the four hundred dollars happened. There is no reason for the guy to lie about it."

"Even if it happened, Mr. Puccio," Leuci said, "don't you think it's possible that I wouldn't know anything about it?"

"No. I don't think it's possible."

Leuci hardly realized he had just been accused of a crime, for he had perceived something much worse: Puccio's plan—to make a case against him—any case—so as to turn him into an Aguiluz.

"Carl Aguiluz is not the same guy I am, Mr. Puccio," said Leuci, angrily. "Aguiluz is implicating his friends and his partners. People who trusted him, lived with him. Before I would do that, I'd kill myself."

A triumphant smile came onto Puccio's face. Leuci saw it, realized its significance, and was appalled at himself. Up to now, Puccio had not been certain. But his doubts had just been removed.

"What are you telling me?" Puccio demanded. "You're telling me flat out that you've done more than you have admitted to."

Shocked, frightened, Leuci made the additional mistake of calling Aguiluz a fucking rat.

"But you're not a rat, is that what you're saying?" said Puccio, nodding thoughtfully.

Leuci made no reply.

"I have a lot of respect for those prosecutors over at the Southern District," said Puccio coolly. "I don't know how they handled you. I don't know what they promised you or didn't promise you. I do know that if you were working for me, there is no way in the world you could get away with whatever you think you are getting away with. If you're not telling the truth, we'll find out. Half the SIU will be coming in here. And they will all cooperate."

"They are not going to cooperate."

"Nearly all of them will cooperate. They're cops. In their hearts, they want to admit their guilt. That's the way cops are. You know that as well as I do."

Leuci was sweating. "Can I leave now?"

Puccio smiled. "I'll be seeing you again."

The next day Giuliani, having spoken to Puccio, called Leuci in once more. "Puccio is about to indict some more people. Do you know a detective named Les Wolff?"

It was a moment before Leuci could speak at all.

"We were partners," he said in a choked voice.

"I know you were partners. Are you sure there's nothing more you want to tell me?"

Leuci shook his head, "No."

"So far," said Giuliani, "every allegation against you, by The Baron and everyone else, is unsupported. But just let one cop come in here and corroborate one dope dealer, and you'll go to jail. There will be no way anyone can save you." After a moment Giuliani added, "What do you think Les Wolff might tell Puccio?"

23

WOLFF, who was then thirty-nine years old, stood six feet tall and was a wiry, well-built man. He had dark, curly hair, and his dark face, somewhat pockmarked from childhood acne, was striking, and full of character. This character was set off by the way Wolff carried himself. He seemed a rather cold man, and he had a strong sense of self.

He came from a Bronx working-class family, went into the army, and served in West Germany. As a Jew in Germany, he was extremely uncomfortable, but he had loved, he often said, German girls. After military service he became a patrolman in the Twenty-fifth Precinct in Harlem.

From the beginning he saw the Police Department as a career. His ambition was to go further in life than his parents had gone, and so he worked harder than most of the cops around him. He made good arrests. He put in overtime. He was also fearless. In Harlem in the middle of the night he thought nothing of checking out cellars, alleyways, backyards alone, his flashlight out, his gun holstered. "These people don't scare me," he often said.

His promotion into the detective division had come after only six years in uniform—faster than most detectives, not as fast as some. As a detective he stayed in Harlem for about three years more, with Dave Cody as his partner, until in 1969, at the age of thirty-four, he was moved up into SIU, and assigned to the Leuci-Mandato team. He had been the leader of every team he ever worked on, he informed Detective Leuci at once, and though he accepted the leadership of Leuci, who was only twenty-nine, he did not like it. He was a competitor. From then on he competed for the job of team leader in almost every case that the newly composed four-man team worked.

To Wolff, being a detective was a business. You did it the best you knew how. It was Wolff who sought to master any new gear that came into the team's possession, principally electronic listening devices and cameras. He became an expert photographer. His paperwork was always perfect. He always had to be the best. He had to win.

After three years in SIU his career had made another upward leap—he had taken on the dangerous undercover assignment for Mike Shaw and the Federal Strike Force, and official reports about his work had been, he knew, glowing.

The fact was, Puccio was not aware of whatever Wolff's current job might be, for the Strike Force's investigation, code-named Project Cleveland, was known to very few men. For most of two years Wolff had worn a wire while recording incriminating conversations with many of the shylocks, extortionists, and hijackers who dominated the garment district, often meeting such men alone in the night in isolated places. His work much resembled what Leuci's had been, except that his target was organized crime rather than official corruption.

Wolff had been given a false name—Les Dana—and a cover apartment on West Ninth Street. Since he was supposedly second in command of a small trucking company, he had demanded appropriate clothes, and was given $300 to buy them. He spent the money and began wearing open shirts with chains around his neck and a lot of chest showing. He looked now not like a cop but like a Jewish hoodlum, and he acted not like a cop but like a trucking company executive. The role was congenial to him, and he began running the trucking company as a business, installing controls, and figuring out ways to cut overhead while improving profits. The detectives who covered him he assigned to unload rolls of merchandise from his trucks. It was the heaviest work imaginable. It was mule work. After one day they wanted off. So Wolff, business being business, unloaded his trucks himself, day after day, and complained to no one.

Whenever he wore his wire into hazardous meetings with hoodlums, he was so cool that no one ever suspected him. He was never patted down. Each time, showing no sign of nervousness, he got his recordings, then left the meetings and went home.

Once a week Mike Shaw held debriefings in the board room at the Morgan Guaranty Trust company on Broad Street. Wolff's manner, while giving his reports, was crisp, direct, totally professional. Shaw admired him. He considered Wolff an absolutely superb undercover detective.

So the first irate citizen Puccio had to contend with was Shaw. By indicting Wolff, Puccio had endangered Project Cleveland, on which the government had already spent hundreds of thousands of dollars. Shaw spoke to Puccio politely, lawyer to lawyer, but he was furious—particularly after he had studied the indictment and seen how thin the case against Wolff appeared to be.

The case dated from November 19, 1970, some three and a half years previously. Together with Aguiluz and five other SIU detectives, Wolff had entered at gunpoint the apartment of a South American drug dealer named Olate. There were three people inside, Olate, his wife, and a friend. A bag of cocaine was seized, evidence enough to arrest all three, but only the friend was taken away under arrest.

It was the details that changed the nature of the case. Puccio had these details from Aguiluz, and they had been verified by two other members of the team who were also cooperating. The seven-man team had fastened onto Olate through illegal wiretaps. They had raided his apartment expecting to find a heavy load of heroin. Instead they had found only money, about $80,000 in all, which they stole. In exchange for this money, the drug dealer and his wife were granted provisional freedom—twenty-four hours in which to leave the country.

Neither Aguiluz nor the two corroborating detectives claimed to have shared money with Wolff, whose portion had allegedly been paid him by one of the three remaining detectives who, so far, had refused to cooperate.

Olate was brought in, and a line-up was hastily arranged. The South American had no difficulty picking Aguiluz and certain other detectives out of this line-up.

But he failed to identify Leslie Wolff.

With that, Puccio had virtually no case against Wolff.

However, for the moment the indictment stuck. Wolff had been arrested and stripped of gun and shield, and Shaw was obliged to drop him from Project Cleveland.

Wolff's anger at what he considered "the government" was so overt that Shaw worried that he might choose to endanger the work he had done under cover, but he never did. Nor did he ever threaten to. He was set to work in an office typing transcripts of the tapes he had made, and all waited hopefully for the indictment to be dismissed.

But when Puccio seemed in no hurry that this should come to pass, the furious Wolff stormed into Puccio's office and threatened to throw the prosecutor out the window. Puccio replied that Wolff could easily avoid trial, possible conviction, prison. All he had to do was cooperate. Tell what he knew.

Leaving Puccio's office, Wolff telephoned Leuci, and requested an urgent conference. They met on the sidewalk in front of Leuci's mother's house in Queens. It was about nine o'clock at night. With Leuci's bodyguards trailing about twenty paces behind, the two former partners walked round and round the block under the budding spring trees.

He would never, never cooperate, asserted Wolff. "I didn't do this. This indictment is bullshit."

"Les, take a lie detector test," pleaded Leuci. "You didn't do it."

Wolff stopped walking and stared at Leuci. "You take the lie detector test. Bob, that Spanish son of a bitch never put a dime in my hand."

As they walked on, Leuci was left to digest the two possible meanings of this statement. Either someone else had handed Wolff the money, or no one had.

"I'll never cooperate," Wolff repeated. But again he

stopped and fixed an anxious glance on his ex-partner's face. They must be pressuring Leuci to cooperate too, he said. What was Leuci going to do?

But his eyes said much more. The two partners were equally vulnerable. Together they were relatively safe. No one could give them up but each other.

"Les, they can cut me up in little pieces. I'm not telling them nothing. That's it. They've had their fun with me."

A cool March wind blew through the night, through the streets of Queens. Round and round the block they walked, but the message they had for each other never changed, and at the end they embraced. They had never done this before. They stood in the street hugging each other until it seemed that, through their overcoats, they could feel each other's heart beating.

As he moved off into the night, Wolff turned and called out, "Bob, I've never felt closer to you than I do right now."

Once Wolff was out of sight, the bodyguard Art Monty came mincing forward and in a kind of falsetto repeated Wolff's curtain line word for word: "I've never felt closer to you than I do right now." Then Monty counseled Leuci, "Don't trust him. He's going down the tubes."

It was perhaps what Leuci himself was thinking. How long could Wolff resist Puccio's pressure? How long could he himself resist it? Which of them would give up the other first?

24

DAY BY DAY the prosecutors, all working independently of each other, bounced Detective Leuci from one office to the next.

Nadjari's men grilled him about the French Connection ripoff. Tell us, detective, was it usual just to sign in with the property clerk and walk out with your evidence? Could you get it just by calling out your name from the back of the line? Is it true that clerks would pass the evidence to you over people's heads, and sign your name to the voucher? What about this affidavit by The Baron that you gave him junk in property clerk envelopes? Invariably they would ask him to leave the room.

"Wait outside, please, detective."

Waiting in the anteroom, pacing the hallway, he would wonder what was happening inside. What were they trying to pin on him now?

Called back in, he would be asked what he thought about this or that cop. "Which one of you fuckers do you think pulled this ripoff?" At last would come the curt dismissal: "You may go, detective."

Puccio took to summoning him every Friday afternoon, the phone ringing just as Leuci, anxious to get home to his family for the weekend, was about to leave for the airport. While Leuci dreamed of escape to Virginia, the prosecutor would engage him in leisurely, aimless conversations.

Puccio knew exactly what he was doing. He would seem friendly. "Bob, I need your help. We have a ton of work here. We've indicted all these detectives. We have to figure out what to do with all these guys. I want you to tell me what kind of men they are."

Shuttle after shuttle took off for Virginia.

"Look, Mr. Puccio, it's Friday night. I haven't seen my family in a week. Would you mind if I went home now?"

"If you prefer, you can come in tomorrow morning. We can finish our conversation then."

When Leuci kept silent, Puccio laughed. "Bob, you'll turn sooner or later."

Back to the Special Prosecutor's office. This time he was interrogated by Nadjari himself, the most feared prosecutor in the city. Leuci, entering his office, was petrified.

But Nadjari proved interested in the French Connection ripoff only. His investigators had focused on former SIU detective Frank King as mastermind. King had been close to Nunziata. Leuci had been close to Nunziata. Therefore Leuci and King—

But Leuci interrupted. "Mr. Nadjari, you want Frank King. You want people who can give you the French Connection case. I've never worked with any of those detectives. I can't give you them. If you don't believe that, I'll take a lie detector test right now. I had nothing to do with the French Connection case. I'm sure you know that."

After a moment, Nadjari said, "We also know that there's more you could tell us."

"How do you know that?" It seemed to Leuci that if he could get past Nadjari, he was safe. "I'm telling you I can't make a case against King. I can't make a case against his partner Jack McClean, who will give you Frank King."

Nadjari looked at him.

"I never worked with McClean," insisted Leuci. "I know nothing specific about him."

Nadjari saw the anguish in Leuci's eyes, but there was a message printed there too, and perhaps Nadjari was able to read it.

Leuci, without speaking a word, was begging Nadjari to receive and understand all that could not be spoken.

Yes, there's more in my past, Mr. Nadjari. But I can't admit to it. I would if I could give you Frank King, or Jack McClean. But what I am concealing concerns only me, and one or two partners. Nothing that is going to mean anything in your picture. Why do you want me to destroy myself? Why do you want me to come in and say the kinds of things Aguiluz is saying. I'll never do it. I'll never hurt Mandato. I'll never hurt Wolff or Cody. I'll never hurt Vinny Russo. Those were my partners. I'm not going to do it.

All this Leuci tried to tell Nadjari with his eyes.

"All right, that's enough for today," said Nadjari, and he showed the tormented detective to the door.

Giuliani summoned him. The Rosner hearing was coming up soon, he said. Leuci would be obliged to respond under oath to each of The Baron's charges. Leuci should begin to think about this.

It was clear to Giuliani that Leuci was losing control.

Giuliani felt sure now that Leuci had committed perjury in the Rosner case, that he was guilty of far more than three acts of misconduct. Clearly Leuci did not know what to do about it. He saw no way out. He was being torn apart, not only at the prospect of testifying against his former partners, but also at the thought that the new friends he had developed—Scoppetta, Shaw, Whitney North Seymour, Giuliani himself—would turn on him.

As for Leuci, the pressure was so constant that he became punchy. He couldn't keep his food down. He couldn't sleep. Fridays were a special nightmare. The call from Puccio. The long wait in Puccio's anteroom, the interview with Puccio, who was in no hurry ever, and who laughed at Leuci's barely concealed terror while one shuttle after another took off, until finally, each week, Leuci would be forced to beg, "Can I go now, Mr. Puccio?"

At last Leuci would board the plane. It would break up through the clouds into the sun, and he would sit back and try to think about going to Virginia. For an hour he would relax—more or less. But on Monday morning, as soon as he boarded the plane for the trip back, the terror would clamp down on him once again. What is waiting for me up there? There were too many people after him now—Puccio, Giuliani, Nadjari. What do I tell them, he asked himself. What don't I tell them? Through the porthole he watched the city as it came up to meet him.

His mind would not stand still. If I go in and tell them,

then I've got to tell the whole story. I can't pick and choose. And if I can't pick and choose, then I can't protect Mandato, I can't protect Wolff, I can't protect Cody. I can't protect Vinny Russo, who is a gentle, honest guy in the true sense of the word, and a decent little guy, and how can I burn Vinny Russo, who really broke me into narcotics? How can I do that to Vinny and to his wife and children?

For the time being, Leuci's resolve remained firm: I'm not going to do it. I'm not going to tell them anything.

The Sergeant Peter Perrazzo case came to trial in the Police Department trial room. Perrazzo, fifty-three, still confined to a mental institution, was to be judged in absentia. The object of the trial was to dismiss him on charges of corruption, because otherwise he would retain rights to his pension, amounting to about $14,000 a year for life. It was incumbent upon the department now to strip these funds from the madman's account.

The trial, before trial commissioner Phillip Michael, lasted about two hours. The chief prosecution witness was Detective Leuci. Only a few people were present, among them Perrazzo's court-appointed guardian and his middle-aged wife, who sat in the front row weeping quietly during the whole of the proceedings. She looked to Leuci like an Italian woman who had sat through a three-day wake and funeral. She resembled any one of his nine aunts, and he was furious with whoever had brought her there. Why should this woman have to hear her husband defamed, he asked himself. Why does she have to know all this?

Perrazzo was convicted and dismissed from the department. Leuci stumbled out of the room, asking himself: What have I done to these people, what have I done?

Another summons from Giuliani. Did Leuci know a detective named Vinny Russo?

Russo, when questioned about a certain illegal wiretap, had denied knowing about it, lying to protect the detectives involved. The plan now was to throw him into the grand jury. If he lied there, then he would be indicted for perjury.

Or did Leuci want to try to talk to him first?

When Leuci phoned Russo at home, it was Maria Russo who came on.

"Maria," he began, "I hate to bother you—"

"You're not going to hurt my Vinny."

"I'm not going to hurt Vinny."

Russo himself took the phone. "What do you want from me?"

"I'll meet you at Sweet's Restaurant next to the fish market."

Russo agreed to this meeting, but when he reached the site, he refused to come any closer to Leuci than the other side of the street. Standing on his side he shouted across to Leuci on the other, "You bastard! What do you want? You want to hurt my family. You want to hurt my kids. You want to hurt me. Why do you want to do this to me? You're here to hurt me."

"I'm not here to hurt you, Vinny," Leuci called across the street. "I want you to come in and talk to them about the wiretap."

"I'm not telling nothing," cried Russo. "What am I going to do? I don't know nothing. I don't know enough that they're going to help me. What am I going to tell them? That I know about a $300 score one time, a $200 score some other time? When I was in SIU, I used to follow a guy for three days. That's all I ever did. I did tails. When the case was over, they'd tell me to go home. I used to go home. I don't know enough. They're not going to help me."

When Leuci reported the results of this meeting, the prosecutors reverted to their original plan—the grand jury for Russo, followed by indictment. Although Leuci pleaded for his friend, the prosecutors remained adamant.

Nunziata, Sheridan, Lusterino, Wolff, Perrazzo, Russo

Leuci went to church because he could think of nowhere else to go. He did not go to the bright modern church in Virginia with its American flags and long-haired priests. That was no good. It was like a Protestant church. Instead he went back to his old neighborhood in

Queens, back to where all the priests talked with Italian accents. He wanted to see candles, to smell incense, to look up at saints. He wanted to talk through a screen to someone who might understand.

Standing in the gloom, he remembered as a child waiting on line outside the confessional on Saturday afternoons. He remembered entering the dark cubicle, confessing his childish sins through the screen, and then coming out into the sunlight again feeling the greatest liberation he had ever known before or since—almost wishing to be killed by a bus immediately, because he was friends with God again and would go straight to heaven.

The confessional he entered now was the same he used to enter as a boy. But when he knelt in the dark and tried to explain to the priest all that tormented him he found that the man didn't want to spend time on it.

We all have our crosses, the priest told him.

Leuci described Nunziata's death, his own remorse.

God decided for Nunziata, the priest told him. It wasn't your fault.

The detective attempted to talk about perjury, but the priest had no clear understanding of the legal meaning of the word. "Did your testimony put an innocent man in jail?" he inquired.

"No."

"It doesn't sound like perjury to me."

When Leuci stepped out of the box into the sunlight, there was no feeling of liberation. He was not consumed with a sense of his own goodness. The old feeling was not there. Nothing was there but emptiness and fear.

Every night now he was relying on Valium to get to sleep. But most nights it did not work well, and some nights it did not work at all.

25

PUCCIO at this time was subject to pressure of his own. It came principally from the Drug Enforcement Administration, in the persons of agents Carros and Taylor, who had come up with a plan. They wanted to threaten Leuci with indictment. Under such a threat, they assured the prosecutor, the detective would crack.

The prosecutor murmured that he had nothing to indict Leuci on. The case of the $400 bribe that they had brought him was not enough. However, he gave permission for the threat to be tried.

And so Leuci was summoned—forthwith—to the DEA offices off Columbus Circle. There he was made to wait in an anteroom. Pacing, he watched people come and go. They wore I.D. cards clipped to their pockets. They walked with great purpose. Leuci was duly impressed. These were powerful people. They were the federal government. He knew who they were, and what they could do to him.

At length Carros came out, ordered the two bodyguards to remain in the anteroom, and led Leuci back to Taylor's office. Taylor had graduated from the Leuci investigation. He was now an assistant regional director. He sat behind his big desk attempting to look important. An American flag stood in the corner. The office, a big one, had a view overlooking much of the city. Carros stood at the window peering out.

From behind his desk, Taylor called Leuci a liar. "I not only think you're a liar, I know you're a liar, and I'm passing on to you a message from Puccio. If you don't tell us everything—what you've done and who you've done it with—by five o'clock this afternoon, Puccio is going to indict you. Do you have anything to say?"

The interrogation, if that was what it was, ran downhill from there. Taylor praised Aguiluz. Obviously Leuci had had this same knowledge. He could have made the same cases.

"Aguiluz has to live with himself for the rest of his life," cried Leuci. "I have to live with myself." Sure he could have made cases against some of those same detectives, he said. But why should he make cases against his friends, when he could make cases against so many other people elsewhere in the system who were equally corrupt—or more corrupt. Aguiluz had shown that there were corrupt detectives in SIU. Leuci had shown there was corruption in every part of the system.

Taylor accused Leuci of caring only about his prosecutor friends in the Southern District. These people had coddled him for years. But he was a crook. Taylor knew it, and so did Puccio in the Eastern District. Either Leuci would reveal all they wanted to know by five o'clock this afternoon, or he would be indicted.

Carros continued to gaze out the window.

Taylor and Leuci began to shout at each other. Taylor called Leuci a liar, a perjurer, a criminal. Leuci called Taylor a buffoon, a jerkoff, a fraud.

"You were a New York City cop for nine years," Leuci said. "And what did you do during those nine years? You bragged about it to me. You hid out in firehouses studying so you could go through college. You got paid by the city for nine years, and then you became an IRS agent, and now you are a big DEA boss. Who are you?"

"I'm the guy that could put you in jail."

"You're the boss of the guys who lost me all the time when they were my backup agents. You don't even know what cases we made. You never even read the memorandums on the cases you were working on."

Back at the offices of the Southern District, Leuci burst in on Giuliani and blurted out his tragic news: "They are going to indict me at five o'clock."

But Giuliani's face failed to register enough surprise. "You knew they were going to run this game on me, didn't you?" Leuci cried. "You didn't give a shit either, did you?"

Giuliani phoned Puccio, and, after a short conversation, hung up. "Puccio tells me that they are not going to indict you today after all," Giuliani reported.

"I'm leaving, I'm getting out of here. I'm going home to Virginia."

"Bob, you have a lot to think about," said Giuliani after a moment.

"Are they going to lock me up, or aren't they? What is going on here?"

"Bob, look at you. You're a nervous wreck. Maybe you better tell me the truth."

Leuci rushed off to Brooklyn Heights to see Shaw. "Mike, what should I do?"

Shaw lay full length on his couch, the lower part of his legs hanging over the far end. "Don't you understand the dilemma I'm in?" Shaw asked. "I can't advise you. I'm a prosecutor. If you make any admissions to me now, I would have to take action."

Shaw could offer nothing but sympathy. "Bob, the only thing I can tell you is that you've got to tell the truth."

Leuci left Brooklyn Heights. It was time for a changeover of bodyguards, Monty and Farley going off, Fritz and Bonifide coming on. "What do you guys think I should do?" asked the tormented Leuci.

The five men were sitting in a car on the same quiet street in Queens where every night the changeover took place. Farley and Monty were Leuci's age. Fritz and Bonifide were older. The younger men advised Leuci to tell the prosecutors nothing: "Those guys are looking to put you in jail."

The older patrolmen advised the opposite. Apparently there was more stuff there, they said. If so, he had best put all his trust in the prosecutors, and quickly. As far as cops in general were concerned, Leuci was already a rat. He had made cases against cops. He was finished. Protecting his former partners was not going to help him with other cops, and he could never go back into the Police Department. He would have to pick sides, and obviously he had better pick the prosecutors' side. It was his only chance. Otherwise sooner or later he would be indicted and arrested.

"They are going to get one guy who worked with you,

and he's going to give you up," said Bonifide. Fritz agreed, saying, "You are the first guy everyone wants to give up, if they have to give up anybody."

They all hate you, the older patrolmen told him. The Internal Affairs people hate you, the DEA agents hate you, the cops hate you, and all the prosecutors hate you, except perhaps for Giuliani.

They told him this with their heads down, not meeting his eyes. He ought to be thinking of one thing, and one only: Gina and the kids. There was no one else who cared about him.

The distraught Leuci ordered himself driven to the airport, and he fled home to Virginia.

The next day Giuliani and Leuci spoke by telephone. The detective's voice was choked, and he was clearly under terrific strain. His reasoning was convoluted, and most of his sentences broke off with their meaning only half complete. But his emotional state was clear to Giuliani. Leuci kept mentioning Nunziata. The decision that was being forced upon him, he said, was one he could not make, and he understood Nunziata's suicide better now. It was perhaps the only way out, not only for Nunziata, but also now for himself.

Giuliani said he would get down to Washington as soon as he could—on the next shuttle. Accompanied by Assistant U.S. Attorney Joe Jaffe, Giuliani rushed to La Guardia Airport and boarded the plane. He was terrified that he would reach Washington too late, but waiting at the exit gate, to his immense relief, was Leuci.

They drove straight to Leuci's house in northern Virginia. Jaffe was left with Gina, who was already preparing dinner. The prosecutor and the detective went for a walk, during which Leuci continued to insist that he was not going to turn on his partners. No one could make him turn on his partners, not Giuliani, not anyone. He wasn't going to do it.

"Don't you see," Giuliani asked, "that what you have just said is already an admission—that there were other acts of misconduct by you, in which your partners were involved? Let me go back, and with your permission, tell them that you are going to come in and tell us everything."

"You're asking me to put to death my best friends," said Leuci, and Giuliani thought he had never heard such anguish in a human voice.

What was Giuliani to answer, except what he took to be the truth—that Leuci's partners, had the situation been reversed, would do the same. Like Leuci, they would have no choice in the matter.

"No, no," Leuci insisted. "They wouldn't do it to me. That's the difference between you and them. They wouldn't do it to me. That's the fact of it. They wouldn't do it to me."

Giuliani told him that he would have to decide either to stick it out alone, or to cooperate completely. He couldn't go down the middle.

When they returned to the house, Gina served dinner, and a good deal of wine was poured, which, for a time, seemed to make everything better. After dinner the prosecutor and the detective descended to the playroom in the basement.

"If I were not a lawyer but a surgeon," Giuliani began, "and you came to me with cancer, and I told you, Bob, let me remove the cancer—what would you do? Because that's what you've got. You've got a cancer. It's eating you up, and if you don't let me take it out, you're going to die. And a lot of people will dance on your grave, good guys and bad guys."

More than three years ago, Giuliani continued, Leuci had set this whole chain of events in motion. He had decided to switch sides. He had come over onto the side of the government; whether he did it for good reasons or bad no longer mattered. Now that he was on this side, he had to play by the rules this side obeyed. "The side you are on," said Giuliani, "is the side where you have got to tell the truth."

When Gina and Jaffe came downstairs into the playroom, Giuliani and Leuci fled upstairs to continue their discussion. When Gina and Jaffe soon followed, they went out of the house and walked along under the trees.

Giuliani said he would love to be able to forget about this matter. He had no desire to force Leuci to reveal information that would overturn the conviction of a miserable son of a bitch like Eddie Rosner. But Rosner was irrelevant now. They had to follow a simple and direct approach. They had to find out what all of the truth was, and publish it. Perhaps Leuci never should have told Scoppetta anything, never should have worked undercover, never should have made any of these cases, never should have agreed to serve as witness. But he had done all that. There was no way now that he could erase the past three and a half years. He was going to have to tell the story of the rest of his misconduct.

At last Leuci began to ask Giuliani specific legal questions. What would happen to him if he revealed things like giving junk to informants or illegal wiretaps? Suppose he revealed that he had made a good many more scores, stolen a good deal more money than he had previously admitted? What would happen to the people he cared about who might have been involved with him? Could they be given immunity?

To all these questions Giuliani had no firm answers and said so. Leuci might be indicted, or he might not. Giuliani would certainly argue strongly against it. Leuci had performed an enormous public service at terrible cost to himself. The Police Department was to a large extent a different place now because of what he had done, the criminal justice system as a whole was cleaner and better, and his credit for this was so tremendous that perhaps he was entitled to make a couple of mistakes along the way. Giuliani would try hard to see to it that Leuci was not indicted. He didn't know. He didn't know how Puccio would react, for instance. He admitted that the Drug Enforcement Administration—Taylor and Carros—was hot after him, and wanted to see him hurt. Those two men could perhaps be calmed down, or held off. He just didn't know.

What would happen to his partners, Leuci wanted to know.

This also was out of Giuliani's control. Mandato,

Wolff, and the others would certainly have to be charged with crimes. There was no way around that. But perhaps something could be worked out, assuming they were willing to cooperate with the prosecutors.

"You set all that in motion when you first went to work undercover," Giuliani said. "Anybody who told you different was misleading you. They were so overwhelmed with what you could do that they never really focused on this part of it. But when you put yourself in the position of being a witness, from that moment on it became certain that everything had to come out."

It was four o'clock in the morning before Giuliani and Jaffe were shown a bedroom. Small beds. The kids' beds, probably. They got into them, and slept for several hours. Then Gina made breakfast, and after breakfast Giuliani and Leuci were alone again and the discussion continued. Giuliani marshaled his final arguments.

"Whether you tell us or don't tell us, we are going to get that information. Just about every detective who ever worked in SIU is going to go to jail. So if you don't tell us about whatever it is you're concealing, then someone else will tell us. Someone else will testify against the partners you're trying to protect, and against you, and the net result will be the same. They'll go to jail. And you'll go to jail."

Around three o'clock in the afternoon, Leuci drove Giuliani and Jaffe to the airport. Just before the two prosecutors boarded the plane, the detective, staring at his shoes, mumbled that tomorrow he would come into the office and tell everything. Giuliani breathed a sigh of relief. They all shook hands, and the two prosecutors walked down the ramp.

Leuci watched them go. By then he had decided to kill himself.

When he reached home, Leuci went for a walk with his son. He wanted to get some sense of how far the boy had come, what he would understand about his father. What did he think about being moved to the Catskills, moved to Virginia? What did he think about having men with machine guns for playmates?

But nothing much had registered on the child's mind. Men with machine guns were good playmates, and were not otherwise significant. The little boy understood nothing at all. He was seven years old. Kneeling, Leuci embraced him, saying goodbye.

He got into his car. I can't just blow myself away like Nunziata, he told himself. What I've got to do is crash my car, so my family can collect the insurance.

He was on the George Washington Parkway, driving fast, trying to figure out how to do it. Hit some other car head on? He couldn't risk killing some nice guy and his family coming the other way. He would have to crash into an abutment. Driving up and down the parkway, he began looking for a good one. He drove past one abutment, past two more. He was driving seventy miles an hour, then eighty, ninety, and a police car came up alongside and pulled him over.

Leuci jumped out of the car, showing his shield. "I'm a New York City cop."

The other cop, as it happened, was an Italian too. The two cops leaned their rumps against the fender and talked. The Washington cop had been in Narcotics once, he said, but he had got out quickly. Narcotics was a crazy scene. He wanted no part of it. He had read about all the Narcotics detectives getting locked up in New York. Were any of Leuci's friends in trouble?

"Yes," said Leuci, "some of my friends are in trouble."

They exchanged home phone numbers. The other cop invited Leuci to the Redskins' games in the fall. He had season tickets. "I got them on the arm," he said.

"Of course," said Leuci, "what else?"

In Florida, Mandato's phone rang. It was Leuci. "How are you doing?" asked Mandato.

"Not very well, Frank."

Mandato knew what this meant.

"Frank, I'm going up to the city tomorrow and—"

It was a call, Mandato realized, that he had half expected for a long time.

"You don't have to tell me. You're going to give us up."

"Yeah, Frank."

"Just call me when you get there," said Mandato, and he hung up. After a moment he turned away from the phone.

26

EARLY THE NEXT MORNING Leuci flew up to New York. It was a holiday. The streets of the city were empty. Foley Square in downtown Manhattan was deserted, no traffic, no people. To Leuci the downtown area had always been a scary place when it was empty like that. It was cold, and not nice—especially today.

He entered the Federal Courthouse and went directly to Giuliani's office. Giuliani and Jaffe were already there. The three men sat down. Giuliani said that Detective Leuci should tell them the worst thing first. When this suggestion was greeted by a heavy silence, he said, "I mean, what do you see as the worst thing you've ever done?"

"That's difficult to say," answered Leuci. "I mean, your perception of what is the worst thing, and my perception of the worst thing are, maybe, different."

"You know what we're asking you?" said Giuliani.

"What are you asking me?"

"Did you kill anyone?"

"No, I never killed anyone. And I didn't have anything to do with the French Connection ripoff, either."

The two prosecutors were relieved. Leuci said, "You guys thought I had something to do with that?"

"It's always possible," said Giuliani.

"I had nothing to do with it."

"That's terrific," said Giuliani. He was ebullient, and for the moment not thinking like a lawyer. But he caught himself at once, and his voice again became stern. "Did you ever sell narcotics?"

"I never sold narcotics."

"What narcotics dealings did you have? Maybe we should talk about The Baron's affidavit first."

"No, let's not do it that way."

It was not going to be easy for him to speak after all. He realized this now, and so did Giuliani.

"Tell us the first thing you ever did," said Jaffe.

"Start from the day you became a policeman," said Giuliani.

And so the long tangled tale at last came out. He described his rookie year in the Rockaway Beach Precinct. No corruption there that he ever witnessed. There was only one bookmaker in the precinct, and if he gave two dollars to a cop once in a while, that was the extent of it. In the Tactical Patrol Force there was no corruption at all. Then he had gone to Narcotics, and had been there for perhaps a year and a half before he began giving nickel bags of heroin to his informants.

The prosecutors wanted numbers. How often had he done this? As often as they had needed narcotics, Leuci answered. Dozens of times. Maybe hundreds of times. Every gift bag had been a sale under the law. Had Leuci known that?

Yes, he had known that.

"All right," said Giuliani, "what was the biggest score you were ever involved in?"

Leuci began to describe what became known as the Riverdale Motel case. This was in early 1968. He and Mandato were brand-new in SIU and had just been assigned to their first detective team. As it happened, the team was a large one, ten detectives in all, including two sergeants. The target was a major drug operation involving both blacks and South Americans, and so the detective team had been split in two. Leuci's team was assigned to work the blacks, while the other team, led by Detective Dominick Butera, had worked the South Americans. Butera's team made such fast progress that it became necessary to put the South Americans under surveillance for seventy-two hours straight, for a heavy package was supposed to arrive at any moment. But the package did not arrive, and with the detectives on surveillance exhausted, part of the Leuci team—Leuci, Mandato, and another detective—was ordered to spell them for a single night.

So the three relief detectives drove to the motel in two cars, then sat in one of them and watched the walls of the motel. Parked out front were two identical Cadillac Eldorados. Presently a South American wearing a cowboy hat got into one of the Eldorados and drove away. Leuci and the third followed. They tailed him into Manhattan, where he moved from bar to bar.

Leuci phoned the SIU duty officer. Was there any word from Mandato in Riverdale?

There was indeed. Mandato had reported that the other South American was loading the other Eldorado. He was carrying suitcases out of the motel room. Clearly the two men were planning to leave town.

Leuci phoned Detective Butera at home, waking him up. What should they do?

Take them, Butera said.

Mandato had left a phone number. Leuci called him back. Was the other South American alone? Well then, could Mandato take him by himself? Mandato laughed. Of course he could. Don't worry about it.

A few minutes later the first South American exited from a bar, took three steps, and found Leuci's arm around his throat, and Leuci's gun in his back.

Leuci handcuffed him, searched him. He also searched the Eldorado. No guns, no drugs. He drove the Eldorado back to the Riverdale Motel, with the prisoner protesting all the way.

Inside the motel room, Mandato sat watching the other South American, whom he had handcuffed to a chair. Mandato too had made a thorough search. He had found no drugs. He did find a gun and he also found something else. "Go take a look in the closet," he told Leuci.

In the closet in a suitcase was the most money any of them had ever seen.

They waited for Butera, the two sergeants, and the rest of the team to arrive. Soon the room was full of detectives, and there were a number of whispered conversations. The South Americans were offering half the money in the closet in exchange for their freedom.

Well, no drugs had been found. One South American could not be held at all and the other could be held only on a gun charge that would probably get thrown out of court tomorrow.

Leuci was sent into the adjoining room to count the money. He spilled stacks of money out of the suitcase onto the bed. Money covered the entire counterpane.

The gun and half the money were returned to the South Americans, and they were ordered to leave the city at once. Later the detectives met to count and divide the score. They had taken $40,000, which had to be split ten ways, including a share for a team member who was off that day—for the number one rule among cops then and always was that a partner got an equal share, no matter what. Cops had their own ten commandments, and the first of them was this: If you are walking along the street and find a dime, your partner gets a nickel.

So Leuci and Mandato the following night took the surprised partner out to dinner and handed him $4,000. He remarked that he had just had a new kitchen put into his house; he had been wondering how he was going to pay for this kitchen. Now you can pay for it, Leuci and Mandato told him.

In accepting the money the partner became guilty of a felony crime, though it was difficult in any sort of realistic world to imagine what else he might have done. The ripoff was over. He had not taken part. He could not give the money back to the South Americans—they were gone. He could not, lacking corroboration, make a case against his partners, even if he wanted to, for it would be nine voices against one. All he could do, if he chose to refuse the money, was to destroy himself before his peers. When the partner faced charges in the Police Department trial room later, Trial Commissioner Luis Neco, citing the foregoing arguments, acquitted him. But Police Commissioner Michael Codd overturned the verdict, cashiered him, and forfeited his pension. The partner has been litigating to get back in the Police Department ever since.

"Let's have the rest of the scores," prodded Giuliani gently.

Leuci recounted about fifteen scores in all, most of them similar, though the money involved now diminished steadily. The principal emotion evoked in the listening prosecutors was not horror, but sadness.

Soon after the Riverdale Motel Case, Wolff and Cody had come into SIU, and had been assigned to the now experienced Leuci and Mandato as partners, and from then on, according to Leuci, all four detectives had shared every score. The "victims" in almost every case were Hispanic drug dealers. Santiago Valdez: drugs seized, arrested, robbed of $12,000. Jose Vasserman: drugs seized, arrested, robbed of $3600; Manual Noa, no drugs found, no arrest, robbed of $20,000. And so it went.

Sometimes the four detectives operated with others, and scores had to be split into extra shares. In all, Leuci said, he had pocketed between twenty and thirty thousand dollars as his share during those years.

The first interrogation of Leuci lasted all morning. No notes were taken, and Leuci's recital was interrupted many times by his need not so much to justify, as to explain. Contrary to what people thought, he insisted over and over again, heroin seized by SIU detectives did not normally go back onto the street. There were two terrible exceptions, the French Connection ripoff, and the five kilos sold by Aguiluz. Apart from that he never heard of a single SIU detective selling heroin.

Nor, the prosecutors realized to their surprise, had they.

SIU detectives, Leuci insisted, arrested more pushers, seized more narcotics than any other agency by far. The SIU guys were great detectives, who committed corrupt acts once in a while. It was just something that happened. It just was there one day, and then it grew.

During the years 1968 to 1971 the Mafia moved out of narcotics—who knew why?—and South Americans took it over. These people didn't speak English. They seemed to consider themselves immune to the law—and most often they were right. They were the flashiest individuals the SIU detectives had ever seen. Their women were literally dripping with jewelry, and wore mink coats to the floor. The men wore heavy gold chains around their necks, and solid gold bracelets on their arms, and gold wristwatches thin as subway tokens.

They had so much money that once they reached court they almost always managed to fix the case, or at least to go free on bail. If necessary, they'd put up enormous amounts of cash bail, a hundred thousand dollars or more, anything just to get out onto the street again, and once there they simply disappeared. They forfeited the bail. Presumably they went back to wherever they came from, and some other dope dealer flew in to take their place.

The SIU detectives, Leuci explained, having conceived an overpowering hatred for these people, began to dispense their own justice. Sometimes they talked of killing one or another prisoner, though this had never been done to Leuci's knowledge. Instead, they simply began to rob them. They would take whatever money the dope dealer had, order him on to the next plane to South America, and applaud themselves for accomplishing what no court seemed able to accomplish, a heavy fine followed by instant deportation.

The only trouble was, it was stealing. But since they were all doing it together, it didn't seem so bad. They were not closely supervised. For the most part they were not supervised at all. There were never older and supposedly wiser superiors there to counsel them. Instead, the hierarchy of the Police Department preferred to close its eyes to what was happening, or even, in many cases, to accept an equal share.

Leuci's recital continued—and it dwindled away an hour or more later with the admission that twice he had given Detective Vinny Russo about two hundred dollars for minor scores in cases where Russo had not been present. "You can't hurt Vinny," Leuci pleaded. "He wasn't even there."

Russo's name was noted.

Giuliani stood up. It was not yet noon, but he was exhausted. They all were. Since it was a holiday, nothing more could be done today. Giuliani told Leuci to go home to Virginia. "We appreciate what you've done," he said, a banal remark that nobody thought was banal at the time. "When you come back, we'll have DEA and IRS people sit down with you and debrief you."

"I want to call Mandato," Leuci said. "I want him to have the opportunity to come in and cooperate."

The prosecutors looked at each other.

"I want to call Cody."

"You can't call everybody, Bob."

"I want to call as many as I can."

"Do you want to get yourself killed?" said Jaffe.

"I want to call my closest partners. I want to call Mandato and Cody, and Wolff."

"Definitely not Wolff." Puccio's indictment against Wolff was still pending.

There was a brief discussion. Finally they decided they would permit him to call Mandato. Cody they wanted to think about. Wolff was out of the question. Leuci should go home now and try to relax. Try to rest. Next week was going to be bad.

From Virginia, Leuci phoned Mandato. "I've told them everything, Frank. If you come up and tell them everything—the truth—you'll be okay."

"Oh? What are they going to do, put me back in the Police Department? What do you mean I'm going to be okay?"

But presently Mandato agreed to fly to New York. "What about Dave and Les?"

"I'm going to talk to both of them."

Mandato said, "All four of us are going to walk in hand in hand, right?"

"That's right, Frank."

"What did you tell them?"

"I told them everything."

"Everything? But Bob, we've done things with people that are dead."

"I told them everything."

"Okay," said Mandato, and hung up the phone without saying goodbye.

The next time the two men spoke was in the corridor in

the Southern District offices. The prosecutors had kept them separated, and were accompanying them even to the bathroom lest they meet and confer. Inevitably they passed each other in the hallway.

"I guess you told them everything, Bob," said Mandato. "These are really nice guys. I can really understand why you would want to tell them everything."

Mandato was not under arrest, and each night he was allowed to go home. He was living in his sister's house on Staten Island.

The prosecutors were playing their cards carefully and well. Not until they were certain that Mandato would cooperate did they permit Leuci to telephone Cody. The idea was to confront Cody with two of his three former partners, proving to him it was useless to fight. He too would begin to make admissions, after which Wolff would be brought in. Once Wolff comprehended that all three partners were prepared to testify against him, he would be forced in his turn to confess, and to cooperate in whatever future trials the U.S. attorney's office might care to prosecute.

Cody was at first amenable. He appeared crushed, and he began to make the admissions of past misconduct that the prosecution team was looking for. He agreed to come back the following morning, and to "cooperate" even more fully. He asked only one favor. Wolff was to be called in the following day. Cody asked permission to talk to Wolff first.

This favor was accorded him, and he left the Southern District offices looking sad, but resigned.

Cody was now forty-seven years old, a frail, gentle kind of man who had lived with his mother most of his life. She had recently died, and he lived alone. His life was centered around cop bars. He met with other cops in bars night after night, exchanging war stories, often drinking himself into oblivion and being driven home by other cops. He had no one else. Apart from his partners—apart from cops—he was alone in the world.

He was forty before he became a detective and was assigned to the Harlem narcotics group, and it was there that he met, became friendly with, and eventually the partner of Detective Leslie Wolff. Wolff was the team leader. Wolff was Cody's strength. It was Wolff who told Cody where to be the next day and what to do when he got there.

For a cop, Cody was an amazingly gentle person. He felt only pity for junkies, whom he likened to alcoholics. He called them sick people. He was never unkind to anyone, not even prisoners, and none of his partners ever saw him angry, even in combat street situations. He was tall and skinny, and looked almost emaciated from years of too much drinking, too many years of improper diet.

That day he met Wolff, and urged his partner to cooperate. Perhaps he used the same words Mandato had used. If the four partners went through this holding hands, they would survive it.

Wolff, however, had no intention of cooperating. Not then, not ever, he told Cody, no matter how many of his friends betrayed him. Wolff was not coming in.

There was no way Cody could handle news like this. If Wolff was going to fight, then Cody would be put in the position of testifying against him in court.

Cody was too weak a man. If he was not able to speak harshly of dope dealers he had arrested, how would he be able to walk into open court and denounce Les Wolff, whom he loved?

He left Wolff, went into a bar, and started drinking. When he was drunk enough, he went across into the park near his apartment in the north Bronx, withdrew his .38 caliber Smith and Wesson Chief from its holster, and fired one shot into his left temple. It was 4:19 in the afternoon.

Within minutes the news swept through the offices of the Southern District. Someone said to Leuci, "By the way, Cody just killed himself."

Leuci had a tube of Valium in his pocket. He gulped down its entire contents, every pill, fifteen of them, maybe more. He wanted his head out of there.

It took him only seconds to lose the bodyguards assigned him that day. He made a right, a left, another right, found himself in front of the judge's elevator, and pushed a button. The doors opened, disclosing a small, middle-aged judge whose expression, as soon as he glanced into Leuci's face, turned to fear. Leuci stepped into the elevator. The judge backed to the rear wall and stood there, saying nothing.

In the street, walking dazedly away from the Federal Courthouse, Leuci asked himself over and over again: What have I done, what have I done?

Someone saw him heading for the Brooklyn Bridge, and rushed up to tell Giuliani. Giuliani knew Leuci was missing. He had already sent agents into the street to find him. Now he sent others rushing toward the bridge. "We've pushed him too far," he told Jaffe.

Giuliani, until recently, had prosecuted corrupt cops with no more compunction than he would accord a bank robber. But his attitude had changed. He could not look at one anymore without compassion. These were men of conscience who had erred, almost every one, and even though they had committed crimes, their consciences remained intact. It was their consciences that, once they were caught, caused them—and the prosecutors—so much trouble. All moral philosophers argued that each man must obey his own concept of good and evil, that his own conscience was paramount. The problem was that each cop's strongest moral principle was loyalty to other cops, particularly partners. It was this principle that the prosecutors forced them to abjure, forcing them to commit, therefore, what were, morally speaking, unspeakably evil acts. Rather than commit such acts, two cops had already killed themselves, one was insane, and Leuci was headed for the Brooklyn Bridge.

Giuliani, though a minor figure early in the Leuci undercover period, had nonetheless been involved—it was he who had driven the car out to arrest Perrazzo. He could no longer be objective. If Leuci went off that bridge, then a part of Giuliani would go with him.

Leuci, by this time, was standing in the middle of the bridge, staring down at the water far below. He didn't remember how he had got there, nor why he had come.

Perhaps he was crying, for he could not see the water very well. He put his hands on the rail. I should do it, he told himself. I'd be doing everybody a favor if I did it. He thought of Mandato, whom he considered more fragile than himself. Frank, when he heard, would definitely whack himself out. No, he would have to go out to Staten Island to save Frank.

Across the bridge was Shaw's house. Shaw would know what to do. He began to stumble on toward Brooklyn. He became confused. A different choice seemed offered to him. He had forgotten jumping, and the pills had only made him stupid. A woman takes pills, he thought. For him it would have to be a bullet.

An hour later he was in the streets of Brooklyn Heights, standing under a theater marquee. Though he still wanted to get to Shaw, he no longer knew the way. A woman passed who looked at him strangely. A moment later she had him by the elbow. It was Margaret Shaw.

Upstairs, Shaw poured strong coffee down him, and made him bathe his fevered face with cold washcloths. Shaw also phoned the Southern District, for they were frantic there, and his most immediate job was to call off the search.

After that he could do little more than listen, and nod sympathetically, as the whole terrible story came spilling out of Leuci.

"Don't you see?" Leuci said, "we're not criminals. We're policemen, and we can't cope with being criminals. When was the last time a Mafia guy committed suicide because he got in trouble? It isn't criminals who kill themselves, it's cops."

"This is such a horror," Shaw said. "This whole thing is so sad, so sad."

Leuci's concern switched to Mandato. Mandato might do something terrible, he said. He wanted to go there, tell Mandato himself.

The doorbell rang, and in walked Assistant U.S. Attorney Joe Jaffe and a federal marshal. It was Jaffe and the marshal who drove Leuci out to Mandato's sister's house on Staten Island. Leuci walked across the lawn and rang the bell.

Mandato himself opened the door. He looked from Leuci to Jaffe and back again. "What's the matter?"

While Jaffe and the marshal waited outside, Leuci entered the house with Mandato. Mandato was alarmed. "Are you okay?" he asked. "You look terrible. Are you okay?"

"Cody killed himself, Frank."

Mandato let out a half-muted scream, and then: "Oh God, Dave, Dave, Dave."

A moment later, the two detectives walked outdoors. Mandato was half leaning on Leuci, half hugging him. They began walking fast up and down the sidewalk. Mandato alternately moaned and screamed Cody's name.

The two detectives were walking so quickly that Jaffe behind them could not keep up. They could hear him muttering, "I will never get involved in this kind of thing again. I will never get involved with cops again." The federal marshal was sitting on the curb across the street watching.

An hour passed. The two detectives patrolled the sidewalk, still clinging to each other.

Jaffe decided to put an end to this meeting. "You've said enough," he told them. "Let's get in the car, Bob."

In the light of the street lamp Mandato studied his former partner. He was beginning to get himself under control, but Leuci, he saw, was as brittle as ever. "Are you okay, Bob? You're not going to do anything, crazy, are you? You're not going to harm yourself, are you? You're not going to leave me to get through this by myself, are you?"

Mandato watched Leuci climb into the car.

Jaffe too was worried. Mandato no longer had a gun, but Leuci did, and the prosecutor, turning in his seat, demanded to know where it was.

"I don't carry my gun. It's in my attaché case." But he refused to give it to Jaffe.

With the marshal at his heels, Leuci stumbled through

the night. He met with Giuliani in one bar, and for a time he sat in another trying to drink himself into a stupor, while the federal marshal watched him nervously from nearby. For a time he may have dozed sitting up in a parked car. Morning came. Unshaven, wearing the same clothes as the night before, he moved through the corridors of the Southern District Courthouse demanding to see Mandato. But his former partner was in an office being interrogated by one prosecutor and three DEA agents, he was told, and a man stood at the office door, barring it and him. Leuci flung the man aside and kicked the door open.

Five startled men looked up at him. It was clear from his face that he was out of control. Nonetheless, the DEA agent nearest the door said, "What the hell do you think you're doing, busting in here like this?"

"Get up out of that chair, and I'll fucking kill you," shouted Leuci.

A stunned silence filled the room. Then Mandato stood up. "I'll take care of him," he said gently, and moved to Leuci's side.

He began to walk Leuci up and down the hall, talking to him in a soft voice.

"I just want to get out of here," Mandato told him. "I want to go back home to Florida. I'm going to tell them what they want to know, and then I'm getting the hell out of here. It's too late to do anything else."

"Frank, I'm not doing it. It's over. I'm calling up Les."

Shaking Mandato off, Leuci went to a phone and dialed Wolff's home number. When Wolff came on, Leuci, in a broken voice, gave way to the grief and remorse that afflicted him.

"Bob," Wolff said, interrupting harshly. "I did my crying last night. I'm done crying for Cody. I'm done crying for you. Fuck you, fuck him. He was a drunk. No one would have believed him anyway." In Wolff's voice Leuci sensed one emotion, and one only, hatred—hatred for the prosecutors, hatred for Leuci and Mandato as well. "If the prosecutors want to believe the ramblings of a drunk, if they want to believe you, let them. They can believe whatever they like, but I'm not coming in there. They're not doing to me what they've done to you guys."

Leuci felt a kind of befuddled admiration for Wolff. He was proud of him. Wolff would defy the entire United States Government.

"Les, you don't have anything to worry about from me, because as far as I'm concerned, you and I never did anything together."

"Don't tell me that," said Wolff coldly. "Tell that to the people you work for." And he hung up.

Leuci stood there a moment, goofy with pride about Wolff. Only slowly did the degree of Wolff's hatred sink in, so that suddenly he saw how it all would end. Wolff would stand fast all right, but he himself would not. When the trial came, Les Wolff would stand in the dock, and Detective Second-Grade Robert Leuci would be sworn in as a principal witness against him.

Leuci went back to the office where the prosecutors waited. Seeing the state he was in, they told him to go home. Mandato was allowed to walk him to the elevator. As he stepped into it, Leuci turned to his former partner and said, "Don't hate me, Frank."

Just as the doors closed, Mandato answered, "Bob, I'll never hate you."

27

GIULIANI, meanwhile, had two problems. The first was how to turn the new Leuci material over to the court, and the second was whether or not Leuci should be indicted.

The first problem was more quickly resolved than the second. Leuci's admissions, including the many counts of perjury, were gathered together by Jaffe and bound into a kind of booklet. The booklet, eighty-four pages thick, was a masterpiece of duplication, cross references, and overkill. Defense lawyers in every subsequent trial would be delighted with it, not only because it would make cross-examination of Leuci so easy, but also for the heavy, satisfying thud it made when tossed contemptuously, theatrically onto a table top, or into the principal government witness's lap. Copies of this booklet were turned over to Rosner's new lawyer, Alan Dershowitz, and to Judge Bauman, who had presided at the original trial, and who would also preside at the hearing he had ordered into The Baron's affidavit.

The compiling of the booklet was a painful thing for Leuci, for he was made by those interrogating him to go over and over acts that were by now up to seven years into his past. He was a different man today than he had been then, or at least he hoped he was, and it was painful for him to be forced to confront the man he had been then—the detective known as Babyface. To talk about Babyface nauseated him. Babyface was his enemy. And yet he remembered the sense of purpose with which Babyface had approached his work in those years— Babyface was never completely evil, or so Leuci wanted to believe, and to repudiate Babyface now, which he had to do and wanted to do, was like repudiating his brother, or his father.

The hearing began. Leuci walked into court, and Judge

Bauman, who had been so friendly and understanding during the Rosner trial, now refused to look at him. Every time the witness, Leuci, looked up at him during the course of the interrogation, the judge swiveled his chair around so that he was facing in the other direction.

The interrogation by Dershowitz went on and on. The lawyer played up each situation, each incident, forcing the witness to provide every detail, to wallow in his own shame.

After a time, afraid he might actually vomit, the witness asked to be excused, and he rushed to the men's room in the hall. When he came out, he found himself suddenly alone in the corridor and face to face with Edmund Rosner. This shocked him, but he dropped his eyes and started to walk past.

"Hey, I'm sorry," said Rosner. "I wish all this had never happened."

Leuci looked at him, "You and me both, pal."

"Can I shake your hand?" asked Rosner.

"Sure." The two men shook hands.

"Good luck," said Rosner.

"Good luck to you," said Leuci.

Then he was back on the stand again. When he looked out into the courtroom, it was to recognize men from Internal Affairs, all wearing half-smiles, notebooks open on their laps, ballpoints busy, taking down every name Leuci divulged. Looking at them was, for Leuci, like looking into a mirror: all the things he had sworn he would never do, he was now doing in open court for posterity forever.

His testimony ended. The hearing ended. And Judge Bauman retired to deliberate. Was Rosner entitled to a new trial?

Even as Judge Bauman studied the new testimony by Leuci and pondered his decision, other arguments resounded up and down the corridors of the Southern District Courthouse. What to do about Leuci? Should he be indicted, or not? There seemed to be three camps, only one of them pro-Leuci. The other two wanted him in jail, though for different reasons.

The Drug Enforcement Administration, as repre-

sented by Tom Taylor and George Carros, not only urged
that Leuci be indicted, they virtually demanded it. The
two agents despised and hated Leuci, that much was clear.
Of all the men the detective had dealt with over the past
three and a half years, these appeared to be the only two
he had not won over.

As they urged his indictment, their voices were loud
and their faces sometimes contorted, but their arguments
could not, on these grounds, be discounted, for in the
everyday functioning of the U.S. attorney's office they
were important men. It was they who assigned the agents
who did the leg work as many of the cases under
investigation were put together. Furthermore, many of
their arguments made sense. "How can you not indict
Leuci?" they would demand. How could Leuci's crimes be
allowed to go unpunished? How could others reasonably
be prosecuted for lesser offenses?

A good many assistant U.S. attorneys were also
pushing for indictment. Their arguments were altogether
intellectual, and for that reason more powerful. The
government, they pointed out, was here faced with a clear
and overwhelming case of perjury. In the Rosner trial
alone, Leuci had lied dozens of times, and that verdict was
now in jeopardy. There had been only one other
trial—that of Perrazzo's two confederates—in which his
perjury had been identical. Add to this perjury the
hundreds of other crimes—the giving of heroin to
informants, the illegal wiretaps, the scores—to which
Leuci had now confessed. These prosecutors too asked,
"How can you not indict him?"

Though most of the lawyers attempted to keep their
emotions separate from their deliberations, this proved to
be difficult. Perjury always made a prosecutor angrier
than any other crime. For one thing, it was the only crime
that, normally, a prosecutor witnessed. For another, it
struck at the root of the prosecutorial system itself. The
courthouse was a kind of concrete temple in which resided
the god of justice, but this temple was built upon the most
fragile of underpinnings, namely the testimony of
witnesses. These fragile underpinnings were protected by

one thing only, the sworn oath. Perjury, they argued, must be dealt with everywhere and always as the most terrible of crimes, because that was what it was.

For purely tactical reasons also, it was argued, Leuci ought to be indicted. It might save the Rosner case. It might save some of the future cases as well, for many had not yet come to trial. It would defuse arguments by Rosner and others that the government had had knowledge of Leuci's perjury and had kept silent. It would prove that the government was furious with its principal witness, and all its arguments before Judge Bauman and others would seem more honorable, more substantial, more convincing.

The decision would be made by the new U.S. attorney, Paul Curran, who knew very little of Leuci personally. He had not been present during the heroics of the undercover phase of Leuci's activity, nor during the indictment and trial of Rosner, nor during the subsequent indictments of so many others. He had no prejudices one way or the other. He looked to his aides for advice, and more advice had come in than he had counted on, much of it conflicting. The weight of it, however, seemed clearly against Detective Leuci. Of his closest, highest-ranking aides, only Giuliani argued firmly for no indictment.

Then Curran's predecessor, Whitney North Seymour, marched through the door. Seymour was a giant of a man, not only in physical stature, but in prestige as well. In the law enforcement community Seymour was a heavyweight, and he argued now in Leuci's behalf. His arguments took the form of a description of the services Leuci had performed for the government. To Seymour, Leuci had tried to do the right thing from the moment he first came forward. Even in lying on the witness stand he had been obeying the dictates of his conscience—he had been trying to protect his partners. This was no doubt reprehensible, but it was certainly understandable, and it was possible even in condemning it to see Leuci's perjury as an act of intergrity.

In calm, measured tones, Seymour underwrote Leuci's character.

He was followed into Curran's office in succeeding days by Scoppetta, and then by Shaw. Shaw, in fact, came twice. The arguments of both men much resembled those of Seymour. Both were trying to keep their counsel on a professional, intellectual plane insofar as possible, but Shaw, finally, was unable to do so.

Inside the U.S. attorney's office, Shaw had always been considered a distant, intellectual kind of man. Often his colleagues went to him with legal problems and he solved them instantly, and they thought of him always as a first-class legal mind. Now, as his plea on behalf of Leuci became personal, even emotional, everyone was surprised.

Shaw was distressed at the way things were leaning in this office, he began. Sure there were rational arguments why Leuci should be indicted, and there were irrational ones too. He categorized the conduct of Carros and Taylor, in threatening Leuci with indictment, as unspeakably evil. Shaw himself had been exposed to Leuci from the very beginning, and to what he had done, and to what it all had cost him. Although Curran hadn't witnessed all this himself, nonetheless he ought to respect it. As the tall, thin lawyer sat on the sofa in Curran's office, the emotions that he usually kept strongly checked rose to the surface. If you appreciated how it started, Shaw said, and what it accomplished, and how understandable his lies were, you couldn't conscientiously bring charges against him. It would not be a fair treatment of this human being.

Giuliani was present during both of Shaw's visits, and from time to time other assistant U.S. attorneys also, and all were surprised at Shaw's understanding of Leuci's character, for on the surface the Harvard-educated rich man's son and the street cop from Queens had nothing in common. "Bob Leuci is one of my heroes," said Shaw.

The decision finally would be Curran's alone. If he decided to indict, whether for perjury or for any other of Leuci's past acts of misconduct, then conviction, given Leuci's confessions, would automatically follow. Curran, as far as Leuci was concerned, was a one-man judge and jury, and on his verdict rode in many respects the rest of

Leuci's life. Indictment would mean at the very least dismissal from the Police Department; it would mean exclusion from any future job within law enforcement as well. To indict Leuci would be to ban him forever from the only world he knew or cared about.

In the American criminal justice system, prosecutors within their jurisdictions are granted absolute discretion. They may prosecute or not prosecute, as they choose. The two decisions, Curran's and Judge Bauman's, were handed down almost simultaneously, though the prosecutor's came first.

The government declined to prosecute Detective Leuci, ruled Curran. The additional Leuci testimony about his own misdeeds had been collateral, ruled Judge Bauman. Collateral is a legal term meaning apart from the central issue, and therefore of no consequence. Rosner's conviction stood.

28

THERE CAME a day when Assistant U.S. Attorney Rudolph Giuliani, trying to put together a major narcotics investigation with new narcotics detectives newly assigned to him, realized that they were all inept. They couldn't tail a suspect without getting made. They couldn't contact a surveillance without calling in that they were lost. They never played hunches.

A great detective, Giuliani thought, should be a man of imagination and fearlessness. A man with a sense of adventure, a man not limited by procedure. In his new detectives, all these qualities were absent, so that he asked himself almost in despair: Where have all the great detectives gone? The answer that came back to him was this one: I put them all in jail.

By then the SIU had been disbanded. Of the approximately seventy men who served in the small, elite unit between 1968 and 1971, fifty-two were indicted. Even this latter figure does not tell the whole story. Nunziata and Cody were never indicted, nor was Bermudez, nor Hubert, nor Leuci himself. Many others were implicated but, for one reason or another, not prosecuted.

Among these was Detective Vinny Russo. It was unlikely, the prosecutors felt, that any jury would send Russo to jail for accepting $150 on one occasion or another, or even for lying in an attempt to protect other cops. Besides, one of the witnesses against him would have to be Leuci. "If you prosecute Vinny Russo," Leuci had told them over and over again, "you'll have another Dave Cody on your hands." Looking at Leuci, as he pleaded for his friend, the prosecutors were struck by the strain that showed in his voice and in his eyes. If they prosecuted Vinny Russo, they might have two more Dave

Codys on their hands. Russo, was, however, forced to retire from the Police Department.

Very few of the detectives against whom charges were brought were acquitted. Aguiluz, after testifying in eight trials, after pleading guilty to felony tax fraud both in the Southern and Eastern Districts, received a suspended sentence and was relocated—no one knew where. His two partners, the Irishman Peter Daly and Joe Novoa, found legally guilty of Aguiluz's five kilo sale, went to Atlanta Federal Penitentiary to smash rocks for ten years.

Novoa had been offered a chance to cooperate; at the last minute he refused it. He was not going to turn on his partners and friends, and he was not going to admit to his children that he was a dope dealer. Aguiluz testified against him, Giuliani prosecuted, and he was convicted. A year or so later he was brought back to New York by the prosecutors to be questioned about another matter; by then he no longer looked like a cop. His shoulders were stooped, he walked with his head down, and he no longer raised his eyes when people addressed him.

Peter Daly had somehow foreseen all that would happen from the moment that Aguiluz was summoned to testify before the grand jury. Daly fled to Ireland at once, for he was safe there. No extradition treaty between Ireland and the United States existed which would touch him. He had made it back home, and he was free. Once he sent a picture of himself to Aguiluz. He was sitting by a handsome lake, wearing a crewneck sweater, waving. There was a pier nearby, and gorgeous Irish countryside in the background.

But his sister got beaten up by her husband in England—and Daly did what any cop would do for his sister—he flew there twice to try to help her. A priest informed on him. During his first visit, Scotland Yard detectives missed him. The second time they did not.

He was flown back to New York with a Scotland Yard detective seated on either side, and in the course of the long flight, one of them asked him the size of the largest seizure of narcotics he had ever made. "One hundred and five kilos," remarked Peter Daly proudly. But only 100 kilos had been vouchered. So at Daly's trial not only did Aguiluz testify against him, but so did the two Scotland Yard detectives. Guilty on all four counts. Ten years.

Detective Jack McClean, everybody's Irish uncle, who had hosted the Nunziata funeral, was sentenced to nine years, along with his partners Ray Viera and Medal of Honor winner Eddie Codelia, for ripping off Hispanic drug dealers. Later their sentences were reduced to four years. Most of the rest of the detectives were prosecuted for income tax evasion, for that was easiest, and the most usual sentence meted out, whether the detectives went to trial or pleaded guilty, was two and a half years.

One or two, among them Sheridan, were made to cooperate in other cases, then were allowed to plead guilty to misdemeanors. At the end Sheridan received a suspended sentence, and escaped jail.

Hardly any detective survived SIU with reputation intact. Imagination, fearlessness, a sense of adventure, a disregard for procedure—SIU men had these qualities in abundance. They were great detectives. Of course it was these same qualities that got them into trouble.

The trials went on month after month—there were so many of them—and the last of these on the schedule was the trial of Detective Leslie Wolff.

29

ON THE NIGHT BEFORE he was to testify against his former partner, Leuci lay in bed in the dark, and remembered how much he had learned to care for Les over the years.

He remembered when his cabin in the Catskills was finished, and it was time to bring a load of old furniture up there. He was in the office complaining about what a hassle this would be, renting a van, loading and unloading the furniture, the long lonely drive up and back. Without being asked, Wolff said, "I'll call you in the morning. We'll go get the van. We'll drive up there together. We'll have a nice day."

He remembered the first time Les and Sandy came to his house for dinner. Les arrived bearing a hand-carved wood head of Christ that he had picked up in an antique shop in Germany when he was in the army there. It was obviously valuable, and Leuci was so surprised that he said, "Les, you must let me pay you for this."

Wolff said, "No, I want you to have it. It's no big deal."

He remembered another dinner at Wolff's house. When dinner was over the Wolffs' daughter, who must have been about twelve that year, played the classical guitar for them all.

He remembered meeting Wolff outside his mother's house after Wolff's indictment by Puccio. Leuci had begun by putting his arm around Wolff's shoulders, at the same time surreptitiously feeling for a wire, so that Wolff, giving his half-smile, said, "Are you searching me? You are the most paranoid guy."

"Are you wearing a wire?"

"No, are you?"

"No. Do you want to search me?"

Again the half-smile. "No, I don't want to search you. I take your word for it."

And then the way the meeting ended: first the embrace, and then, "Bob, I've never felt closer to you than I do right now."

Wolff rarely showed affection. He rarely laughed either. He was always worried about what people thought of him. Which was probably why he had chosen to go to jail. If convicted he could always claim he had been framed. But to plead guilty would be to admit to his two children, who were now teenagers, that he had been a corrupt cop.

And so tomorrow Leuci would be forced to give testimony that might send Les to jail. Leuci got out of bed, felt his way to the bathroom, spilled Valium out into his hand, and gulped down the pills in the dark.

But back in bed he still could not sleep, and the old faces began to parade before his tightly closed eyes: Nunziata, Cody, Lusterino, Butera, Hourigan. Butera had taken part in the Riverdale Motel score, had been arrested, indicted, suspended, his gun and shield taken from him, and then for six months the prosecutors had pounded him. He dropped dead of a heart attack one day while on his way to meet the prosecutors of the Eastern District. He was forty-two years old. Hourigan had taken part in one of the ripoffs for which Wolff would go on trial tomorrow. Once arrested, he had begun to drink, and before the year was out had drunk himself to death. He too was forty-two years old.

These were the dead, but in the dark Leuci kept visualizing the faces of the living whom he had ruined, as well. Poor crazy Perrazzo, Vinny Russo, Mandato, and now Les Wolff.

The Valium was no help. He could not sleep, and at last he got up and paced until morning came. Haggard, exhausted, he drove to the courthouse, where he swallowed more Valium and then stepped into court, mounted the witness stand, and was sworn in.

The prosecutor was Tom McDermott, and he was another in the long line of those who, almost despite themselves, now cared very deeply about Detective Leuci

Leuci and Wolff were staring at each other across thirty feet of intervening courtroom. Both faces, to an outsider, would have appeared expressionless, but McDermott thought he could discern a thousand messages flashing back and forth between the former partners. Stepping into the line of sight, he interrupted this anguished exchange, and began his questioning.

Step by step he led Leuci back over the three events for which Wolff was now on trial.

1. Armed with warrants, Leuci, Mandato, Cody, Wolff, a lieutenant, a sergeant, and the lieutenant's driver raided the bar and apartment of a major narcotics dealer named Santiago Valdez. They arrested him and seized his drugs. While Leuci was searching the bar, Wolff came down and said he had found money in the apartment upstairs. The sergeant, who had seen the money too, suggested that they skim off a couple of hundred dollars to cover legitimate expenses incurred in making the case—the Police Department reimbursed no expenses ever. According to Leuci, Wolff said, "There's a hell of a lot of money up there, and I'm not giving it to this dope pusher."

So they worked out a way to get the money out of the house. They synchronized their watches. Wolff went back upstairs. After precisely 90 seconds, Leuci stepped out onto the sidewalk, and the money came flying out of the upstairs window in a hatbox, Leuci caught the hatbox, walked to his car and drove off. Later the seven detectives split $12,000.

2. Leuci and his teammates obtained a warrant for the arrest of Jose Vasserman, another major narcotics importer. Again their work was flawless. Vasserman was supposedly armed and dangerous, and his door was surely barricaded. Hit that door with shoulders, and two things would happen. The drugs would go down the toilet, and one or more detectives might get shot. So Leuci and his team talked the building superintendent into shutting off Vasserman's water and electricity simultaneously. When Vasserman peered out into the hallway to see

if the building lights were out too, the detectives grabbed him without a struggle.

Inside the apartment they found that Vasserman had been packaging heroin in the presence of a second man they didn't know. Under the law the second man, who had not been part of the investigation, was as guilty now as Vasserman—who promptly offered them $3600 to let the man go. After talking it over, they accepted the money. They then arrested Vasserman, and seized and vouchered his drugs.

About two weeks later Leuci got a phone call from Lusterino, who said that Mikey Coco wanted to see him. Leuci and Mandato met Coco in the Holiday Inn on Fifty-seventh Street. The mobster said, "There's a bail bondsman who has got $20,000 to fix this case for Vasserman."

The two detectives said there was no way Vasserman could beat the case.

"Take this $10,000," said Coco. "If the guy goes to jail, give it back to me, because I'm going to have to vouch for this money. If the guy beats the case, you get another $10,000."

Leuci and Mandato took the money, and the next day talked it over with Cody and Wolff. Leuci said, "If Vasserman goes to jail, we're going to have to give this money back, because Coco is vouching for it." He added, "I don't want to be in the position of owing a guy like that money."

According to Leuci, Wolff said, "Let him sue me. Fuck him."

Vasserman was sentenced to seven years. Coco's $10,000 was not returned.

3. The four detectives had been trying to make a case against Manuel Noa, another major narcotics mover. But Noa never touched drugs unless paid in advance. The detectives decided to order the drugs themselves, then arrest Noa for possession. But for this they needed $9,000 front money. The Police Department did not have that kind of money. If they went to the feds for it, the feds would take over their case—and probably blow it. To SIU

detectives, federal narcotics agents were one and all buffoons. So they went to an informant—a second major dealer—who agreed to order the drugs and put up the money.

At length Noa informed the informant that the shipment was in. The informant informed the detectives, who drove up to Noa's West Forty-ninth Street apartment armed with warrants. Inside, they found drug paraphernalia and records of drug transactions, but no drugs, though they tore the apartment apart. They did find a picnic basket full of money, an enormous amount of money, a hundred thousand dollars or more, and they owed their informant $9000.

Negotiations ensued. The five detectives (Leuci's team plus Sergeant Hourigan) left the apartment with a paper bag full of money. They returned the $9000 to their informant and shared the rest, which came to about $2000 each.

30

ALTOGETHER Leuci was on the stand for two full days. As soon as Prosecutor McDermott was finished with him, Wolff's defense attorney, Paul Goldberger, rose and approached the stand. From the defense table, Wolff watched passively while Leuci, under cross-examination by Goldberger, was accused—and accused himself—of the acts for which Wolff was being tried. The case—Leuci's whole life—had come full circle, and sitting before the jury in the thirteenth floor courtroom, he seemed to be fulfilling two roles at once: he was prosecutor and defendant both.

Goldberger started with nicknames. Did Leuci have a nickname? Was Babyface his nickname?

Leuci: "Babyface was a common nickname given to young-looking narcotics detectives. When I was first starting in the Narcotics Division I was a lot younger than I am now—"

Goldberger: "Detective Leuci, will you answer the question? Did anybody call you by the nickname of Babyface?"

Leuci: "Junkies in the street used to call me Babyface, yes. No detective would refer to me as Babyface, counselor."

Goldberger: "Why, because they were afraid of you? Were you a tough guy in the street? Did you use a lot of physical force in the street?"

Goldberger: "You used to carry narcotics around with you in Brooklyn, didn't you? As a matter of fact, you had a little magnetic box that used to hook up under the dashboard, and you used to keep some bags of narcotics in it, is that right?"

Leuci: "A little key case that I used to keep narcotics in for my informants, that's correct."

Goldberger: "You used to carry something else with you, some other white powder occasionally?"

Leuci: "I used to carry packages occasionally of pancake flour."

Goldberger: "And with the pancake flour you threatened to flake some junkie in the street, is that right?"

Leuci: "I would threaten to put it in his pocket if he tried to swallow some narcotics on me when I approached."

Goldberger: "So where did you carry this white powder, in your pocket?"

Leuci: "Sometimes."

Goldberger: "Felony weight?"

Leuci: "It was pancake mix, counselor."

Goldberger: "Would it have been felony weight if it had been drugs?"

Leuci: "It could have made twenty pancakes."

Goldberger: "But your testimony is that you never did flake anybody? Never framed anybody?"

Leuci: "Much too easy to arrest them."

Goldberger: "Now, would you say it's a fair statement that from time to time you and Mandato would cover for each other?"

Leuci: "Yes."

Goldberger: "Mandato was in the habit of taking a lot of time off when he was supposedly on the job, wasn't he? Mandato would wind up at a motel with some girl as opposed to being on the job on some occasion? Wouldn't he?"

McDermott: "Objection, your honor."

Goldberger: "Are you familiar with the Jade East Motel in Queens?"

Leuci: "Am I familiar with it?"

Goldberger: "Yes."

Leuci: "Yes."

Goldberger: "Mandato been there?"

Leuci: "I heard Mandato was—I heard Mandato mention the Jade East Motel to me."

Goldberger: "Were you ever at the Jade East Motel when you were supposed to be on duty?"

The Court: "May I make a suggestion, Mr, Goldberger? I may be a little obtuse. I don't at this point think that the sexual—"

Goldberger: "I'm not at all interested in the sexual appetite, judge."

The Court: "—have any relevance to these proceedings."

Goldberger: "Mandato, from time to time, had psychiatric problems, is that correct?"

The question, according to the rules of courtroom procedure, demanded only a yes or no answer, so Leuci was obliged to reply in the affirmative. He looked across at a jury that was already hostile to him, that had not even met Mandato yet, but already despised him, and he wanted to explain that Mandato, when forced out of the Police Department, had experienced a depression so deep and long-lasting that he had not known what else to do besides trying a psychiatrist.

But Goldberger had already begun a new line of questioning. "Did you come to know a person by the name of Jacobs? And did you come to know a person by the name of Johnny Ryan? Did you give Johnny Ryan heroin to simonize or wash your car in front of the Brooklyn Supreme Court?"

Leuci: "I don't remember giving heroin to Johnny Ryan at the Brooklyn Supreme Court. I had given heroin to Johnny Ryan many times around the Narcotics Bureau headquarters downtown, and he washed my car along with all the other detectives' cars in Narcotics. That was the only way Johnny Ryan would ever get drugs. Johnny Ryan was a burnt-out informant. Our cars may have been washed the day before. We didn't need it. He had to feel he was doing something. He was a guy that just hung around the Narcotics Division and he couldn't buy drugs in the streets any more and narcotics detectives took care of his habit as best we could."

Goldberger: "And when you gave drugs to Ryan, or gave drugs to Jacobs, did you understand that you were committing a crime at that time?"

Leuci: "Did I understand that to be a crime, the fact of giving drugs to someone? At that time? Yes, I guess so, I guess so."

Goldberger: "You guess so?"

Leuci: "Yes, I guess so. I'll give you that, counselor, sure. I knew it was a crime."

Goldberger: "So when you gave drugs to Johnny Ryan, and to Joe Jacobs, you were selling them drugs under the law, is that right? So the answer is yes, you had sold drugs?"

Leuci: "No, I did not sell drugs. I never gave anyone drugs for money, and that's what you are saying, counselor. I never did that."

Goldberger: "How many times would you say that under the law you sold drugs?"

Then Goldberger started a new line of questioning: the scores to which Leuci had just admitted in open court, and for which Detective Wolff, sitting silent and unmoving at the defendant's table, was on trial.

Goldberger: "And the money you made was cash money, right? Green dollar bills, is that right? You took them home with you?"

Leuci: "Yes."

Goldberger: "You built a trap in your house in Kings Park?"

Leuci: "I had a trap. That was built into my house in Kings Park to put my guns in, Counselor. I had two little children and I had a trap built into the house and there was also money in there, but it was a very tiny little trap."

Goldberger: "A tiny little trap that got filled up with lots of money."

McDermott: "Objection."

Goldberger: "Do you take medication before you testify?"

Leuci: "At times."

Goldberger: "Did you take some tranquilizers yesterday?"

Leuci: "Yes."

Goldberger: "What kind of tranquilizers do you take before you testify?"

Leuci: "I take a Valium every once in a while. I

don't—yesterday I did. I took a Valium yesterday."

Goldberger: "Did you take a Valium this morning?"

Leuci: "Yes."

Goldberger: "It calms you down before you testify?"

McDermott: "Objection."

The Court: "Sustained."

Goldberger went off in still another direction. Did Mandato or Wolff or Cody or Hourigan or O'Brien speak Spanish? Leuci answered that they did not.

Goldberger: "So pretty much you are the man. If there was a Spanish drug dealer to talk to, and he could only speak Spanish, he'd pretty much have to talk to you, is that right?"

Leuci: "Plenty of Spanish dealers were ripped off by guys who couldn't speak Spanish, my friend."

Goldberger: "I ask that that be stricken, judge, as unresponsive to the question."

Night came. Again Leuci lay awake in the dark. He could not stop thinking about Les, and about the trial. This cross-examination, which would continue in the morning, was the most savagely personal he had yet undergone—the nickname, the pancake flour, the trap, the Valium, the Jade East Motel. Goldberger had been supplied with information only a partner could know. To be subjected to such a cross-examination was a sickening experience. But he didn't blame Les. Les was fighting for his life.

I'm doing this for my family, Leuci told himself, for my kids. Then he thought: Does Les love his children any less than I love mine?

Lying there, he realized how much he still cared for Les Wolff. He wanted Les to come out of this trial okay. At the same time, he didn't want to lose the trial, because this would mean he had gone through these years, this trial all for nothing. His thoughts were a jumble. He didn't want Wolff convicted, and yet if Wolff were acquitted, then would not the jury, in effect, be condemning him in Wolff's place?

When dawn came he was still trying to work it out.

Later he was back on the witness stand, his questions

unresolved, his emotions no clearer, his brain foggy from two nights of no sleep.

Goldberger: "And what of your testimony yesterday that Detective Wolff went over to the picnic basket and put his hands in, and he says something like: 'This is for us,' or 'This is for me?'"

Leuci: "The picnic basket is opened up. The defendant walked over to the basket, reached in, and it was—with a smile on his face, and I was laughing. We were all laughing. We thought it was kind of funny. Noa didn't think it was so funny, I don't think. He said, 'We're going to take this money,' and Noa said, 'No, no, no,' and we smiled, and the defendant put the money back in the basket."

Goldberger: "Is it a fact, sir, is it the best of your recollection that you never testified at a grand jury concerning Les Wolff going over and picking up any money out of a picnic basket?"

McDermott: "Objection."

The Court: "Sustained."

From time to time Leuci glanced over at the jury. He saw no sympathy there, no understanding of any kind. At the defendant's table, Wolff watched him impassively, while his wife Sandy, in the first row of the courtroom, mouthed curses in the direction of the witness stand.

At last Leuci was allowed to step down and former detective Frank Mandato was sworn in in his place. Under questioning by Prosecutor Joel Cohen, Mandato's descriptions of the three ripoffs differed from Leuci's in no significant detail. His cross-examination by Goldberger was also almost identical. The former detective testified in a flat, emotionless voice, and when he gazed across at Wolff from time to time he too seemed to be trying to send messages, one of which seemed to be: Perhaps I can do you more good up here than I could sitting beside you in the dock.

Other witnesses followed, including Domingo Coca, the informant who had put up the $9000, Wilfredo Risco, José Vasserman's friend, who had bought his freedom for $3600, and Manual Noa's ex-wife. Coca had just pleaded guilty in a drug sale case, and had been sentenced to five years in prison. Risco, whom they had let go, was a worse man than Vasserman by far, though they hadn't known this. Risco had shot one cop in Ecuador, had bribed his way out of prison there, was currently in jail for armed robbery, and was about to go on trial for the murder of another cop in Puerto Rico.

When the turn of the defense came, Goldberger called only character witnesses, a series of them, the most important being William Aronwald, who had succeeded Shaw as head of the Strike Force. Aronwald testified that Wolff had an outstanding reputation for honesty and integrity. As for Leuci, he was "not worthy of belief." A second Strike Force attorney, Steven Frankel, testified that Leuci "has an awful reputation for truthfulness . . . you can't believe the things he says to you."

The trial was halted while a second group of prosecutors was brought in to praise Leuci. Scoppetta, now a deputy mayor, came. Whitney North Seymour came. E. Michael Shaw came. Rudolph Giuliani, now an associate deputy attorney general, flew up from Washington. Their presence, as well as their words testified to the extremely rare thing Leuci had done in coming forward of his own accord, testified to his truthfulness, testified to his integrity. Yes, he had perjured himself in two trials, but only to save his partners—to save Leslie Wolff.

It was no longer a trial of facts. It was Leuci against Leslie Wolff, partner against partner. The jury was asked to choose one partner or the other. It filed out and began deliberations. It was, Leuci realized, six years almost to the day since Leuci's first conversations with Scoppetta. Had those six years atoned for anything?

Leuci himself seemed to be hoping for a verdict that would justify not only his testimony against Wolff, but his testimony against everyone else, too—a verdict beyond the competence of this jury or any other.

It was 2:05 P.M. the next day when the jurors filed back into the courtroom and took their seats.

The verdict was not guilty on all counts.

As it was announced, Sandy Wolff leaped to her feet,

screaming and clapping. Wolff himself smiled faintly at the jury. Otherwise he showed no emotion.

A few days later, Wolff stood trial on the same charges in the Police Department trial room before Deputy Commissioner Francis Looney. There were few witnesses, few spectators. Looney's verdict, later endorsed by Police Commissioner Michael Codd, was guilty on all counts. Detective Third-Grade Leslie Wolff was ordered dismissed from the Police Department, and his pension forfeited.

There was one final meeting between Leuci and Wolff.

Leuci was assigned at this time to the First Deputy Commissioner's Special Force in an office at 280 Broadway, across Police Plaza from headquarters. When a call came in summoning him to headquarters, he glanced around for someone to walk him over. But there was no one available, and he realized suddenly that he had not walked alone in the city in over four years.

The commanding officer of the Special Force, Deputy Inspector Harold Hess, told him he could wait, or else he could go alone. "Sooner or later you're going to have to go out alone," said Hess.

On the elevator, going downstairs alone, Leuci was in the grip of a sudden fear which he did not understand, and he wanted to turn back. Instead he began walking fast across Police Plaza, head down. When he looked up, who was coming toward him on an intersecting path but Les Wolff. Leuci saw that he had very few choices. He could stop in his tracks, he could go back to 280 Broadway, or he could continue on to Police Headquarters. But if he did continue, he would come face to face with Les Wolff in the middle of this vast open plaza.

A quick glance showed that Wolff had changed neither speed nor direction. Abruptly, Leuci decided that he wouldn't either. He also decided that when their paths intersected, he would let Wolff speak first. But his feet became leaden. Glancing up, he saw that Wolff had slowed also.

And so they came together. They looked at each other, and for a moment Leuci thought that Wolff began to smile. An instant later he realized he was wrong. That crease on the side of Wolfe's cheek was not a smile. Leuci looked straight into Wolff's eyes, and saw only coldness there, only hatred. Then Wolff's eyes dropped. Shaking his head from side to side, he walked on.

Some months later, when asked to describe Wolff, Leuci said, "Les Wolff was tough, strong—much stronger than I am—calculating, devious. Les Wolff had ice water in his veins. I don't believe for a second he ever cried for Dave Cody. Les Wolff never cried for anyone but Les Wolff. He was the coldest man I've ever met. I respect Les, and—" A catch came into Leuci's voice: "—and I miss him."

31

LEUCI WAS OFFERED a new name and relocation, but he chose to remain instead a New York City cop. Even before the trials were finished, he had sold the house in northern Virginia and bought another in a distant New York suburb. From then on he commuted to work by Volkswagen, unaccompanied by bodyguards.

But he remembered to carry his attaché case on his person more often than in the past, and he tended also never to zip it shut. He tried not to think of further attempts on his life. Mikey Coco was still in jail, but would be getting out soon. The lawyer Benny Caiola was already out. Edmund Rosner, his last appeal exhausted, had just gone in, so presumably he was no longer a threat, if in fact he ever had been. On the other hand, the various ex-policemen had begun now one by one to trickle back into the sunlight again. Were any of them threats? Leuci chose to think not.

The undercover phase of his life had lasted sixteen months. The trials had lasted four and a half years after that, and though they marked the end of many lives, they could be said to have signaled the beginning of his. It would be a long road back, and he knew this. He did not expect it to be easy. But if only he could remain a cop, he believed he could get through it. Being a cop was a part of his physical protection. To kill him would be to kill a cop, and no one would do that lightly but a crazy man. But being a cop was part of his psychic protection too.

Only if he could remain a cop was there any hope to build a new Bob Leuci, or so he believed.

It would not be easy.

In the midst of the trials he had been assigned to a newly formed integrity unit, The First Deputy Commissioner's Special Force. This unit was staffed to a large extent by integrity-minded officers who had already served for many years in the Internal Affairs Division. Leuci had never hoped to be received by such cops as these with open arms, but surely they would grant him at least a grudging acceptance.

They had not done so. When he came into the office the first day no one welcomed him. No one even smiled at him. Men looked up from their work, stared at him, and then looked away. Leuci was assigned to a lieutenant and to a sergeant. There was no warmth there, none of the camaraderie that he had always sought and found in other police units in the past. He had never experienced such coldness before, and he did not know how to cope with it.

Deciding to try to win them over, he began to come in mornings carrying containers of coffee on the lid of a box, or he went out in mid-morning and brought coffee back. He put a container down on the desk of each of the men he worked with, and the containers stood there untouched, all day. There even were times when men got up from their desks and came back a few minutes later carrying coffee containers of their own. They sat down and drank from these, without a word to Leuci.

Finally he had decided to attempt a man-to-man talk with the two lieutenants and the sergeant whom he considered the most influential officers in the unit. But as he led the three men into a small office, he had no idea what he was going to say to them.

They sat down and asked him what this was all about.

His life was difficult enough, Leuci told them. He lived in a kind of no man's land. He thought maybe they would have some kind of empathy for him. Apparently they didn't. At least he needed to know why they felt about him the way they evidently did. Perhaps it would help if they understood where he was coming from and why he had acted the way he had.

The middle-aged sergeant, James Meehan, said, "Leuci, I don't give a fuck about you. I don't give a shit what your story is."

"I think maybe you misunderstand me," said Leuci hesitantly.

Sergeant Meehan cut him off. "You are a fucking rat. I don't like rats." He got up and left the room.

The two lieutenants remained a short time longer. One explained that he had spent twenty-six years in the Police Department, and that, while assigned to the Special Force, he would do his job. He would never judge Leuci for what he had done. On the other hand, Leuci should not expect to be treated as his friend. And he left the room.

The lieutenant who remained was the best educated of the three. He wore an enormous college ring. His approach was more philosophical. He didn't know Leuci's whole story, he admitted. He understood that no one had caught him, that he had "cooperated" of his own accord—which was all to the good, he supposed. Now Leuci should do his job here, and if he did it well, no one would bother him. "But if you're here to make friends," the lieutenant concluded, "you may as well forget it."

"What am I supposed to do?" asked Leuci, "come in here and not talk to anybody? I can't go through every day like that."

"Your life is away from the Police Department now," said the lieutenant. "It's not part of the department any more." And he walked out.

Left behind, Leuci tried to convince himself that he was not as evil as these men seemed to think. He would win them over. There were good people in the Police Department. He wanted to be part of them, to feel the affection and closeness that he had known in the old days as a patrolman in TPF—and that he had known as a corrupt detective in SIU, too.

From then on, if a job had to be done that no one else wanted, Leuci would say, "Look, I'll do it." Although he was not a drinker, he would stand with them in bars at the end of the working day, buying rounds of drinks, listening to their conversation, rarely taking part except, sometimes, to agree with them. As the months passed he began to win smiles from time to time. They had problems being nice to him, but eventually couldn't help themselves.

The day came when Sergeant Meehan's son, a young patrolman in the Ninth Precinct, was indicted.

Sergeant Meehan believed passionately in many right-wing causes. He believed in the American flag. He played Sousa marches on the phonograph in his office, and "The Stars and Stripes Forever" was one of his favorites. His son was his pride and joy. After distinguishing himself in combat in Vietnam, the kid became a cop, and he was his father's image. He worked in one of the toughest precincts in the city, he survived a gun fight, he received commendations. Like his father, he was a rugged street guy, a tough, tough cop who, however, would never curse in front of a woman.

James Meehan, Jr., was exactly what his father had wanted.

But Internal Affairs had been conducting an investigation of corruption in the Ninth Precinct, and six cops were quietly indicted. Sergeant Meehan was never told that his son was among them until the day came when Jimmy Meehan, Jr., was to be arrested.

Sergeant Meehan by this time had reached the stage where he was willing to engage in long conversations with Leuci. He could understand cops making money, he said, for he had seen it happen many times in his years in the job. What he couldn't believe was that any cop would take money from a dope dealer.

Leuci tried to explain. An erosion took place that was exactly similar to what happened to cops who worked against known gamblers, and who got caught up in the corruption of taking money from the gamblers. In fact, probably the gamblers' money came from junk, Leuci said. The cops who took the money never thought that far.

Usually these discussions ended with Meehan walking out, slamming the door behind him. To take money in a narcotics case was the lowest thing in the world. How could any cop do that, and call himself a cop?

It was the job of Inspector Hess, who headed the unit,

to inform Sergeant Meehan that his son was to be arrested. Meehan walked in the door that morning, a big smile on his face, wearing a plaid suit, with a red and green tie that didn't match the suit, and big heavy brown shoes. Hess said, "Jimmy, I have to tell you something."

As he listened to Hess, the blood drained from Sergeant Meehan's face.

"My son's no thief," Meehan cried, when Hess had concluded. "I know he's not."

He began to talk about lawyers. He would hire his son the best lawyer in the country.

Leuci said to him, "Jimmy, whatever you need, just ask me. Anything I can do to help."

For a moment Meehan only stared at him. Then his arm went around Leuci's shoulder and he said, "Don't worry, I take care of my own children."*

Leuci's acceptance by members of the Special Force dated from that day. It had taken, literally, years.

After Wolff's trial, it became necessary to reassign Leuci elsewhere. If, in the upper echelons of the Police Department, any deep thinking was done on the subject, it was never made public. In a routine change, he was transferred to Internal Affairs, a unit that had always been, within the department, a separate place, cut off from the mainstream, cut off from other cops. He was assigned a desk, and regular working hours, and he began teaching courses in surveillance as part of the training program which Internal Affairs conducted.

When he stood up in front of his first class of students, he was introduced only as a man with eleven years of detective experience, an expert on surveillance techniques. He began to speak about leapfrogging, and block-squaring. To conduct a proper surveillance, Leuci explained, one needs four cars ideally and—

In the middle of the classroom a hand shot up. "What did you say your name was?"

"Detective Leuci."

---

*James Meehan, Jr. was later acquitted, and was ordered reinstated as a police officer.

"Are you *the* Detective Leuci?"

"I'm Detective Leuci."

"I don't think I have anything to learn from you," said the student, who was a detective lieutenant. He got up and walked out of the classroom and did not come back.

Of course certain cops told Leuci they were proud of what he had done. And many others were new, and had never heard of him.

He was a policeman again, he told himself. It was his opinion that a man could only be a policeman if he was accepted as such by other policemen. These men accepted him here. He was back in the Police Department, more or less. He missed the street, believing that that was where he operated best, and he realized that probably the department would never trust him in the street again. He went on teaching. I'm not in combat, he told himself, but not everyone can be.

Deep down he wanted to believe, and he wanted the world to believe, that he had done what he had done because he was a policeman, because he had seen evil growing before his eyes, evil that he himself was part of, and he had moved to end it by the only means open to him. He had come forward not as a rat, but as a cop. He had acted not calculatingly, but emotionally. And of all those he had destroyed, he had destroyed the old Bob Leuci most of all.

His most recurrent nightmare is this one: that he should be asked to leave the Police Department. To remain a cop, moving among other cops, is the only life for him that he can conceive, and he is taking it one day at a time.